SCOTLAND AND THE FICTIONS
OF GEOGRAPHY

Focusing on the relationship between England and Scotland and the interaction between history and geography, Penny Fielding explores how Scottish literature in the Romantic period was shaped by the understanding of place and space.

The book examines geography as a form of regional, national and global definition, addressing national surveys, local stories, place-names and travel writing, and argues that the case of Scotland complicates the identification of Romanticism with the local. Fielding considers Scotland as 'North Britain' in a period when the north of Europe was becoming a strong cultural and political identity and explores ways in which Scotland was both formative and disruptive of British national consciousness.

Containing studies of Robert Burns, Walter Scott and James Hogg, as well as the lesser-known figures of Anne Grant and Margaret Chalmers, this study discusses an exceptionally broad range of historical, geographical, scientific, linguistic, antiquarian and political writing from throughout North Britain.

PENNY FIELDING is Senior Lecturer in the Department of English at the University of Edinburgh. Previous books include an edition of Walter Scott, *The Monastery* and *Writing and Orality: Nationality, Culture, and Nineteenth-Century Scottish Fiction.*

This series aims to foster the best new work in one of the most challenging fields within English literary studies. From the early 1780s to the early 1830s a formidable array of talented men and women took to literary composition, not just in poetry, which some of them famously transformed, but in many modes of writing. The expansion of publishing created new opportunities for writers, and the political stakes of what they wrote were raised again by what Wordsworth called those 'great national events' that were 'almost daily taking place': the French Revolution, the Napoleonic and American wars, urbanisation, industrialisation, religious revival, an expanded empire abroad and the reform movement at home. This was an enormous ambition, even when it pretended otherwise. The relations between science, philosophy, religion and literature were reworked in texts such as *Frankenstein* and *Biographia Literaria;* gender relations in *A Vindication of the Rights of Woman* and *Don Juan;* journalism by Cobbett and Hazlitt; poetic form, content and style by the Lake School and the Cockney School. Outside Shakespeare studies, probably no body of writing has produced such a wealth of response or done so much to shape the responses of modern criticism. This indeed is the period that saw the emergence of those notions of 'literature' and of literary history, especially national literary history, on which modern scholarship in English has been founded.

The categories produced by Romanticism have also been challenged by recent historicist arguments. The task of the series is to engage both with a challenging corpus of Romantic writings and with the changing field of criticism they have helped to shape. As with other literary series published by Cambridge, this one will represent the work of both younger and more established scholars, on either side of the Atlantic and elsewhere.

For a complete list of titles published, see end of book.

SCOTLAND AND THE FICTIONS OF GEOGRAPHY

North Britain, 1760–1830

PENNY FIELDING

CAMBRIDGE
UNIVERSITY PRESS

CAMBRIDGE UNIVERSITY PRESS
Cambridge, New York, Melbourne, Madrid, Cape Town, Singapore, São Paulo, Delhi

Cambridge University Press
The Edinburgh Building, Cambridge CB2 8RU, UK

Published in the United States of America by Cambridge University Press, New York

www.cambridge.org
Information on this title: www.cambridge.org/9780521895149

First published 2008

Printed in the United Kingdom at the University Press, Cambridge

A catalogue record for this publication is available from the British Library

Library of Congress Cataloguing in Publication data
Fielding, Penny.
Scotland and the fictions of geography : North Britain, 1760–1830 / Penny Fielding.
p.   cm. – (Cambridge studies in romanticism)
Includes bibliographical references and index.
ISBN 978-0-521-89514-9 (hardback)
1. Scottish literature–18th century–History and criticism.   2. Scottish literature–19th
century–History and criticism.   3. English literature–Scottish authors–History and criticism.
4. Place (Philosophy) in literature.   5. Geographical perception–Scotland–History.
6. Literature and society–Scotland–History.   7. Literature and society–Great
Britain–History.   8. Human geography–Scotland–History.   9. Romanticism–Scotland.
10. Romanticism–Great Britain.   I. Title.   II. Series.
PR8555.F54 2008
820.9'9411–dc22
2008025661

ISBN-978-0-521-89514-9 hardback

For Heather Murray and in memory of Linda Bradley

Contents

Acknowledgements

I am grateful to the Arts and Humanities Research Council for funding a period of leave that allowed me to bring this book to completion.

My research had one of its earliest outings during a year I spent at the University of Pennsylvania. I thank all my friends there, and particularly John Richetti for his generous hospitality and for arranging the talk at which my North Britain project started to take shape. I am also very grateful to Stuart Curran for introducing me to the poetry of Margaret Chalmers. Other parts of the book benefited greatly from exchanges following talks or conference papers, and I especially want to thank Janet Sorensen for organising a very stimulating and congenial visit to Chicago and Indiana that helped me finish the book. I am very grateful to James Chandler for innumerable insights into Romanticism (and the rules of baseball). I have learned a great deal from conversations with and the work of Leith Davis, Ina Ferris, Nigel Leask, Yoon Sun Lee, Alison Lumsden, Caroline McCracken-Flesher, Fiona Robertson, Anne Rowland, Maureen McLane, John Plotz, Erik Simpson and Graham Tulloch. As is the case for everyone working in Scottish Romanticism, I am greatly indebted to the great intellectual generosity and friendship of Ian Duncan, and would particularly like to thank Peter Garside for his help with and support for this project.

Many people answered specific queries, and I thank Gill Hughes for her unfailing and invaluable supply of information about Hogg; Ian Campbell Ross for help with eighteenth-century novels; and Charlie Withers, for answering questions about proper geography. My colleagues at Edinburgh were unfailingly supportive. Bob Irvine, Susan Manning and Alex Thomson have consistently enlarged my understanding of Scottish Romantic writing, and Randall Stevenson's help and patience were very much appreciated. Claire Colebrook, James Loxley, Lee Spinks and Andrew Taylor were wonderful sources of encouragement, information and conviviality.

My research was greatly assisted by the staff at the National Library of Scotland, and it is a real pleasure to work there. Linda Bree at Cambridge University Press made the editorial process run very smoothly. Linda Tym tracked down the last recalcitrant notes and lightened the load of preparing the manuscript.

For forms of help, support and inspiration too numerous to mention, heartfelt thanks go to Iain Ashman, Pam Beasant, Dermot Cavanagh, Aileen Douglas, Paul Fielding, John Lyon, Sally Mapstone, Milo Paich, Jen Richards, Barbara and Dan Traister and Karina Williamson.

An earlier version of the first section of Chapter 2 appeared in Leith Davis, Ian Duncan and Janet Sorensen (eds.), *Scotland and the Borders of Romanticism* (Cambridge: Cambridge University Press, 2004). A few paragraphs of the last section of the same chapter appeared in *The Eighteenth Century: Theory and Practice* 39 (1998): 25–43. Part of Chapter 6 appeared in *Studies in Hogg and his World* 9 (1998): 45–63. I am very grateful to the editors for permission to use this material.

Introduction

Arriving in Aberdeen in 1773, Samuel Johnson addresses his readers, the inhabitants of 'our own island':

> To write of the cities of our own island with the solemnity of geographical description, as if we had been cast upon a newly discovered coast, has the appearance of very frivolous ostentation; yet as Scotland is little known to the greater part of those who may read these observations, it is not superfluous to relate that under the name of Aberdeen are comprised two towns standing about a mile distant from each other, but governed, I think, by the same magistrates.[1]

For Johnson, the phrase 'our own island' does not denote equality of national belonging among a modern, educated readership. Scotland may as well be 'a newly discovered coast' for the majority of his readers, but it can be rescued from its state of primitive obscurity by 'the solemnity of geographical description.' The work of geography, then, will reveal not only Scotland's place in the Union but also its emergence, or discovery, as part of the modern, civilised world, here represented by the reassuring information that Aberdeen is legally regulated. It is through geography, in Johnson's mind, that Scotland can be understood as part of a national narrative and given form and function within British history.

A second example makes this recourse to the epistemological security of geography more explicit. The English topographer and antiquarian Richard Gough, complaining that he knows little about Scotland, and for good reason, speculates: 'Whether it be for want of materials or application, the nationality of our northern neighbours suffers the natural and artificial fate of their country to lie as undescribed as their poverty once left it unimproved and unadorned.'[2] Gough's coupling of geographical knowledge and economic progress is instructive, as Scotland's geography was bound up both in its own sense of political and historical character and in a cultural identity which became general currency in Enlightenment Britain. Geography was both the tool that would deliver economic improvement across the nation, and the means by which the nature of historical progress itself could be understood.

Scots participated enthusiastically in rendering their nation legible through geography and making it visible to the economic, scientific and historical eye. The impetus to construct a complete survey of the nation, proposed by David Erskine, Lord Buchan, in 1781, was to gather together statistics of population and agricultural production from all the parishes of Scotland in order to 'exhibit a noble and complete survey of this part of the united kingdoms, and enable any remote or collateral heir to an estate, who could not reap any advantage from his predecessor's experience and observation, to have access at once to every necessary elucidation towards the improvement of his property', while 'at the same time, this collection would be a most interesting and useful national attainment.'[3]

If geographical knowledge could provide the means to economic improvement, it was also the way for Scotland to be understood not only in terms of its own history but also as a model for history itself. Scottish Enlightenment stadial history was deeply imbricated in geography. The internal divisions of Scotland into mountainous Highlands, fertile Lowlands, and newly thriving central cities was a very broad and schematic simplification of the complex spatial and temporal relations of Scottish localities. Increasingly, a cartographic representation of Scotland came to subsume smaller divisions and to offer a geographic canvas upon which the broadest strokes of human development could be painted. Scotland seemed to offer in miniature the key to a complete global understanding that would make time and space simultaneously available as a subject of inquiry, made famous by Edmund Burke's remark in 1777 about global identities:

But now the Great Map of Mankind is unrolld at once; and there is no state or Gradation of barbarism, and no more of refinement which we have not at the same instant under our View. The very different Civility of Europe and of China; The barbarism of Persia and Abyssinia. The erratick manners of Tartary, and of Arabia.[4]

The first thing we notice is Burke's aerial position, giving a place to stand from which he can view the globe while remaining himself outside it, a position that was to come under persistent pressure in the Romantic period. But more importantly for my subject here, Burke's 'Map of Mankind' perfectly enfolds history into geography. Global difference is to be imagined as something that happens in time as well as space; it is a matter of 'gradation' and 'refinement'.

Though not invented by Scottish thinkers, the historical relations of barbarism and civility became the constant theme of the Scottish Enlightenment. Scotland not only developed stadial history – the movement of peoples from tribal hunting, through agriculture, to commercial modernity – the very geography of the nation demonstrated it. The bleak landscape and clan society of the Highlands, the agricultural improvements of the Lowlands and the flourishing cities of Edinburgh and Glasgow, bourgeois centres of commerce and the professions, could be read as a kind of living museum in which all stages of society could be exhibited to the historical observer. Scotland's geography was already inscribed with broad historical and social meanings in ways that could be seen to determine its inhabitants: fierce, barbaric Highlanders and industrious, commercially sophisticated Lowlanders. Not surprisingly, Montesquieu's *Spirit of the Laws* was influential on Scottish philosophy and historiography, grounding the very possibility of regional variation and the consequent differentiation of societies by means of social and legal organisation on a spatial framework. Put bluntly, Highlanders were tribal and feudal and their mountainous territory chiefly suited for hunting, while Lowlanders were civilised and democratic, their societies produced by the leisure afforded by agriculture and commerce.[5]

It was not, of course, that England lacked a complex and varied geography that could exemplify historical patterns. As Franco Moretti's *Atlas of the European Novel* shows, the geography of all parts of the nation-state can be mapped in ways that demonstrate 'its peculiar geometry, its boundaries, its spatial taboos and favorite routes.'[6] But Scotland, in the Romantic period, was *already* seen to be exemplary in terms of its geography. Its internal divisions between Highlands and Lowlands, and its remote islands, seemed to offer a paradigm of the relations between history, geography and social organisation. Again, this is not to say that England did not have exemplary regions, but there was no routine comparison of the statesman farmers of mountainous Westmorland to tribes of North American Indians, as was the very common case with Scottish Highlanders who were thus made to stand for entire stages of human development. In order to understand the specific cultural work of the Scottish geographical imagination that is the subject of this book, we can, for heuristic and introductory purposes, continue to contrast it with what was available for English writers of the period. Needless to say, there is a considerable area of overlap between England and Scotland, not least in the ways – which we are now coming to understand – that Scottish models of bardic verse or minstrelsy can illuminate the cultural work of English Romantic poetry.[7] I do not propose an absolute separation between 'English Romanticism' and 'Scottish Romanticism', but a comparison between some English and Scottish approaches to space will highlight different availabilities of spatial models. We still need to account for the fact that most Scottish writers do not turn as readily to certain forms of affective, individual or phenomenological relation to space as can their English contemporaries but, rather, assume the already-historicised character of geography.

For Wordsworth, paradigmatically, attachment to place is a form of self-determination. Even his *Guide to the Lakes*, although giving travel directions to the Lake District, is not primarily interested in wider forms of location. The appeal of the landscape, he argues, is that a 'concentration of interest gives to the country a decided superiority over the most attractive districts of Scotland and Wales.'[8] The visitor to the Lakes is invited to consider the landscape in terms of its special qualities, focused on singular points and expressed as an intensification, or 'concentration', of affect, rather than on its geographical position. The inhabitants have an enviable autonomy that demonstrates the unique qualities of the place rather than its representative ones. English Romantic poetry, to generalise for a moment, allows a sense of the local as affective, a humanist notion that presupposes the centrality of the subject and assumes his or her experiences as an organising principle. Histories are generated by these localities not in the sense of geographical determinism, in which social organisation is a result of climate and terrain, but as an expression of the experiences of the local population. Narratives describe a locality gene-rated and maintained by the stories told about it. William Wordsworth's 'Michael' or 'The Brothers' and Dorothy Wordsworth's 'Narrative of George and Sarah Green' construct place from the relationships and memories of its inhabitants.

It is not surprising that Wordsworth should have been the focus of Heideggerian approaches to the idea of dwelling in a particular place. John Kerrigan has written of Wordsworth's 'need to find a dwelling-place which would not fade.'[9] Jonathan Bate claims that, for Wordsworth, 'poetry is something that happens at a particular time and in a particular place.'[10] John Lucas identifies in Wordsworth's landscape a property which 'has to do with endeavour, work, and all that is contained in the key terms "occupation," "abode," "dwelling." '[11] In addition, John Barrell has described Clare's sense of place as 'increasingly preoccupied with the being "local," and [. . .] concerned with one place, Helpston, not as it is typical of other places, but as it is individual; and individual not because it is different, but because it was the only place he knew.'[12] English Romantic poets, then, pursue the singularity of place as an experiential quality. It is possible for Coleridge, sitting beside his baby in his cottage, to record the impressions of his locality as pure phenomena:

> Sea, hill, and wood,
> This populous village! Sea, and hill, and wood. (ll. 10–11)[13]

Of course, if we know the social history of Nether Stowey, or the fact that Coleridge was suspected of radical activity there, or we wonder about the potential political meanings of the frost's 'secret ministry', we can produce many compelling, historically situated readings. And it goes without saying that the historicisation of Romantic-period studies has done much to reinsert the social or industrial objects that find themselves written out of Romantic landscapes. Indeed, Michael Wiley has demonstrated the many ways in which we can read Wordsworth's landscapes in terms of their social geography.[14] But my point is that it was possible for Coleridge to list his surroundings in this purely experiential way, moment by moment, in a manner that was not at all as readily available to Scottish writers of the Romantic period. For Coleridge, the term 'populous' is not *primarily* a comment on the statistical growth of the village and its place in a national economy in the way it was for Scott, describing Edward Waverley's feelings of pleasure at the reconciliation of a divided Scotland after the 1745 rebellion: 'He then, for the first time since leaving Edinburgh, began to experience that pleasure which almost all feel who return to a verdant, populous, and highly-cultivated country, from scenes of waste desolation, or of solitary and melancholy grandeur.'[15] Although both Wordsworth and Scott lived in areas that could be described as the north of Britain, Wordsworth infrequently uses the term 'north' outside a standard poetic register of epithets like 'north wind' or 'frozen north'. For Scott, on the other hand, the north of Britain has an already inscribed political identity as North Britain, a subject I shall discuss in the next chapter.

It was not, of course, that Scottish writers were uninterested in the description or representation of individual places. On the contrary, the local is of primary importance in Scottish Romanticism as it develops the idea of regionality in the tradition of the National Tale, drawing a distinction between 'peripheral' places and metropolitan centres and dramatising the journey between them. Or we might point to the importance of local beliefs in the ballad and the Gothic short story, or the listing for a wider British readership of hitherto unheard-of villages in Scott's *Lay of the Last Minstrel* and the tales of James Hogg. But, even for locally designated writers such as Burns and Hogg, the Ayrshire Ploughman and the Ettrick Shepherd, as I shall argue in Chapters 2 and 6 of this book, the problematic relation of the singular to larger structures always disrupts the idea of the singularity of place. Even the most phenomenological of Scottish writers, the Shetland poet Margaret Chalmers, whom I discuss in Chapter 5, is equally interested in space as a national and global structure as she is in describing her sense of dwelling in it.

For Scottish writers, then, to experience a familiar landscape is to read the ways in which it is historically inscribed. The travel writer William Thomson imagines the modern citizen of Edinburgh's New Town surveying in panoramic mode the Firth of Forth and the Grampian mountains: 'The objects seen from hence are not only fitted to please and soothe the imagination, by their natural sublimity and beauty, but such as associate in the mind of a Scotchman, the most important passages in the history of his country, and are, on that account, doubly interesting.'[16] The Scot, in Thomson's mind, cannot experience the sublime in its pure, empirical form but is always one step removed, caught up by questions of national history. Wordsworth and Scott offer another exemplary difference here. Although it starts off with two reivers discussing a border raid, Wordsworth's play *The Borderers* is more interested in the abstraction of borders as an internal condition than in the external history or topography of the region. Wordsworth was later to comment:

As to the scene & period of action little more was required for my purpose than the absence of established Law & Government—so that the Agents might be at liberty to act on their own impulses. [. . .] I read Redpath's history of the Borders but found there nothing to my purpose. I once made an observation to Sir Walter Scott in which he concurred that it was difficult to conceive how so dull a book could be written on such a subject [. . .].[17]

Perhaps Scott (never one to be deterred by wearisome reading matter) was just being polite on this occasion, for he had made use not only of George Ridpath's *Border-History of England and Scotland* but also of a host of even drier titles, including William Nicolson's 1705 collection of treaties, *Leges Marchiarum, or Border-Laws*, for the extensive legal information in the notes to his *Minstrelsy of the Scottish Border*, his *Essay on Border Antiquities*, and his Borders-set novels *The Black Dwarf*, *The Monastery* and *The Abbot*. Unlike Wordsworth, who seeks to clear a space for 'impulse' amid the constraints of law, Scott, not short of impulsive Borders characters in his own work, was fascinated by the Border laws in themselves (as I discuss in Chapter 3) and the ways in which they interacted with Borders society.

We can develop this sense of the already-written quality of Scottish places if we take as an example the figure of people returning to land to which they have an attachment. When Leonard Ewbank returns to Ennerdale in 'The Brothers', it is to find that he can no longer be a part of a community based on shared, unwritten understandings between the villagers. Place is affective and interpersonal – Leonard returns to sea at the end of the poem not because of any great historical shift that has alienated him from the social or economic function of the village, but because his attachment is severed with the confirmation of the death of his brother James. In 'Michael', Michael's relation to place is similarly grounded in the individual. The site of his relationship with his son does not change – in fact it becomes infused with a tragic stasis as Michael repeatedly returns to the unfinished sheepfold – but his emotional investment in it does. We might compare these examples with Scott's first two novels. In *Waverley*, the hero visits and then returns three times to the place that will become his home – the estate of Tully-Veolan, seat of the Jacobite sympathiser Baron Bradwardine. On his first return, ill and confused, he fails even to recognise the place. On his second, the house has been sacked by the Hanoverian Army in their pursuit of the Jacobites and the 'accessaries of ancient distinction' of which Baron Bradwardine had been so proud to have been 'treated with peculiar contumely.'[18] Finally returning to marry Rose Bradwardine in the newly restored house, Edward is able to recognise himself as part of a new political order in the similarly restored and renewed Union of England and Scotland. It is as if the redirection of Scottish history after 1745, the novel's declared subject, brings the meanings of the house into view, or, put more simply, it is history that makes place legible.[19]

In Scott's second novel, *Guy Mannering*, the lost heir Harry Bertram returns to his ancestral estate of Ellangowan without remembering the circumstances in which he had originally gone missing, or indeed without being aware that he is lost. At first, the key to awakening his past seems to lie in personal memory. He recognises a folk tune sung by one of the servants, and, in what seems like a purely affective relation to place, is guided through the location of his kidnapping by the Gypsy Meg Merrilies. But these romance figures are in the service of a larger historical development. The restoration of personal memories becomes part of the greater historical fantasy of a conservative myth of restoration following the displacement of the revolutionary and Napoleonic years. And the need for this wider political restoration is made explicit in the text through the interventions of the lawyer Pleydell, without whom the restoration of Harry to the Ellangowan estates would not be possible.[20]

For Scott, the personal relation to any individual place is always part of a historical dialectic, and one way of thinking both about the special qualities and the doublings and fissures of the sense of location in Scottish writing is to identify Scotland's complex relation to the local. Cairns Craig argued that Scottish culture is dogged by a perception that '[its] achievement is necessarily local' and, worse, is threatened by 'the infection of the parochial'.[21] This may have been the case in the later years of the nineteenth century, but in the years covered by this book, ideas of the local – and even the parochial – emerged that gave to the local a position of great importance and one that speaks to ways in which Scots thought of themselves as instrumental in the understanding of Britain, Europe and the globe. The local is, in fact, a useful way of understanding how Scottish geography works at a cultural level and the complex position that it occupies.

Given Scottish geography's interest in the structural, it was not surprising that Scotland should form the subject of Britain's first great modern work of statistical analysis, John Sinclair's *Statistical Account of Scotland*, published in twenty-one volumes between 1791 and 1799, which took up where Lord Buchan's proposal had left off. Sinclair's aim was to break down the social and economic geography of Scotland into manageable units and to present the information as a resource for central government to improve the economy of the country and the welfare of its people. Sinclair himself was to call his method a branch of 'the philosophy of modern times', which consisted in 'analysing the real state of mankind, and examining, with anatomical accuracy and minuteness, *the internal structure of society*.' The local – the individual parishes which were all different from each other – functioned as a point on a network that demonstrated larger patterns of similarities as well as differences. But Sinclair's bold claim for structural objectivity and accuracy sits alongside his method of inquiry and his insistence that it should be empirical, 'the sure basis of investigation and experiment.'[22] Although it was to end in the abstraction and uniformity of the structural mapping of Scotland, the *Statistical Account* had its roots in the conterminous growth of interest in local knowledge. William Thomson points out the variable nature of such information, depending as it did upon the observations and opinions of individual informants, and that no individual is unbiased. Even to select ministers as the least partial informants, as Sinclair had just done, was not

objective enough for Thomson, who advocates that all statistical information should be regulated by 'a Council chosen annually by deputies,
representing the most respectable part of society in that kingdom.'[23]

Generically, we can see two modes of inquiry, with different geneses
and forms, interwoven in the later decades of the eighteenth century as
the impulse to map space mathematically interacts with the experiences of
the individual traveller. Thomas Pennant's two *Tours* of Scotland are
what their titles suggest, but they are founded on the same method as
Sinclair's *Statistical Enquiry*. In 1772, Pennant advertised in the *Scots
Magazine* his intention to take a second tour in Scotland, asking the
magazine's readers to direct him to interesting objects. His expected
informants were typically ministers, who contributed their ideas on local
topography, natural history and political economy. Pennant had a pre-
determined set of points to be addressed:

QUERIES, Addressed to the Gentlemen and Clergy of *North-Britain*, respecting
the Antiquities and Natural History of their respective Parishes, with a View of
exciting them to favor the World with a fuller and more satisfactory Account of
their Country, than it is the Power of a Stranger and transient Visitant to give.[24]

Pennant's work is inductive, moving away from the deductive work of
environmental determinism, but it is designed to co-opt the local into a
larger picture. Pennant was himself part of the flourishing of natural history in the period as it sought to put together taxonomies of the national
and global natural world. He at once privileges the local as a source of
authentic knowledge communicated by individual subjects and subsumes it
into a larger structure. The local – here specifically the parochial – becomes
identified by its difference from other localities in a given national whole,
rather than by its singular quality derived from the observing subject.

Conversely, Robert Jameson's first major geological work (following
his study of the Shetlands and Arran), the *Mineralogy of the Scottish Isles* of
1800, is a confident attempt to give a history of Scotland in rock, showing
underlying continuities not only between different parts of that country
but also between European and global formations. What appear to be local
phenomena are revealed as a part of a much larger underlying structure.
Mineralogy, he claims, is 'a ground-work, without which the observations
of the geologist, and the labours of the miner, will be ever uncertain, and
of little utility.'[25] Yet, for all its scientific assurance, Jameson's work is
anxious about its reception. He is concerned to distinguish himself, a
proper geologist, from mere travellers who 'satisfy themselves, in their
geological observations, by following a very superficial and absurd mode

of investigation' as they 'sit in their carriage and view the rocks as they pass along.'[26] Given his attitude to the tourist, it is perhaps then surprising that Jameson should decide himself to record his observations in the literary form most usual for the late-eighteenth-century *Tour:* the diary:

It is a fitter task for me to record faithfully what I have myself examined, and to give a fair report of the materials which were collected, than to expose myself, by the form or arrangement of the work, to the danger of having the facts twisted and perverted by hypothesis, the rage for which is as remarkable in this as in the other sciences.[27]

There is thus a third position between the informants of the *Statistical Account* and the scenes of Wordsworth's childhood that acknowledges – in fact grows from – a tension between the first two. If the local depends upon its singularity – the unique set of associations that the subject experiences – then it cannot take its place in a larger structure of historical geography. Rather than working as a reproducible point in a nexus, it is continually recreated through the experiences and representations of its inhabitants and altered through the accretions of memory. But if, on the other hand, the local can be predicted by virtue of its situation in a national topography, then what makes it specifically local? What is the connection between a named place and the unique space that it inhabits? In this book, I try to untangle some of the complex representations of place in Scotland and as Scotland in the Romantic period. We can read this as an expression of a more general problem: that of Scotland's relation to Britain. Scotland is deemed to stand in a secondary relation to England, added on in 1707, but it is also what completes Britain's wholeness.[28] The local is necessary to understand where one is in the nation, but it is not always easy to assimilate it into the nation. In various contexts and forms of writing, we can see how this problem was tackled in different ways: attempts to level out the awkwardness of the local through the centralisation of power, to assimilate it into a larger network or to posit it as a place so dependent on subjective associations that it cannot be physically located at all. For Scotland, the very impulse to know the nation in geographical terms results in an instability in how it is measured, and it is these tensions and instabilities in Scotland's cultural spatiality that I will explore in this study.

The structure of supplementarity that configures national spatiality will inform my next chapter as I discuss the ways in which Scotland becomes representative of Britain. Britain emerges as a northern nation in a general turn from the Classical south to a growing interest in the origins of

British culture and language in primitive northern European tribes. At the same time, 'North Britain' becomes a pejorative term for Scotland seen as a nation struggling to catch up with England's economic progress. Within this inherently unstable structure, Scotland becomes both the spatial embodiment of the north as a foundational British identity and a 'peripheral' locality, a north that acts as England's other.

The second chapter introduces the capacities and problems of geography itself and looks at the idea of place in three geographical contexts important for the book as a whole, using Robert Burns, Scotland's icon of locality, as an example of how literature can destabilise the structures of geography. First is the idea of Burns as a 'local' poet, raising the question of how specific a place must be to be deemed local. Second is the relation of Burns to eighteenth-century theories of larger schemes of placement, as he situates himself on an environmentally divided globe that saw 'northern' and 'southern' climates as social determinants. These two ideas demonstrate the interrelation of the local and the global, which is given a national context in the third part of the chapter. Throughout this book, I argue that Scotland's identity as 'North Britain' must include the *graphē* of geography, which evokes both geographies of place and geographies of language, and here I look at how north–south relations are discernible in theories of the global movement of languages.

Chapter 3 turns to travel narratives and to Scott's *Rob Roy* as they map ways in which the national, as constructed through Scottish Enlightenment theories of stadial progress and a commercial *telos*, comes under the pressure of the local. I explore how the a priori conclusions of stadial history come up against the inductive observations of the empirical traveller. Looking at the tropes of roads and borders, I show how these spatial measurements are divided both internally and against each other. The geometry of the nation reveals a tension between a state made commensurable by its legal and commercial practices and the varying functions of the local in both supporting and dissolving this structure.

In Chapter 4, I return to the geographies of language discussed in Chapter 2 and look more specifically at how writing generates concepts of the nation and the origin of the modern commercial state. Focusing on antiquarian ideas about the geographical distribution of place-names, I discuss how Scotland could be foundational for the ancestry of Britain and how this ancient past is produced by Scotland's own sense of modernity. Scott's *The Antiquary* draws on antiquarian ideas about toponymy and numismatics to show how linguistic nationalism works like a modern currency, based on exchange and representation. The novel imagines history as a form of credit that, rather than reproducing past events, draws attention to their circulation and consumption in the present.

The final two chapters are case studies for the way in which Scotland's cultural topography in the early nineteenth century produces, challenges and rearranges Enlightenment spatiality. Where the previous four chapters look at the way the north is mapped and inscribed through geographies of place and language, these concluding chapters explore accounts of being at the north – of Scotland, of Europe and of the world. Chapter 5 compares two contemporaneous accounts of the northern islands of Orkney and Shetland which investigate the national limits of the north and the function of Scotland in circumscribing the island of Great Britain. In comparing Scott's 1814 tour of the northern coastline of Scotland with the 1813 volume of poems by the Shetland author Margaret Chalmers, I explore how very different ideas of national identity and languages of spatiality can be produced by the same locations. Scott's apparent 'vacation' into new space turns out to be inscribed with the discourses of cultural identity he had thought to leave behind, while Chalmers, despite her acknowledgement of a 'peripheral' position, is able to exploit the spatial ambiguities of the north in order to subvert the distinction between centre and periphery.

The last chapter is about James Hogg and returns to the problem of the singularity of the local. Hogg registers the difficulty of asserting a unique place when geographical knowledge must come from the recognition of correspondences, while simultaneously picking apart the larger structures of national and global space that this book has reviewed. I look at stories set in three geographical positions, moving northwards but recognising that the north is an asymptotic position which cannot be reached. Hogg's geographical range travels from the impossibility of locality in a Scotland associated with tradition and folk beliefs, to warfare in northern Europe where Hogg exposes the failure of either environment or national borders to determine social subjects, and finally to the North Pole, both the epitome of the north and the most problematic point of all – one which both challenges Enlightenment mathematisation of space and dissolves the idea that the human subject can occupy a singular space.

CHAPTER I

North Britain

In 1737, Thomas Gray, then a student at Peterhouse, Cambridge, was called upon to write some Latin verses to be issued at the University Tripos ceremony. In response, he produced 'Luna Habitabalis', a whimsical study that depicts a moon inhabited by various peoples curiously similar to those on Earth. At the instruction of one of the muses (presumably Urania, Muse of Astronomy), the speaker of the poem surveys the moon through a telescope while she directs him to 'Look to the north!', and he describes the course of his gaze:

> Jam Galli apparent, jam se Germania latè
> Tollit, et albescens pater Apenninus ad auras:
> Jam tandem in Borean, en! parvulus Anglia nævus
> (Quanquàm aliis longè fulgentior) extulit oras:
> Formosum extemplò lumen, maculamque nitentem
> Invisunt crebri Proceres, serùmque tuendo
> Hærent, certatimque suo cognomine signant: (ll. 64–70)

Presently the Gauls appear, then wide-spreading Germany rises into view, and white-topped father Apeninus towers aloft; finally, behold! Look to the north! tiny England, no bigger than a beauty spot (although brighter far than all other lands), offers its shores to view. Straightway throngs of princes come to see this lovely radiance, this shining dot, and continue looking far into the night; and each one vies eagerly to distinguish it with his name.[1]

Gray's early flight of optical fancy as he 'look[s] to the north' has implications beyond its occasional purpose, and his positioning of England at a certain 'north' usefully brings together some of the themes of this book, hinting both at the aspirations behind the urge to locate and at the difficulties of location itself. First there is the problem of identifying the nation both as a 'dot' or island, and as England, which is plainly not an island, thus pointing to tensions between the sense of an imperial island nation and its own internal divisions between its north and south components. Second, Europe, as we will see throughout this chapter, is the product of historical, linguistic and geographical change – of a series of peoples (the Gauls), and changing vistas ('wide-spreading Germany') – rather than a fixed or given position. National borders (France or Prussia) are subsumed or rubbed out in this shifting historical perspective. Geography and chronology exist in an uneasy relation not only of mutual dependence but also of incompatibility. Furthermore, radiant, imperial England/Britain is so 'tiny' that it must be made known through a complicated series of representations: projected onto an imaginary, reflective moon and sighted only through a telescope. Britain is never fully present to the naked eye, or the empirical gaze. And this Britain is also identified as the object, rather than the architect of imperialism – a curiously nameless land waiting to be mapped by the names of its colonisers, a point that is both *here*, recognisable through the history of the viewer, and *nowhere*, a space awaiting inscription. Urania's telescope has the effect not only of reducing geographical distance but also of telescoping time, apparently projecting into modern Britain an earlier, as yet unwritten country awaiting the narratives of invasion, immigration and absorption which will, paradoxically, produce the distinctly located nation.

These ideas, some of which Gray was to develop in his later poetry, both establish Britain as a northerly part of an imagined whole and undermine that act of identification. Through Gray's telescope we not only see a miniaturised version of the ways in which Britain could be imagined geographically but are also reminded how geography is staged, or inscribed. And the particular problem that Urania sets is: what should we look for when we 'look to the north'? As the muse implies, eighteenth-century Britons had a generalised sense of being in the north, perhaps in some ways similar to our modern, and equally general, category of 'the west'. But, more than any contemporary understanding of living in the west, northerliness was a condition that was continually analysed and reinscribed in a geographical sense. Being northern was a matter not only of cartography but also of toponymy, myth, language history, climate, empirical travel. In this chapter, I will outline some of the modes and structures that produced a geography of the north for British subjects and also enveloped the nation in wider European and global geographies. But even before such a position might be isolated, the north is already divided by Britain's internal national boundaries: England and Scotland are both northern nations, but one is more northerly than the other. 'North Britain' and the north of Britain are not the same place. Scotland is the north itself, yet also a site north of another northerly power. It is at once an icon of northerliness for imperial, military, commercial Britain and a country marginalised by its northern position, and it is to these norths that I will first look.

To think of Scotland as 'North Britain' is already to shape it geographically. 'North Britain' is a term that at once homogenises and divides, and does so in various ways. First, it confers a unity upon both the nation-state of Britain and a Scotland whose internal divisions are thereby blurred. 'North' becomes a general signifier for Scotland in the decades preceding its adoption as a common term for the north of England following the industrialisation of parts of that region.[2] Although 'North Britain' was a commonplace term for Scotland throughout the eighteenth century, its meanings were not straightforward, and the term 'north' was loaded, divided and sometimes ambiguous. In an early political satire describing the loss of the American colonies and the political instability at home leading up to the 1784 election, Robert Burns plays with the term as one which moves between the geographical and the political. 'North' is both Scotland and Lord North, whose coalition with Charles James Fox was finally seen off, as the poem sees it, by the electoral choice of the people of both England and Scotland, 'Suthron' and 'Caledon'. Pitt, who became Prime Minister, can thus himself be 'be-northed' with Scottish loyalty to counteract the ill effects of North:

> Behind the throne then *Gr-nv-lle*'s gone,
>   A secret word or twa, man;
> While slee *D-nd-s* arous'd the class
>   Be-north the Roman wa', man:
> [. . .]
> But, word an' blow, *N-rth*, *F-x, and Co.*
>   Gowff'd *Willie* like a ba', man,
> Till *Suthron* raise, an' coost their claise
>   Behind him in a raw, man.
> An' *Caledon* threw by the drone,
>   An' did her whittle draw, man [. . .].[3]

The inclusion of Lord North's name here is, of course, occasional, but even without this particular resonance, we can see how carefully Burns names Scotland and how its position as North Britain is already geographical and political. On the one hand, Scotland is a place to be travelled to from the south, a journey that takes one into the unknown, beyond the ancient national barrier of the Roman wall. Yet, on the other, Scotland is *Caledon*, a Romano-British nation in its own right, and one to which England, which does not have its own name, is southern and secondary. The specific cultural geographies of ancient Caledonia will form part of Chapter 4 of this book, but already the supplementary logic of British geography is working its effects. Scotland is secondary in a nation-state governed from Westminster, yet it is also British in a primary sense; both added on to England in the Act of Union in 1707 and necessary to express the nation's complete identity.

The doubled status of Scotland is exemplified in its identity as North Britain. The term points to a geographical equivalence, the idea of a locality defined entirely by its structural position and thus politically neutral. But, to put it more precisely, such geographical neutrality is itself a political statement. 'North Britain' *was* used in a casual way as a term for Scotland, but its equivalent term, 'South Britain', was less common. One of the latter term's most frequent users is Tobias Smollett – both North and South Britain appear regularly as equivalent national names in *The Expedition of Humphry Clinker*, a novel designed to illustrate the necessary wholeness of Great Britain. And the terms carry a particularly strong political valance in the light of Smollett's journalistic career. The definition of North Britain took on a political urgency with the publication of John Wilkes's satirical newspaper *The North Briton*, which continued for forty-six issues in 1762–3 and was immediately reprinted (with some of Wilkes's other productions) in a three-volume set.[4] *The North Briton* was Wilkes's riposte to the perceived partiality of the Prime Minister, Lord Bute, who was generally held to favour his fellow Scots now appearing in increasing numbers in London. Following Bute's appointment of Smollett, London's most prominent literary Scot, to edit his propagandist paper, *The Briton*, Wilkes counter-attacked with his virulently anti-Scottish *North Briton*.

The imagined editor of *The North Briton* is a Scot not shy of admitting his quest for patronage:

What I have to say of myself, shall be soon dispatched. I thank my stars, I am a *North Briton;* with this almost singular circumstance belonging to me, that I am *unplaced and unpensioned:* but I hope this reproach will soon be wiped away, and that I shall no longer be pointed at by my sneering countrymen.[5]

This Scottish 'editor' is 'unplaced' in more ways than one. In the early issues of the paper, as Wilkes (sometimes assisted by his equally Scoto-phobic friend Charles Churchill) assembles his satirical targets, Scots emerge as subjects who disrupt the political geography of the nation. First, hordes of Scots are displacing themselves (as Wilkes never passes up an opportunity to point out) by deserting their given place of Scotland and assuming an artificial relation to their new locality as 'placemen' under Bute's nepotistic patronage. A 'placeman' is necessarily alienated from the place he occupies by the impropriety of the political reasons for his being there. But more than this, Wilkes suggests that Scots do not have a properly felt relation to place to start with. The properly patriotic subject is attached to his or her country through a national sensibility that extends beyond physical absence, but the Scots are seemingly incapable of this:

Like the Jews, we are spread over the face of every country, (except *our own*) and of this in particular. I regret it exceedingly, and the more, as I am afraid the evil is without a remedy; for I have never heard of any one of my countrymen being attacked with the *patrialgia*, the *maladie du Suisse*, (the *home-ach*, as it has been happily called) and in consequence languishing till he returned to *Scotland*.[6]

Scots, Wilkes implies, are not really a people at all – the comparison with the Swiss denies them not only a relationship with a small, famously independent nation with which Calvinist Scotland sometimes compared itself, but also nationhood altogether.

In a later issue, a cautionary tale unfolds of two Scots, a father and son, on a visit to London. On being shown round Westminster Abbey, they encounter the Stone of Scone, the ancient coronation stone of Scotland appropriated by Edward I, and they excitedly recall the prophecy that Scots will reign wherever the stone is found. The two Scots' lack of proper patriotic feeling, a modern civic virtue, is filled by a primitive, superstitious spatiality (the idea that the inanimate stone will magically transform its own surroundings) and by an improper, 'uncivil' emotion: 'The completion of this glorious prophecy had so intoxicated their understandings, that they could not behave commonly civil.'[7] Despite their (Scottish) host's pleas for moderation, the father exclaims: 'Sir, we have as geud a right to this country as yoursels; and let me tell you Sir, there is nae such thing as an *Englishman*, and I hope shortly the very name will be annihilated.'[8]

Melodramatic as this is, it touches on a cultural phenomenon that was gaining ground. Not only was 'English' having to compete with new meanings of 'British' as a defining term, but scholars of language and history were increasingly turning to Scotland as the site of British origins. As we will see in Chapter 4, although the name of England was hardly 'annihilated', the name of Scotland/Scotia/Caledonia was to prove a particularly interesting question for historians, while England had to share its usual alternative name, Albion, with Scotland.[9] There was a lively debate among antiquarians about the temporal relations of the English language in Scotland and in England. In the example of Wilkes in the 1760s, whose editor (in common with many actual Scots) self-consciously boasts of his ability to avoid 'Scotticisms', English is the dominant language and Scots a secondary, deformed derivative. But in subsequent decades this developed into an argument about which language was a 'dialect' of which and how cultural productions could be mapped onto national origins.

On the one hand, Scots is situated as an offshoot of English, which has latterly pursued a temporary diversion but which will, under the guidance of the Scottish intelligentsia, return to its original course and become once again identical with English, its parent language. A reviewer of John Pinkerton's *Ancient Scotish Poems* takes issue with Pinkerton's naming Scots a sister language of English: 'the Scottish is a branch from the English stem; and the *daughter* rather than the *sister.*'[10] This is also where Hugh Blair positions Scots: 'The Language spoken in the low countries of Scotland, is now, and has been for many centuries, no other than a dialect of the English.'[11] James Beattie likewise insists that even when it was a court language, Scots 'was a dialect of English, as the Dutch is of German, or the Portuguese of Spanish.'[12] English is here anterior to Scots, but in another perspective, Scots and English change places, and the perceived *dialect* turns out to contain the origins of the mainstream *language*. John Sinclair, compiler of the first statistical account of Scotland, observes that 'the two languages originally were so nearly the same, that the principal differences at present between them, are owing to the Scotch having maintained many words and phrases which have fallen into disuse among the English.'[13] In *The Expedition of Humphry Clinker*, the spokesman for this theory is the old soldier Lismahago, who appropriates not only the language but also British literary history for a Scottish origin:

He said, what we generally called the Scottish dialect was, in fact, true, genuine old English, with a mixture of some French terms and idioms, adopted in a long intercourse betwixt the French and Scotch nations; that the modern English, from affectation and false refinement, had weakened, and even corrupted their language, by throwing out the guttural sounds, altering the pronunciation and the quantity, and disusing many words and terms of great significance. In consequence of these innovations, the works of our best poets, such as Chaucer, Spenser, and even Shakespeare, were become, in many parts, unintelligible to the natives of South-Britain, whereas the Scots, who retain the antient language, understand them without the help of a glossary.[14]

As Janet Sorensen points out, 'in Lismahago's portrayal [Scots] haunt the present with their fullness of understanding of [London's] past language and canonical literature, now lost to Londoners.'[15]

The question of language illustrates the unstable order of priority between England and Scotland in the formation of a sense of Britain. At the same time that Scotland is seen as a supplement, yoked to the greater power of England at the Union and beginning to exploit that union, it is also becoming an origin for Britain as a whole. In the next chapter, I will look in more detail at the geographical distribution that underpinned language history, but here I want further to draw the contours of the sense of northernness from which Scotland, and Britain, could take their identities. Scotland might be called 'North Britain' in a pejorative sense by Wilkes, but the idea that Britain was itself a northern country, of which Scotland was the most northerly part, continued to grow in strength as a form of cultural location.

So far from being secondary to England, a latecomer to the Union, Scotland offers a source for Britishness itself. The 'North' in 'North Britain' becomes not only an adjective that describes Scotland in particular and in relation to England but also the location of Britain in general, and its cultural significance. At a most primary level, philologists contributed to the establishing of Britain as a northern country identified as such by its very name. Scholars of language were wont to claim that the name of the country itself referred to its northerly location: John Cleland comes up with the derivation '*Bori*, the northern island, thence *Boritannia*, and by a contraction common to most languages, *Britannia*.'[16] George William Lemon backs up Cleland by suggesting that 'Bori' is cognate with 'Boreas', the north wind, and he further associates the concept of northernness, by a complicated syllogism, with things of value. The ancients, he explains, connected the left, or sinister, side with bad luck, because they looked for good omens from the northern, or right-hand side of the sky: 'in our language, we seem to understand it in the sense of the Greeks; for as their happy omens came from the right, *the sinister omens* must have been *unfortunate*, because they came from *the left*; i.e. from the South.'[17]

These derivations come from the more fanciful school of eighteenth-century etymology, but they are nevertheless an important expression of a wider sense of the north as a place from which modern civilisation can derive its origins and sustain its social values and cultural experiences. In 1800, Madame de Staël's *On Literature Considered in Relation to Social Institutions* declared an affective preference for 'the literature of the north'. De Staël's literary north is a composite one, drawing together

English, Scottish, German and Scandinavian works, but the most frequently named is Macpherson's *Ossian* poems. She accumulates a number
of features, which were commonly used to characterise not only northern
literature, but also northern subjectivity in general. Northerners, mainly
as a result of their climate, are hardy and resilient, equipped to withstand
not only the elements but also political oppression. An ideal love of
liberty and independence with a practical ability to achieve them were
characteristic of northern societies. Although the Athenians sought
independence, de Staël argues, Greeks were in general easier to subjugate
than northern peoples. She characterises this spirit of self-determination
further:

A certain pride in the soul, an indifference to life, born of both the harshness of
the earth and the gloom of the sky must have made servitude intolerable; and
long before the theory of constitutions or the advantages of representative
government were known in England, the warlike spirit, which the Gaelic and
Scandinavian poetry sang with such enthusiasm, gave man an elevated notion of
his individual strength and force of will.[18]

This affirmation of northernness could give a clear political resonance
to the terms 'North Britain' and 'South Britain'. The Scottish political
economist James Anderson, in a reversal of the common idea of the
feudal backwardness of the Scots, sees *England* as a country rescued from
its slavish tendencies by the spirit of industry: 'It is thus that South
Britain, that once poor despised country,—the prey of every invading
power, and slave of many successive conquerors, has at length become the
envy or the dread of all the nations around it.'[19] Scotland, on the other
hand, having got over the temporary aberration of its anarchic clan past,
can now reap the benefits of its natural tendency to 'the blessings of
liberty, and the spirit of independence.'[20] But the most common distinctions between north and south were in the fields of literary history
and environmental theory. As many commentators have observed, the
growing interest in literary history in the eighteenth century is coterminous with a turn to the north as a site of literary interest. Progress
poems imagine the flight of the muses, dismayed by political corruption,
from the classical south to a new home in northern Europe, or, specifically, Britain. The most well known example, Thomas Gray's 'Progress of
Poetry', describes this northward journey:

> Till the sad Nine in Greece's evil hour
> Left their Parnassus for the Latian plains.
> Alike they scorn the pomp of tyrant-Power,

And coward Vice, that revels in her chains.
When Latium had her lofty spirit lost,
They sought, oh Albion! next thy sea-encircled coast. (ll. 77–82)[21]

The move from Greece, to Rome, and then to England or Britain was the usual pattern, but one which increasingly came to accommodate Scotland. For Wilkes, in the 1760s, the idea that Scotland might be the logical conclusion of this northerly trajectory – a final hop from England to Scotland with an outgrowth of Scottish thistle choking the English rose, and Scottish political corruption choking what he saw to be exclusively English liberty – was a cause for alarm and something to be put down by satire:

> Hail SCOTLAND, hail, to thee belong
> All pow'rs, but most the powr's of Song;
> Whether the rude unpolish'd *Erse*
> Stalk in the buckram *Prose* or *Verse*,
> Or bonny RAMSAY please thee *mo'*,
> Who *sang sae* sweetly *aw* his woe.
> If ought, and say who knows so well,
> The second-sighted Muse can tell,
> Thy happy LAIRDS shall laugh and sing,
> When ENGLAND'S GENIUS droops his wing.
> So shall thy soil new wealth disclose
> So thy own THISTLE choak the ROSE.[22]

But Wilkes was already too late. As we shall see in the next chapter, Allan Ramsay was not the only author and editor of Scottish song to be popular throughout the island, and Macpherson's *Ossian* poems, much loathed by Wilkes, were circulating not only in England, but also in Europe. By the beginning of the next century, North Britain was to be not only a literary curiosity, but also a centre of publishing which supplied the whole English-speaking world. Walter Scott would become both 'The Wizard of the North', inspiring a local tourist industry in his home town of Melrose, and an international best-seller who, by the end of his career, could transcend location altogether: 'In torrid climes, in regions cold and bleak, / In every land and language wilt thou speak.'[23] For Madame de Staël in 1800, the progress of literature was already turning back on itself. Instead of describing the turn from the classical south to the north, she sees an alternative point of origin in the north itself, identified as 'the Scottish bards, the Icelandic fables and the Scandinavian poetry.' From this northern origin, the virtues of northern literature can spread south. More specifically, in de Staël's narrative, Scotland can be the origin of English poetry: 'The English poets, successors of the Scottish bards, added to their pictures the reflections and ideas that these pictures inspired, but they kept the imagination of the north that delights in the seashore, the sound of the wind, the wild heaths; that which carries the world-weary soul into the future and into another world.'[24]

Progress poetry incorporates not only a northerly journey, but also a northern origin. The trope of northern tribes moving across Europe could still signify the collapse of Roman civilisation, but increasingly they came to stand for the birth of European civilisation itself, the original peoples of Europe and the inaugurators of language and culture. In 1784, Edward Jerningham published his *Rise and Progress of the Scandinavian Poetry*, a work intended to demonstrate 'that spirit of war and enterprize which runs through the whole Scandinavian minstrelsy.' The poem is an account of cultural and political evolution which, rather than reaching Scandinavia from the south, has its own northern origin in 'the rude Genius' who inaugurates a new poetic language and summons, as if from the earth itself, the 'living fathers of the Runic rhyme':

> When urg'd by Destiny th'eventful year
> Sail'd thro' the portal of the northern sphere
> Of Scandinavia the rude Genius rose
> His breast deep-lab'ring with creation's throes:
> Thrice o'er his head a pow'rful wand he whirl'd,
> Then call'd to life a new Poetic world.[25]

Jerningham's northern muse, the spirit of war and enterprise, is part of a reinforcement of northern Europe as a unified political identity. Paul-Henri Mallet was originally commissioned to write his *Northern Antiquities* (its English title) as an ancient history of Scandinavia designed, as Sam Smiles puts it, 'to re-orient European history around a northern axis'.[26] And in his preface to the English translation, Thomas Percy asks: 'Is it not well known that the most flourishing and celebrated states of Europe owe originally to the northern nations, whatever liberty they now enjoy, either in their constitution, or in the spirit of their government?'[27] The distinction between Celts and Goths and other subdivisions of the original tribes of Europe generated a great deal of argument and the details of the many and varied disputes would take up more space than this book permits. Differences – in language, religious practices and social organisation – were certainly carefully documented, but, as Colin Kidd points out, the opposition between 'the pragmatic, freedom-loving Teuton and the mystical, sentimental, but improvident Celt'[28] took a long time to evolve, not entering into rooted 'racial' stereotypes until later in the nineteenth century. The separation of Celt and Goth in the Romantic period was occasional and strategic, generally at the expense of modern Highlanders, or, increasingly in the nineteenth century, Irish immigrants. Individual arguments were violently contested, such as John Pinkerton's and George Chalmers's quarrel about the origin of Scottish place names, which I explore in Chapter 4, or the eighteenth-century dispute about Gothic and Celtic tribes as the originators of British culture. But all these disagreements rested on a prior agreement: that the cultural supremacy under discussion was one that had superseded the classical authority of the south. Nick Groom, in a discussion of the problem as it was figured by Macpherson and Percy, summarises the key question: 'which northern race had carried letters, and by implication poetry, from the fabulous heats of the East to the moody epic wastes of the North?'[29] In *Fingal*, the epic battle between the Caledonians and the Danes is, as Fiona Stafford points out, more like the encounter between the Greeks and the Trojans than an attempt to establish radically different ethnicities,[30] and in James Hogg's comic rendition of the same theme, *Queen Hynde*, the warring tribes of Celts and Scandinavians do not differ much in their social practices. Gray's 'The Fatal Sisters' merges all Britain's northern spaces as it recounts a meeting of the Scandinavian Fates which takes place in Ireland and is witnessed by a native of Caithness in the far north of Britain, whom the sisters instruct to spread their message throughout the rest of Scotland:

> Mortal, thou that hear'st the tale,
> Learn the tenour of our song.
> Scotland, thro' each winding vale
> Far & wide the notes prolong. (ll. 57–60)[31]

Northernness is thus a prior cultural identity but one which can be subdivided for political and contingent purposes. Northernness was a sufficiently vague ethnic identity to absorb the all-constituent peoples of Scotland – Lowlanders, Highlanders, and the peoples of Sutherland and the northern isles who were increasingly associated with Norse origins – but also one precise enough to identify itself against a Celtic west. Many depictions offer a generalised Scot or Caledonian, whether the starving, avaricious figure of Wilkes's and Churchill's satires, or the all-purpose freedom-loving warrior. Alternatively, details of social organisation blur the distinction between Celtic and Norse influences, seeing both as complex civil societies, who could defend themselves militarily, hold diplomatic meetings and engage in trade.

Scotland's northerly location is a divided and doubled one, both distant from a political centre and central to an emergent social and cultural identity. In the next chapter, we shall see in more detail how these northerly identities worked in contradictory and sometimes paradoxical ways, but in the second part of this chapter I want to explore further the more general and abstract geographical ideas that produce the north in the late eighteenth and early nineteenth centuries.

MODERN GEOGRAPHIES

In the first sentence of the preface to the first edition of his *Modern Geography*, the Scottish scholar John Pinkerton asserts not only the 'importance of geography as a science' but also 'the exuberant variety of knowledge and amusement which it exhibits'.[32] This 'exuberant variety' appears in his own book as a rich mixture of topography, political history, economics and natural history, all prefaced by some remarks on astronomy. It characterises a sense, which had flourished throughout the eighteenth century, that geography was not only an overarching discourse for material knowledge but also well placed to serve the needs of modern Britain in what was often regarded as a happy marriage between theory and practice. New systems of navigation facilitated a confidence in global cartography and were seen as instrumental in voyages of exploration and commercial exchange. The systematic surveying of the nation was understood as a means to its economic improvement.

The eighteenth century saw a flow of geographical textbooks but, as Charles W. J. Withers points out, knowledge of place is 'not just about the situated production of geography in public classes, private drawing rooms, school rooms and texts'.[33] Withers goes on to examine surveys, mapping and landscape painting, and to these I would add the importance of travel writing, the history and distribution of languages and the discourses of romance and myth. The intersection of these systems of location is a frequent point in the Romantic-period geography that I explore in this book; the production of a modern nation, underpinned with science and the commercial advantage of geographical knowledge, is also an auto-ethnography of the nation-state's drawing up narratives of inclusion and exclusion as it strengthens its own imperial power. The story of the British North is one of peoples and languages, the consolidation of myths about national origin and the establishing of a Romance past that will interact in various ways with a nationalist rewriting of modernity. As I suggested in my introduction, Scotland's function as a site of the local plays a key part in this process: the meaning of places can both reveal the specificity of particular practices, beliefs and stories and underscore the totality of the nation for which these practices provide a history.

No figure illustrates this duality better than John Pinkerton himself, antiquarian and polymath, for whom few arguments were too small to ignore and who could lose friends as quickly as he could make them. The title of *Modern Geography* encompasses the ideas not only that his book is a modern updating of world geography but also that geography itself is an expression of modernity. The preface to the first edition in 1802 announces boldly:

No period of time could be more favourable to the appearance of a new system of geography, than the beginning of a new century, after the elapse of the eighteenth, which will be memorable in all ages, from the gigantic progress of every science, and in particular of geographical information; not less from the surprising changes which have taken place in most countries of Europe, and which of themselves render a new description indispensable. Whole kingdoms have been annihilated; grand provinces transferred: and such a general alteration has taken place in states and boundaries, that a geographical work published five years ago may be pronounced to be already antiquated.[34]

Geography is modern here because it is technical and scientific, and thus can only be accurate or authentic following the scientific revolution of the Enlightenment. But it is also modern because it is of the present and, thus, subject to political change and the need constantly to redefine itself in order to reflect changing borders and alliances.[35] Geography can describe the integrated nation, but it can also threaten that integrity by revealing the provisional, shifting nature of boundaries and limits. Coterminous with the historical modernity of modern geography is an appeal to an ancient past, the guarantee of cultural tradition and incremental national identity that could shore up the instability or unboundedness of the modern nation. It is no coincidence that the author of *Modern Geography* was also the editor of *Ancient Scotish Poems*, as Scotland was one of the hinges that united British modernity with a sense of its ancient past. Pinkerton was a Unionist, critical of Scotland's pre-Union past, but early Scottish culture was something he could not leave alone. His antiquarian researches produced a number of books of pre-modern, or ancient history including the two-volume *Ancient Scotish Poems* in 1786, a collection of poetry from the manuscripts of the Maitland Collection, consisting mainly of the work of William Dunbar, Gavin Douglas and Richard Maitland. Pinkerton's aim seems at first to prove that these Scottish poets are as good as the English Chaucer, but he is soon finding that they are even better, lacking Chaucer's 'nastiness', displaying much greater 'elegance and opulence', and proving an excellent source for the modern reader who wishes to improve his or her conversational or writing style: 'For knowledge of the primitive and progressive powers of words is the only solid foundation of that rich and terse style which posterity pronounces classic.'[36] Ancient poetry, in short, is an asset for anyone making their way in modern, literary, civic Britain. And the ancient geography that underpins this poetry is helpfully vague, being generally Scottish while not insisting on a clear distinction between England and Scotland: ancient bards are generally said to be 'all of the *north countrie*' because the northern English and Scots languages were so similar.[37]

Pinkerton often goes out of his way to insist on the imprecise geography of the north in general and a number of his publications (including *Ancient Scotish Poems*) include a section on the inaccurate mapping of not only of Scotland but also of northern Europe in the ancient world. In his *Dissertation on the Origin and Progress of the Scythians or Goths* he traces an indistinct north, its shores 'marked by uncertain fame',[38] and the spatial ambiguities of Ancient Roman geography even linger into the eighteenth century when it comes to setting out the parameters of the north: even the eighteenth-century cartographer d'Anville (whom Pinkerton admired) has not yet finalised the matter:

The bounds of ancient knowledge on the West and Wouth are fixt and clear. On the East D'Anville has fully settled it [. . .]. But the Northern, the most important of all to the history of Europe, D'Anville leaves as Cluverius ignorantly puts it; and has thus left a prodigious task to succeeding geographers.[39]

The doubled geography of the north produces place both as a precise location, predictable and reproducible, and as something much less defined, made legible by the individual narrations of myth or story. It is a structure of which Scotland is a very clear example, but I want to argue now that it is also something deeply embedded in the course of eighteenth-century and Romantic-period cultural geography in general. The eighteenth century offers two very different ways of ascertaining the position and function of the north, but they are ways whose histories are intertwined, sometimes surfacing in the same text. The first has its roots in Enlightenment natural theology: a scientific, causal account of origins that traces the foundation of all social life to the primary tilting of the axis of the Earth, originating seasonal variation and climate change.[40] This moment of material determining occurs both in scientific texts and in more literary ones, often with the variation (as in James Thomson's version in *The Seasons*) that the globe had enjoyed a uniform climate until the flood had mysteriously caused the axis to incline. As Thomson describes it: 'great SPRING before / Green'd all the year', but after the deluge climatic conditions are 'in restless change revolv'd'.[41]

Jean-Jacques Rousseau locates his discussion of this phenomenon in a section of the *Essay on the Origin of Languages* that describes the movement of language from south to north. It is the tilting of the Earth's axis, in Rousseau's account, that ushers in not only seasonal change but also cultural difference, the formation of distinct peoples and, in short, history itself (here in Rousseau's pessimistic account of the corrupting force of social organisation):

He who willed man to be social, by the touch of a finger shifted the globe's axis into line with the axis of the universe. I see such a slight movement changing the face of the earth and deciding the vocation of mankind: in the distance I hear the joyous cries of a naïve multitude; I see the building of castles and cities; I see the birth of the arts; I see nations forming, expanding, and dissolving, following each other like ocean waves; I see men leaving their homes, gathering to devour each other, and turning the rest of the world into a hideous desert: fitting monument to social union and the usefulness of the arts.[42]

Societies, politics and history are brought into being by the creation of a north–south polarity, and this global geography, with its divine origin, is the primary determining factor for subjects occupying the globe. Position here is scientific and inevitable, held in place by two clear points, north and south, which allow Rousseau to make absolute distinctions in this section between northern and southern languages. I shall look further at precisely what those distinctions were in the following chapter, but here I want to juxtapose Rousseau's mappable globe with a contrasting eighteenth-century account of locating the north, from Pope's *Essay on Man*:

> Ask where's the North? at York, 'tis on the Tweed;
> In Scotland, at the Orcades; and there,
> At Greenland, Zembla, or the Lord knows where
> No creature owns it in the first degree
> But thinks his neighbour farther off than he.
> Ev'n those who dwell beneath its very zone

Or never feel the rage, or never own;
What happier natures shrink at with affright,
The hard inhabitant contends is right.[43]

So far from Rousseau's fixed, determining polarity, Pope's north is the very model of relativity, a shifting position that recedes before the geographical imagination. Attempts to map a polarised globe into 'zones' have no bearing on the inhabitants of that globe, to whom location is a subjective alignment. The first degree, the symbolic origin of cartography, cannot be 'owned' by any creature but is a subject position, produced by experience. Where Rousseau's northerners are determined by their location, with Pope it is the other way round. Rousseau's north is structural, where Pope's is local.

These two models resurface at various points throughout the eighteenth and early nineteenth centuries, and they generate different forms of the discourse of space and place. A physically determined north, governed by climate and located by global position and scientific measurement, is underpinned by the mathematisation of space in the eighteenth century and a geography that had been developed and taught alongside astronomy. Tracing the philosophical history of place and space since Plato, Edward S. Casey identifies the emergence in the late seventeenth century of the third term of *position*: 'For if it is true that space is determined entirely by its relations, then what matters most is not the size or shape of space, its capacity or volume, but the exact positions of the items related to each other in a given spatial nexus.'[44] As Casey points out, position becomes central to the Enlightenment ordering of spatiality. At its most straightforward level, the availability of position is part of the mathematisation of space that accompanies advances in navigation and exploration. After decades of experimentation, and a number of successful models of his shipboard chronometer, John Harrison was finally awarded the Longitude Prize by Act of Parliament in 1773. The globe was now officially mappable as a network of intersections. For the global traveller, it was possible to think of place as a relative point within an absolute structure, and for John Pinkerton, it marked the division between ancient and modern geography and a chance accurately to describe the location of Scotland: 'How could the ancients take longitudes, or latitudes, with any exactness? Ptolemy's geography of Scotland is, above all singularly defective.'[45] And for the national geographer, like John Sinclair, the local could also be a position – a statistical synecdoche for a nation understood as an economic system.

A socially contingent north, identified through metonymy, myth and local observation, calls upon literature and cultural history as geographical markers.[46] We have already seen in the first part of this chapter a number of examples of the mythic or legendary north, easily portable between Scotland and Norway, or Scythia and Sarmatia, or Britain as a whole and Scotland in particular. As I will argue in subsequent chapters, the 'North Countree' of the ballads could be either part of, or distinct from, the ancient nation of Caledonia, and, in the tangle of competing histories of language origins, 'north' could refer to the entire body of Gomerian peoples (descendants of Noah's son Japhet who had populated Europe) or a specific dialect of English. Needless to say, these structures rarely maintain a strict opposition. The deterministic north and its shifting, imaginary counterpart are really the same place, each expression depending on and merging with the other. The distinction between a climatically determined north and south, seemingly a scientific pattern, is itself dependent on Eurocentric assumptions. The 'torrid zone', for example, a commonplace phrase in poetry, was technically the area between the tropics of Cancer and Capricorn, and thus equally northern and southern, but the phrase is usually shorthand for the south because it was south of Europe. A single north–south opposition, because it is clearly bipolar, holds out a temptingly scientific certainty but one that can be difficult to sustain amid cultural theories that also drew on the less geographically exact terminology of east and west. William Falconer, author of the most substantial British work on climate, insists on an absolute north–south divide:

Some writers have made a distinction between those people who live towards the East or West. But this is of no consequence; and the differences they remark, may be ascribed to other causes. The distinctions of this kind, found in the ancient writers, which are in some measure still kept up in modern expression, evidently refer to a difference in climate. The ancients looked upon the East, as well as the South, as the region of heat, from the countries in that quarter, with which they were acquainted, lying in a hot climate.[47]

The theory that poetry has its origin in a mystical eastern location is less commonly articulated than, and often subsumed in, the more visible, polarising geography of north and south. Thomas Warton, a subscriber to the theory of eastern origins, starts his dissertation 'On the Introduction of Learning into England' with the observation that, 'The irruption of the northern nations into the western empire about the beginning of the fourth century, forms one of the most interesting and important periods of modern history.'[48] It is the ancient north that produces modern society.

I would now like to turn to two poems (both by Scottish writers) which illustrate not only the recurrence and range of northerliness in British writing of the period but also the mixed, or sometimes even contradictory, modes that produce this idea of Britain's northern identity. First is Robert Colvill's Ode 'On the Winter-Solstice' (1765).[49] In many ways, this is a conventionally patriotic poem, volunteering the ideas that all nations love Britain under the benign rule of King George, literature in English is superior to all others, and God is Heaven's Architect. As a progress poem, it traces the flight of the muses from Parnassus, to England, and then to Scotland. Colvill relies on conventional geographical structures but does so with a particular exuberance as he dispatches his freewheeling muse to survey and compare states of existence in different global regions. Influenced by Thomson's *Winter*, Colvill's perspective is even more airborne as his muse sweeps above the globe, observing zones and peoples. This global perspective draws on different modes of geographical representation. On the one hand, Colvill's north is a vision of hostile vistas and frozen oceans, drawn from Gothic art and imaginary landscapes. On the other, he confidently predicates his global distinctions on the scientific certainties of climate.

Despite its global range, Colvill's poem assumes itself to be set in a generally northern location and is a useful example of the sense of northernness as a defining subjectivity. In the broadest of senses, the north, in Romantic-period Britain, was where 'we' are. This was confirmed at a quotidian level by representations on maps and globes and by travel directions: the hemispheric north is where one travels from. It is at the top of the map or compass, at eye level on a globe, in a specific space which is the same as that which we occupy. It is what is 'there' compared with the newly discovered, or as yet unmapped seas and islands of the south. Colvill's geography establishes, on the one hand, a globe determined by its physical chorography, mathematically accountable and divisible into equal northern and southern components, and, on the other, a cultural north which has a different structure from the south. The north is the location from which culture precedes, legible not only because of its distinction from the south but also because the north is itself the centre of knowledge, containing within it all the social and natural distinctions which define human life and of which the south is the other. The poem's first line establishes seasonal variation itself – Rousseau's primary cause of history – as a northern quality: 'Hail Winter! hail grim tyrant of the North!'[50] The north is a position from which it is possible to understand how people are distributed over the globe according to climatic variation.

In a structure drawn from climate theory, Colvill contrasts the plague-ridden, hot South and its inevitably enslaved populations with the free peoples of the colder north:

> O lands unbless'd! where fev'rish strife
> Embroils the purple tide of life:
> Where banish'd from the breezy North
> Devouring Pest'lence oft walks forth:
> Where Freedom's joys are sought in vain,
> While savage tyrants sternly reign;
> And never heard, their subjects cry,
> As vex'd beneath the scourge, of their inclement sky. (p. 7)

The south is the opposite of the north but also contained within it in a sort of north–south version of Orientalism. Colvill imagines a second south, in contradistinction to the social, readable one, about which nothing can be known. This is a south where nothing lives, whose horrors are 'unknown', and from where northern explorers are repelled. Colvill calls upon his muse to sing

> What horrours dire, unknown, may vex th'antartic sky.
> When northern climes returning summers hail,
> There heavy darkness holds her dreary reign:
> [. . .]
> Ill fated he who tempts the shore,
> That BRITAIN's daring navy tore;
> When caught on Winter's raging main
> Bold ANSON's art was all in vain [. . .]. (pp. 6–7)

This south is a mythological place that defeats not only individual explorers but also science itself. The British Navy's modern 'art', its systems of navigation during George Anson's 1740–4 circumnavigation of the globe, are no match for the infernal moral lessons of South America:

> Where dreadful storms defend the coast,
> Of burning flame, and starving frost;
> Infernal plagues and horrous dire,
> To guard forbidden climes, and damp Ambition's fire. (p. 7)

Coming at the beginning of my period, Colvill's doubled geography sets a pattern which we can detect at various points in the subsequent decades. A Eurocentric north both produces the systematic structures of navigation that seem to give geographic mastery of the globe but also undermines the possibility of a global geometry by imagining a local or mythological north, unfettered by precise locations. In my next poem, published nearly fifty years after Colvill's, we can see how these two modes of location produce modern Europe, and where Scotland's own northerly position resides.

The recognition that Britain was a northern nation, already emerging in literature and antiquarian histories, is given a further, modern political context in the geographies of Britain's involvement in the European wars of the Napoleonic era. At a time when national and imperial boundaries were under attack or dispute, the assumed underlying geographies of climatic distribution could shift with them to address political claims and notions of national identities. We can see how these flexible geographies operate in Anne Grant's patriotic poem *Eighteen Hundred and Thirteen*, written in response to Anna Letitia Barbauld's poorly received *Eighteen Hundred and Eleven* (1812) which had been hostile to British military policy and had prophesied the end of the British commercial empire. In Barbauld's poem, as Suvir Kaul has noted, neither Europe nor its constituent nations are named, and the work has an abstract, even ahistorical quality.[51] But where Barbauld looks forward to the symbolic rise of a new order of liberty in the west of the New World, the Scottish Grant employs a complex and highly detailed geographical scheme to reassert the dominance of the British north, with Scotland as its *locus classicus*.

Eighteen Hundred and Thirteen does not have the sophistication of Barbauld's poem – it is a long work with a tendency to ramble, but it is this rambling that allows Grant to shape or reconfigure European and British correspondences and geographies without too strict an adherence to causality. The poem works by means of unannounced shifts, digressions and juxtapositions which can blur geographical positions, and even historical figures, into each other, and, in doing so, demonstrates some of the qualities of the north, as it is produced by British writers, that I have been describing in this chapter. First, Grant moves her geographical discourses between what we might loosely call Rousseau's north and Pope's north; that is, between a scientific, environmental division, and an imaginary inscription. Second, *Eighteen Hundred and Thirteen* shows how these discourses shade into each other and are contingent and political. The poem slips between geography and metaphor, between military events and a cultural imaginary, and between a politically determined and an idealistically realised Britain. Grant's north is one produced both by scientific and by imaginative discourses, the two repeatedly taking each other's places. And finally, Grant, herself a patriotic Scottish author, exploits Britain's and Scotland's own northerly positions to establish the north as the pre-eminent political and cultural place to be.

The poem maps out French-dominated Europe with clear, visual brushstrokes, imagining a quantifiable globe with natural markers and divisions, a fixed, visible north and south with distinct climates:

> From where the North pours forth his waste of snow
> To where the Sun his brightest beam bestows,
> From the chill regions of eternal frost,
> To Nature's garden, fair Italia's coast [. . .].[52]

In her account of Napoleon's retreat from Moscow, Grant, in common with many early eighteenth-century writers, draws a parallel with Charles of Sweden's Russian campaign.[53] Yet she emphasises not only the historic parallel but also the difference between Charles's 'iron Swedes, to polar climes inured' who lasted longer and displayed a more heroic resistance to the 'frozen soil' of northern Europe than Napoleon's French, who put up a much poorer show:

> Like timorous deer, who midst the smothering snows
> Fall thick beneath Siberian hunters' blows,
> Gay, boastful children of a southern sky,
> Low sunk on earth the Gallic squadrons lie.
> [. . .]
> Though o'er their heads the shifting splendours fly,
> The bright Aurora of a northern sky,
> No genial heat these vivid beams impart
> To thaw the life-blood curdling round the heart [. . .]. (p. 16)

The repeated rhymes and the parallelism of 'southern sky' and 'northern sky' make use of the polarisation of climate theory. The message is clear that it is the French Army's southern characteristics – national pride and personal vanity together with lack of physical courage – that fail them in a northerly climate. These were precisely the characteristics ascribed to them by William Falconer who claimed that southern nations suffered from an excess of pride, manifesting itself in the French as a form of vanity, which makes them particularly unattractive in war:

Strabo describes the vanity of the French nation, and its effects on their conduct, in terms that exactly suit their present character. They have, says that writer, added to their ignorance and ferocity, a great degree of arrogance and folly, and affectation of ornament. [. . .] In consequence of this levity of disposition, they are, when superior in war, extremely insolent and overbearing; but when defeated, stupid and helpless.[54]

Although Grant's Europe is in this sense zonally fixed, in another sense, it is geographically very flexible indeed. 'Britain' is at once a northern nation and outside spatial and temporal restrictions altogether. It becomes a transhistorical force with the power (in a quotation from Gray) to pass 'the flaming bounds of space and time' (p. 6). Because Britain is a nation of colonisers, Britishness is not confined to a particular geographical location but rather becomes a free-floating concept, generated by but not restricted to location.

The poem's northerly focus is, in fact, its most surprising aspect as all of Wellington's victories in 1813 had been in southern Europe. In June of that year, he had broken the back of the French presence in Spain at the Battle of Vitoria, and the following month had seen off Marshal Soult's counter-offensive through the Pyrenees at the Battle of Sorauen. Finally, the long-drawn-out Peninsular War, so costly to the British taxpayer, had been settled in favour of Britain. Yet, these events are contracted into a single verse-paragraph, which they are obliged to share with General Moore's heroic death at Corunna in 1809. What seems to be more important to Grant is the Allied victories in northern Europe, but, as the poem's hero Wellington omitted to take part in any of them, the poem has to perform an imaginative leap in order to install Britain as a pre-eminent northern nation. Wellington is manoeuvred into a symbolic northerly position by a trick of metaphor. His Spanish victories are summarised. The local resistance seem hopeless:

> Till Wellington to head the conflict came,
> With cool experience sprinkling Valour's flame;
> And British legions lent their tempered fire
> To rash resolves that blaze but to expire. (p. 13)

The poem then detours through an extended metaphor in which Wellington's pyrogenetic activities are compared to a forest fire which lies dormant for a season before reappearing, in the style of James Thomson, to the amazement of the 'baffled rustic':

> By British aid an impulse thus was given
> To sparks enkindled by the breath of Heaven.
> The new-born glories send a lustre forth,
> Guild Europe's gloom, and warm the frozen North:
> The germ of future conquest nourished here,
> Expanding, flourished in this wondrous year [. . .]. (p. 14)

The poem thus locates European identity as a war played out in the north, but a north brought into existence by a British originary presence. Written after the Battle of Leipzig (the so-called 'Battle of the Nations') of October 1813, the poem inserts Britain into a Europe defined by its northern powers: the armies of Sweden, Russia, Austria and Prussia, 'the stern avengers of the North' (p. 25) who defeated the French at Leipzig, as well as earlier encounters between the Swedish, Poles, and Russians (pp. 30–1). The modern north is seen to replay the history of the classical south, but with greater honour, strength and unity. Austria, Sweden and Russia form a triumvirate that outlasts and outperforms the betrayals of the Roman model in which each member 'Gave up his best-loved friend to bloody fate' (p. 31). In contrast to weakened imperial Rome, the Northern allies stand as a model for national organisation and cooperation:

> Not so this union of consenting power,
> Like stars that meet in some propitious hour,
> Combine in happiest aspect all their rays,
> And see the lower world delighted gaze. (p. 32)

Having by these various means established Britain as Top Northern Nation, Grant moves Scotland more specifically into her geographical schema. Here again we can pause to see how the development of Scotland as the British north had changed a great deal since the days of the *North Briton*. A northerly climate had been used to target the Scots as backward and starving, unable to progress beyond their environmental limits. Charles Churchill's *Prophecy of Famine* (dedicated to his friend Wilkes), casts his Scottish peasants as naked and helpless in the face of their 'native' climate:

> *Here*, for the sullen sky was overcast,
> And summer shrunk beneath a wintry blast,
> A native blast, which arm'd with hail and rain
> Beat unrelenting on the naked swain [. . .].[55]

The best that can be said for Jockey and Sawney, the heroes of Churchill's mock epic, is that they are 'from their youth enur'd to winter-skies' and have no desire for the fancy clothes they are unable to afford in the first place.[56] But in Grant's poem to be 'to polar climes inured' (p. 15) is a good thing. In these circumstances, to be northern is to be strong and martial – both qualities celebrated in the model of the Scottish soldier and typified by the Highland Regiments raised for the British Army in the years following the Jacobite rebellion. More than just a means of strengthening the armed forces for the wars with France, this was also a way of incorporating and absorbing into cultural conformity the earlier myth of the savage Highland warrior. Wilkes had cast the Scot as an unpleasant mixture of servility and aggression, and the Jacobite rebellion as an attempt to enslave the British nation. The English were obliged to deal with 'their fellow subjects of *Scotland*, who were forging chains for both nations; and, worse than the infamous Cappadocians of old, not only refused the liberty they might enjoy themselves, but endeavoured to entail *their* vassalage and slavery onto the whole island.'[57] Yet, by the following decade, although Wilkesite anti-Scottish prejudice persisted throughout the century, the Scots had come also to stand for the opposite of their characterisation in the *North Briton*. Robert Colvill's *The Caledonians* (1779) offers a typical example. Thirty-three years after the Jacobite threat had been defeated, the Caledonian soldier can be recast as a protector of the island against external invasion rather than the cause of internal wars:

> Oft has the blood-stain'd Caledonian sword
> Repell'd Invasion from her sea-girt shore;
> In fields of death bright Liberty explor'd;
> Her gifts redeem'd from fang of lawless pow'r.[58]

And just before the publication of Grant's poem, Walter Scott's *The Vision of Don Roderick*, written in celebration of the French retreat in 1811, singles out the Scottish soldier for praise:

> And O! loved warriors of the Minstrel's land!
>   Yonder your bonnets nod, your tartans wave!
> The rugged form may mark the mountain band,
>   And harsher features, and a mien more grave;
> But ne'er in battle-field throbb'd heart so brave,
>   As that which beats beneath the Scottish plaid [. . .].[59]

Although Grant is unable to manoeuvre a company of Scots to Leipzig (or rather omits their likely but unheroic presence as mercenaries), they are nevertheless instrumental in restoring a proper distribution of European power, again through their northern situation. In the 1760s, Wilkes had viewed the Scottish influence at Westminster as a destabilising pressure on British power in relation to Europe: the 'North British administration' is likely, in his view, to strike up unpropitious associations with other European powers, particularly with Britain's old enemy, but Scotland's older ally, France. An imbalance of power within Britain will, he claims ironically through his Scottish editor, reconfigure 'the whole continent':

I will only add, how greatly must this island, and above all *our dear country*, now figure to the whole continent? The most real union among all the parts of government, and the whole body of the English nation, no less joined with us in *hearts* than in *interests*, rising up, like one man, to support the new *Scottish* pillar of the state! What satisfaction has the *Czar* expressed in our *firm* and *united* councils! What unbounded confidence has the *King of Prussia* in this new *North British* administration! and with what unfeigned rapture will *France* receive the news that there is no longer a first minister in this island from their *ancient enemy* England; but from their firm and unshaken ally, SCOTLAND.[60]

Grant's poem, by contrast, configures a Scotocentric Europe as the very model of political stability and national independence as she dwells on connections between Britain and Holland, using the latter as a unifying, mediating influence on England and Scotland as northern nations. Grant describes the exile in Britain of the Prince of Orange, son of William V, and his education not only in Cambridge (scene of 'The deep researches of the British mind') but also on a visit to Scotland, inspired by Scott's narrative poem *The Lady of the Lake*: 'The poet's song thy wandering footsteps drew, / Till all Loch Catrine opened to thy view' (p. 42). From here, it a short step for Grant to insert Scotland into the centre of her vision of free Europe as she describes the restoration of the Dutch monarchy following the revolt against French rule:

> Led to the contest by the gallant Graham,
> Who sheds new lustre on that splendid name,
> To friends as dear, as terrible to foes,
> As Scotland's pride and ornament, Montrose,
> The Orange Standard shall one more advance
> To carry terror to the heart of France. (p. 45)

The modern-day heroic Scot is Thomas Graham, Baron Lynedoch, who had previously appeared as one of the hero commanders in *The Vision of Don Roderick*. In Scott's poem, Graham (Scott calls him 'Graeme' to emphasise the Scottish pronunciation) is a global warrior, equipped to fight 'from clime to clime' although Scotland is always 'his thought in march and tented ground'.[61] In Grant's epic, the universal martial Scot takes on more specific geographical qualities. Although suffering from ill health, Graham had reluctantly commanded a British force to secure the return to the Netherlands of the Prince of Orange. Contrary to Grant's rousing account, the expedition was an uncertain one; Graham's army was assembled hastily out of substandard units not deemed good enough for Wellington, and, although victorious at Merxem, he failed to take the fortress of Bergen-op-Zoom and sustained heavy losses.[62] Undeterred by these events, Grant enhances not only Thomas Graham's reputation but also that of James Graham, Earl of Montrose, commander of the Royalist faction in the civil war in Scotland. With typical sleight of hand, Grant manages to combine not only the two Grahams but also, more startlingly, a seventeenth-century Royalist, fighting for the Stuart family, with the very House of Orange who would supplant them. Scotland's divided past is smoothed out; Montrose, also known less flatteringly as 'Bloody Claverhouse' for his suppression of the Covenanters, is here an unequivocally modern hero; any trouble involving the Stuarts is obliterated; and the ideal figure of the military Scot takes centre stage in routing the French and restoring Europe to its northern hegemony, typified in the alliance between Scotland and the Netherlands.

In an updating of the Progress of Poetry mode, Grant imagines a Europe whose southern regions have fallen silent in response to the oppression of the Napoleonic Empire. Only the mountains of northern Spain (newly liberated by Wellington) can raise an 'unpremeditated song' of liberty, but, as the ancient muses had discovered, this song cannot be sustained and, 'like a passing vision, melts in air' (p. 95). But all is not lost: immediately afterwards, the music of liberty transfers to Britain, replete with the mythic history of its 'constellation of high-gifted bards' (p. 95) and the first three stops on this modern literary progress are the banks of the Teviot in Scotland, scene of the old 'high heroic song' of the ballads, next Lord Byron on a visit to 'his Scottish grandsires' (p. 95) and then Scott, in his 'wizard Minstrel' guise (p. 100). Ancient Scotland is the cultural touchstone for modern northern Britain, dominant in the political order of Europe. *Eighteen Hundred and Thirteen* ends with Britain's hand adjusting the scales of European power, as peace 'To Europe all its wonted bounds restores' (p. 144), and the geographical contortions of the poem are assumed to be resolved. Grant's Europe then is both a cultural and a physical space, its north–south divisions claiming a material, somatic inevitability that underscores Scotland's claims for political and artistic importance and, by means of Grant's literary conjuring tricks, moving a seemingly peripheral northern nation to the centre.

North Britain, then, can erase or extend its boundaries to accommodate the political and cultural purposes of Scottish authors. It is always at least two places at the same time: both Scotland and Britain, an ancient or imaginary space and a modern political force, synecdochal for north-ernness in general and a singular position generating its own national character. In the subsequent chapters, we shall see how the demands made upon this extendable, flexible geography produce Scotland as a doubled locality whose relations to systems of placing demonstrate the problematic spatiality of national contours in the period.

CHAPTER 2

Burns, place and language

James Currie, the biographer and first editor of Robert Burns, associates the distinctive character of Scottish song with a sense of place:

Many of the love-songs of Scotland describe scenes of rural courtship; many may be considered as invocations from lovers to their mistresses. On such occasions a degree of interest and reality is given to the sentiments, by the spot destined to these happy interviews being particularized. The lovers perhaps meet at the *Bush aboon Traquair,* or on the *Banks of Etrick;* the nymphs are invoked to wander among the wilds of *Roslin,* or *the woods of Invermay.*[1]

Currie's juxtaposition of 'interest' (the application of a personal feeling) and 'reality' (the recognition of an external condition) introduces an idea that highlights the unstable nature of Romantic place as he suggests that the local may not just be familiar and thus specific to those who live there, but may also exemplify familiarity itself as a general principle. Although it was unlikely that most British readers in 1800 had much empirical acquaintance with the banks of Ettrick, the fact that songs may be set there confers on them, according to Currie, a sense of 'reality'. This in turn calls up the position of North Britain within Great Britain: on the one hand, Scotland is geographically other, a place of curiosity to inspire the external reader's 'interest', while, on the other, Scottish places are imbued with the universal inner 'reality' of nature that underpins the social organisation of modern Britain through sensibility and neoclassicism: 'these rustic bards [. . .] are guided by the same impulse of nature and sensibility which influenced the father of epic poetry.'[2] And, of course, no rustic bard exemplified this more than Robert Burns, whose growing status as an icon of locality drew attention to the place of Scotland in the national cultural geography of Britain and to places within Scotland as forms of the local.

Early accounts of Burns, however, had difficulty in squaring the circle of Burns's universal localness. Currie seems to have been a little embarrassed by Burns's choice of local landmarks, asserting that their specific identity can be sublimated into something more general and, by consequence, 'superior':

Many of [Scotland's] rivers and mountains, formerly unknown to the muse, are now consecrated by his immortal verse. The Doon, the Lugar, the Ayr, the Nith, and the Cluden, will in future, like the Yarrow, the Tweed, and the Tay, be considered as classic streams, and their borders will be trod with new and superior emotions.[3]

Henry Mackenzie's 1786 unsigned encomium in the *Lounger* was the review that made Burns's name, but despite his claim that one of the new poet's names was 'the Ayrshire Ploughman', Mackenzie knew that precisely to locate Burns for a wider British market required some careful adjustment of geographical terms:

The person to whom I allude is ROBERT BURNS, an *Ayrshire* Ploughman, whose poems were some time ago published in a country-town in the west of Scotland, with no other ambition, it would seem, than to circulate among the inhabitants of the county where he was born, to obtain a little fame from those who had heard of his talents. I hope I shall not be thought to assume too much, if I endeavour to place him in a higher point of view, to call for a verdict of his country on the merit of his works, and to claim for him those honours which their excellence appears to deserve.[4]

Burns is to be introduced, according to the title of the review, as an 'original genius' as if his poetic talents sprang directly from a specific place. But rather than clarifying Burns's position, Mackenzie's spatial terms and metaphors, as he seeks to 'place [Burns] in a higher point of view', shift between localities and meanings. As the Ayrshire Ploughman, he is intimately related to the soil itself, rooted in a particular material locality. Yet, he is also bounded by arbitrary administrative borders, the 'county where he was born'. The repeated word 'country' shifts in meaning from *rural* to *national,* suspending Burns somewhere between autochthonic 'original genius' and a new status as National Bard. The question of where Burns is thus introduces a tension into the earlier eighteenth century's smooth absorption of a fertile, productive, aristocratic landscape into national identity. As rural locality becomes associated with emotions and private virtues, it raises the question of singularities that cannot easily be subsumed into larger political structures. As I discussed in the Introduction, the local emerges against the background of the eighteenth-century impulse to understand space through macro-structures. Coupled with growing interest in social diversity, geographic theory seeks to explain local difference through global structures in the division of the globe into climatic zones, consolidated into an opposition between north and south and their attendant forms of social and somatic determinism.

This chapter traces Burns's participation in three overlapping ways of thinking about late-eighteenth-century geographical context. First is the idea of place in its preliminary form: the nuts and bolts of location itself, the task of differentiating one place from another, and the even more difficult question of isolating place from a wider concept of space. The second section then looks at Burns's involvement in conjectures about systematic geography and climatic zones and his engagement with eighteenth-century theories that attempt to read the singular either through its local associations and sensibilities or through its position in global structures of scientific determinism. Finally, I explore the relations of the local and the national in the geographies of language itself and Burns's response to linguistic theories that traced the movement of speech from south to north. In all these contexts, we can see how Burns resists and complicates the models of placing that sought to divide and structure the globe.

INSCRIPTION

Eight years before the publication of Burns's *Poems, Chiefly in the Scottish Dialect*, James Dunbar, Professor of Moral Philosophy at Aberdeen, imagined the first speech of 'a mind, somewhat elevated above common life'. This representative rational subject poses first of all the question: 'Where am I! Whence my original! What my destiny! – Is all around me discord, confusion, chaos! or is there not some principle of union, consistency, and order?'[5] The primary knowledge sought by Dunbar's ideal speaker raises the question of being in a specific place – the fundamental question 'Where am I?' – but it is immediately followed up by the recognition that place can only be understood by its position in a structure. What, for Dunbar, was a question about natural theology is also a problem of spatiality that has very contemporary resonances. 'Place', in a formal sense, is not an easy concept to think about. Place demands distinctions, otherwise everywhere would be experienced as the same, yet the borders that define it are always porous and provisional. Despite our knowledge that maps are always arbitrary, place nevertheless seems to require physical contiguities and meetings. As Doreen Massey has pointed out, the popular definition of place tends to shade towards 'community', but communities, unlike places, do not need to be identified by means of locality.[6] Similarly, 'region', as the name implies, evokes a specific form of regiment or government to demarcate it, whereas our ability to experience 'place' does not depend on its specific political organisation.[7] Burns provides us with models for thinking about both these terms – his tax-afflicted drinking companions in Poosie Nansie's and other hostelries, or the figure of Coila, the muse appointed to Ayrshire. But the idea of place also holds out for him the possibility of the ahistorical, the synchronic and the spatial, the chance of identifying a locality understood not only through the contingencies of history.

We should be careful about thinking in terms of Burns as a 'local' poet, not least because of the extremely flexible uses to which that term has been put in Burns's afterlife. Along with all the paraphernalia of the Victorian reinvention of Scotland that persist today, Burns is pressed into service to stand for various divisions: Scotland in general, the Lowlands, and the south-west of the country. Another danger presents itself if we associate Burns's locality with his status as labouring-class poet and both with a nostalgic sense of ideal community. This is place imagined as the lived, the empirical and the communicable, the place of shared experience, and tends to be defined in contradistinction to an abstract 'space' of alienation:

In pre-modern societies, space and place largely coincide, since the spatial dimensions of social life are, for most of the population, and in most respects, dominated by 'presence' – by localised activities. The advent of modernity increasingly tears space away from place by fostering relations between 'absent' others, locationally distant from any given situation of face-to-face interaction.[8]

The lure of 'face-to-face interaction' is – here, explicitly – its logocentrism, the belief in the immediate, communicable vitality of speech and the sense of loss that comes with the absence of projected otherness. But the case of Burns underscores how impossible it is to preserve these distinctions. In his songs, apparently imitative of the kind of 'pre-modern' modes of which Anthony Giddens writes above, the face-to-face is already imbricated in the absent other. 'The Northern Lass', as traditional a love song as any of Burns's, draws hypotheses of global absence: 'Though cruel fate should bid us part, / Far as the Pole and Line' (123, ll. 1–2).[9] 'On a Scotch Bard Gone to the West Indies' explicitly predicates the '*merry roar*' (100, l. 9) of social interaction in a community defined by its localised activities on an imaginary future absence in another hemisphere – here, Burns's own projected but never realised emigration to Jamaica.

Burns still finds himself with a double reputation for being the most famous local poet who is also expected to deliver sentiments of universal application.[10] Such a structure of equivalence usually identifies each term with the other: Burns is universal *because* he is also local, each singular locality being alike in its very singularity, untouched by the differentiating and alienating forces of history and politics. Burns speaks, to put the matter in the most commonplace of eighteenth-century terms, with the voice of nature. The local identity of the Ayrshire Ploughman rests on two prior problems: how can the singularity of any place emerge from a perceptual field, and how can this singularity be made known in textual form? To understand these questions, we need to look not only at Romantic ideas about the creative imagination and its topographic function but also at the evolution of ideas about place, writing and difference throughout the eighteenth century.

Burns has many ways of inscribing location. 'Tam O' Shanter' alone uses a strikingly wide range of referents: technical measurement (the 'lang Scots miles' [321, l. 7] between the inn and home); local narrative (the place 'Whare *Mungo*'s mither hang'd hersel' [321, l. 96]); European comparisons (the witches' dance is 'Nae cotillion brent new frae *France*' [321, l. 116]); and the location of natural phenomena expressed as a global direction (the 'borealis race' [321, l. 63]). The poem reminds its readers that place is a matter of selective delimitation and that the possibility of a discrete space defined absolutely by its boundaries is purely imaginary, occurring only in the supernatural world where evil spirits cannot cross running water. Burns's own representations of a named locality are adaptable, and even Coila, his local muse and descendant of many generations of poetic *genii loci*, is not as easily 'bounded to a district-space' (62, l. 193) as she claims to be in 'The Vision'. Coila does not embody locality so much as screen it; her representation of localised Scotland is projected onto her mantle in a bewildering scene that evokes not the bounded nature of the 'district-space' but the openness of the sublime: 'Here, rivers in the sea were lost; / There, mountains to the skies were tost' (62, ll. 73–4). This is not the sublime as moment of origin but rather a prior inscription; as muse, Coila does not provide a spark of inspiration but a strategic link to the written past and to places already in '*Scottish Story* read' (62, l. 87). Locality cannot be experienced at first hand but only as a literary structure, and, in fact, Burns has already identified Coila's territorial delimitation not as a positive value but as an empty space as yet undiscovered by Scottish writers. In the verse epistle to William Simson of Ochiltree, Burns laments that Ayrshire, again identified with Coila, has not been recognised by earlier poets:

> She lay like some unkend-of isle
>   Beside New Holland,
> Or whare wild-meeting oceans *boil*
>   Besouth *Magellan*. (59, ll. 39–42)

The as-yet-unwritten is a space already cleared by writing; indeed, Ayrshire's 'unkend-of' status can only be made known *through* writing. In topographical terms, the pre-existence of Coila's territory can only be understood in the geographic discourses of eighteenth-century exploration: a globe mapped by the names of its surveyors and a New World imprinted with the names of the Old.

The shifts in this poem between a narrowly identified point (Ayrshire) and a global expanse (the newly mapped continent of Australia, then known as New Holland, and the Southern Ocean) are frequent in Burns's poetry as he restlessly considers the markers by which place can be read. His references to recent exploratory activities in the South Seas draw attention to eighteenth-century concerns about geographical organisation and navigation: the possibility of knowing at what 'point' one might be situated on a global structure, a particularly pertinent question for late-eighteenth-century Britain as it consolidated its naval powers after the fixing of the measurement of longitude.[11] The ship-board chronometer allowed the globe not only to be mapped but also to be isotopically fixed with imaginary lines that gave the impression of objective precision, and drew time into the service of place to create an apparently stable, navigable structure. Such mathematisation of space reminds us of divergences in the idea of place in the second half of the eighteenth century. New confidence in a globe that could be 'accurately' mapped as spatial extension renders place as a point or position in unified space. But, as I have argued, the sense of the formal, mappable unity of global space is coterminous with the emergence of place as locality, known not by its formal position but by its unique relation to the experiencing subject. This tension raises questions about empiricism and epistemology: can spatial relations offer structural certainties that transcend any particular moment of experience? Or can place be understood *only* through experience? One set of answers to these large philosophical questions can be found in a surprisingly small textual place: eighteenth-century inscription verse.

The fashion for the inscription of verses onto physical objects – trees, rocks, seats, windows – constitutes what Geoffrey H. Hartman has called 'a dependent form of poetry [. . .] conscious of the place on which it was written'.[12] We might further say that it is the place that is dependent on the poetry, its singularity an effect of the writing that calls it into being. This acts as an attempt to establish 'place' as it is defined by Michel de Certeau when he writes that '[a] place (*lieu*) is the order (of whatever kind) in accord with which elements are distributed in relationships of coexistence. It thus excludes the possibility of two things being in the same location (*place*)'.[13] The act of inscription, then, identifies the place as singular and unique. At the same time, it works against any principle of rigorous exclusion; the apparent homology of place and writing in fact sets up an imaginary interiority which has already been breached by the very process which calls it into being. In order to recognise any place or point, there must already be a *structure* of identification. The role of the inscription as signpost or guide drives a wedge between subject and object, reminding the viewer of the external ways of seeing that make the scene comprehensible and of the gaze that disrupts the calm unity of place and writing.

Hartman goes on to argue that with its development by Wordsworth, the poetry of nature-inscription undergoes an imaginative transformation that binds text and place in an ideal coexistence with the Romantic observer/author: '[t]he setting is understood to contain the writer in the act of writing: the poet in the grip of what he feels and sees, primitively inspired to carve it in the living rock'.[14] But Burns's inscriptions are not like this. They form an uneasy and disparate set that seems to recognise the impossible ends of the inscription form. Some follow the customary eighteenth-century pattern of summoning up a particular moment to describe a highly conventional scene. A poem with the title 'Written with a Pencil over the Chimney-Piece, in the Parlour of the Inn at Kenmore, Taymouth' (169) invites the reader to contemplate the unique moment of its inscription, yet this leads to a very standard prospect of Augustan nature with a homily on how the personifications of human experience can find solace in landscape. Other poems displace their original setting by turning it into a metaphor for the afterlife. 'Verses Written on a Window of the Inn at Carron' expresses the hope that the failure of Burns's party to obtain entry to the inn may be a sign of things to come: 'Sae may, shou'd we to hell's yetts come, / Your billy Satan sair us!' (165, ll. 7–8). Four 'Lines Written in the Kirk of Lamington' make the same move, complaining about the coldness of both church and minister and warning 'Ye 'se a' be het or I come back' (256, l. 4). These poems argue not for the singularity of inscription but for its iterability – its capacity to be uttered with different significances in a different place. If Wordsworth, as Hartman argues, uses inscription-writing to bind the poet to the place, then Burns draws in the contexts of future readings to mark the impossibility of that binding.

In similar vein is 'A Verse Composed and Repeated by *Burns*, to the Master of the House, on Taking Leave at a Place in the Highlands, Where He Had Been Hospitably Entertained' in which Burns hopes that 'just [such] a Highland welcome' will be awaiting him in Heaven (173, l. 30). At three words longer than the verse itself, the title pulls the text away from its inscribing function (exaggerating a necessary process for the genre in general). The very supplementarity of the title invades the autonomy of the act of inscription: if the poem can invoke a complete synthesis of place and observer, then there should be no need of the additional layer of description. Inscription, so far from demarcating the singular locality, shows that place can never preserve a self-sufficient and discrete interiority.

While the miniature-work of Burns's inscriptions demonstrates the impossibility of a topography of presence on a small scale, he is also interested in the wider system of reference of which each individual act of inscription is a part. Burns turns to this larger scale in a poem on Scotland and its national and global positions. 'Caledonia' is a rollicking celebration of Scottish history as martial force that conceals its more complex relation to the forms of otherness that constitute nationalisms. Narrating a sequence of attempted invasions driven back by the Scots, the poem structures itself around geographical patterns of interiority and exteriority. But if nationhood is to be defined by a principle of inclusion/exclusion, then the poem renders these choices difficult, both in the question of Scotland's relation to England and Britain and in that of the possibility of any fixed geographical position in the first place. Burns's personified Caledonia is a kind of supplementary Britannia whose protecting borders describe and contain Island Britain whilst undermining the completion of Anglocentric Britain. More inward-looking than her imperial sister, Caledonia is largely concerned with resisting attacks from outside her borders in the form of Roman, English and Scandinavian onslaughts from which she emerges 'bold, independant, unconquer'd and free' (253, l. 41). Yet, in preserving this discrete existence for Scottish nationhood, the poem glosses over its earlier declaration that Caledonia is already descended from a Scandinavian source in the form of her 'grandsire, old Odin' (253, l. 11). What should be excluded from Scotland is already part of its constitution. Just as any totality represented by Britannia is undermined by Caledonia's supplementary yet necessary role, so Caledonia herself fails to preserve discrete boundaries.

The poem seeks to reconcile the myths of an originatory generation that can repeat itself in time and of eternal presence. Caledonia is, at once, within history, existing in a series of definable moments, and outside it. When Burns writes that her 'heavenly relations there fixed her reign' (253, l. 7) two readings are possible: that Caledonia's governance of Scotland descends from her divine ancestry, and that her position is fixed in space and time by a set of cosmographical and mathematical relations. 'Relations' are thus both historical and generational, and structural and synchronic. This secondary meaning is picked up again at the end of the poem when Caledonia is positioned in a right-angled triangle that seemingly reconciles time both with place and with eternity:

> For brave Caledonia immortal must be,
>   I'll prove it from Euclid as clear as the sun:
> Rectangle-triangle the figure we'll chuse,
>   The Upright is Chance, and old Time is the Base;
> But brave Caledonia's the Hypothenuse,
>   Then, Ergo, she'll match them, and match them always. (253, ll. 43–8)

Burns's apparently throw-away reference takes us towards some very large epistemological questions concerning time and space. In its Enlightenment context, the geometrical figure was an ideal object that could be known even though it had no material or empirical character at all. Both the sun and Euclidean geometry had appeared together in Hume's *Enquiry Concerning Human Understanding* as examples of different kinds of rational enquiry. The right-angled triangle, Hume argues, represents a mathematical axiom which remains true in the absence of any material examples in the observable world: 'Propositions of this kind are discoverable by the mere operation of thought, without dependence on what is anywhere existent in the universe. Though there never were a circle or triangle in nature, the truths demonstrated by Euclid would for ever retain their certainty and evidence.'[15] What is true here is not empirical fact but structure (what Hume calls 'the relation between [. . .] figures'), and he draws a categorical distinction between relations of ideas and matters of fact.[16] The latter are not relational but must seek verification outside their rational structure in the empirical world. Hume gives the example of the sun's rise: '*That the sun will not rise to-morrow* is no less intelligible a proposition, and implies no more contradiction, than the affirmation, *that it will rise*'.[17] It is only custom and experience that allow the observer to predict the sun's reappearance. From here, we are quickly in the difficult territory of cause and effect and the problems of philosophical scepticism. In Hume's terms, then, the sun is not clear at all but a matter of precarious inference.

At first glance, then, it seems that Caledonia is impervious to history, simply waiting around in eternity until she can be understood by rational method, her origins not dependent on any temporal configuration. Her status as the hypotenuse makes her equal to the territories governed by time and chance and tames and controls them, resolving both causal and accidental versions of history in a fixed and eternal stasis, much in the same way as the chronometer seemed to have achieved the resolution of time and space for navigation. But, of course, the poem is *about* history, its Humean context establishing a ground upon which abstract and transcendental structures can be seen to have a finite origin. No structure can exhaustively explain itself from within itself, in the same way that Euclidean geometry cannot be clear as the sun; to think through the possibility of a transcendental structure requires its incarnation in writing or representation. Burns announces this when he writes that the right-angled triangle is 'the figure we'll chuse' to represent Caledonia-in-history: if the triangle is really a perfect, eternal structure, then it should not have to depend on any passing poet to 'choose' it. In fact, the poem asserts, the 'figure' of the triangle is just that: a figure, a trope, an inscription. Geometry – or any ideal structure – is already inscribed in the empirical because it must be produced as writing.[18]

It is Burns's awareness of the complex structure of place that inform his engagement with the troublesome relation of empirical points, the general structures that allow them to be known, and the historical forces that give those structures their determining force. Neither a 'national' nor a 'local' bard, Burns's complex investigation of topography allows us to consider the political and epistemological structures of late-eighteenth-century geography which produce 'place' as inscription. His verse recognises that although it is impossible to think the local or particular without some form of conceptual generality, the general cannot itself act as a self-explanatory and objective totality; there is always something else at stake. What is at stake here is the whole system of Enlightenment theories of environmental determinism, the subject of my next section.

CLIMATE

As Burns was toying with the geometrics of space, a simpler form of mathematisation had become a standard way of thinking about global divisions and human societies as points on a larger structure. Throughout the eighteenth century, environmental determinism had offered itself as a way of accounting for the regional variation of peoples in a way that could also satisfy a more generalised science of man.[19] It was a way, in effect, of explaining the local through an increasing confidence in global totalities. Environmental determinism required the conceptualisation of space as a field whose divisions, or 'zones', marked a mathematical precision independent of human experience or activity. 'Climate', though tending towards its modern meaning, was still primarily a spatial term, referring to the zones between the equator and the poles rather than directly to prevailing atmospheric conditions, and thus offers a more fixed and categorical structure than might ideas about the unpredictable agency of weather.[20] Climate theory was not local or contingent but depended on a scientific and spatial overview that asserted that local difference was produced by objective global structures.

Climate theory had started as a kind of experimental positivism upon which social history could be based. Montesquieu had conducted his preliminary enquiry into the effects of heat and cold by experimenting on a sheep's tongue, but by the end of the eighteenth century the theory had taken on somatic identities as a given. Although it was still held by its supporters to give a somatic basis for empiricism, the theory being that heat relaxed the 'fibres' of the body, exposing the nerves to external influence and making the subject more susceptible to external impressions, little attention was paid to these details. Opponents claimed that climate theory had no place in empiricism or any respectable philosophy at all and that it consequently had to be passed off as a 'secret' phenomenon whose effects could never be witnessed. Hume writes disparagingly of 'qualities of the air and climate which are supposed to work insensibly on the temper,'[21] and John Millar claims that the study of physiology has not kept pace with the extravagant claims of the climatologists:

We are too little acquainted with the structure of the human body, to discover how it is affected by such physical circumstances [. . .] and in the history of the world, we see no regular marks of that secret influence which has been ascribed to the air and climate.[22]

By the end of the eighteenth century, a well-worn global network of climatic difference had been established, no longer dependent on experimental proof.

To give primacy to climate is also to acknowledge geography as the causal agent of social history. Zonal theory argued that whereas geography is determining in a primary way, history itself is a product of climate: hot countries do not have history, which is a product of cold nations. Adam Ferguson writes: 'The torrid zone, every where round the globe, however known to the geographer, has furnished few materials for history'.[23] Cold peoples are more ready to admit the influence of political history because they are less instinctively attached to custom. Peter the Great, according to William Falconer's *Remarks on the Influence of Climate*, 'accomplished an almost entire change in the manners and customs throughout the vast empire of Russia'.[24] So subordinate is history to geography that Falconer here manages to subvert with perfectly logical insouciance Hume's argument that it is political and 'moral', not physical, causes that determine human behaviour. The very possibility of political change, claims Falconer, is part of the differential structure of climate.

Despite the boundless confidence of climate theorists that their structure of global totality was immune to the vagaries of history, their strategies are always undermined by historicity itself. Even as he declares it to be a way of pointing up the 'natural' divisions of the globe, Falconer demonstrates how a scientific system is culturally specific: 'The works of the great Linnæus will always remain as the pride of northern literature. He established the utility of systematic arrangement, both in natural history and medicine' (p. 65). Falconer frequently uses the terms 'north' and 'south' as if they were homologous with 'cold' and 'hot' although his work recognises elsewhere that the poles are equidistant from the equator. This repeated straying from the rigorous binary of cold/hot, which had given climate theory its original basis in empiricism, runs throughout Falconer's book. Although he accepts that island nations were different from those with contiguous borders, the main structural force of climate theory was the bipolar axis, as it was, after all, the tilt of this axis that had brought about climatic difference in the first place.

As I noted in the previous chapter, Falconer believes that the distinction between north and south is very different from that between east and west: 'Some writers have made a distinction between those people who live towards the east or west. But this is of no consequence; and the differences they remark, may be ascribed to other causes' (pp. 169–70). But in banishing east and west to the realm of the imaginary in favour of the objective, scientific difference between north and south, Falconer is already in the territory of cultural definitions, although, despite his claim that 'England appears to be the country best fitted for observation, of any with which we are acquainted' (p. 73), he never acknowledges the relativity of the compass points produced by his Anglocentric view. North and south are as much a cultural vocabulary as east and west, and, in fact, Falconer quite often himself grafts the familiar conventions of eighteenth-century Orientalism onto his vindictive, violent, cunning, indolent southerners. The cultural significances of the Eurocentric west are equally difficult for him. American Indians, by this time already becoming identified with the imagined tribal social organisation of Goths and Celts yet seeming to confirm the racial othernesses of the south, slide into both northern and southern characteristics, and Falconer has to contain them in their separate climatic region defined as humid, living, as they did, in a country 'over-run with woods and marshes' (p. 165).

We can see this tension between geography and history in the environmental delimitation of societies. Climate theory preferred to deal with peoples rather than with nations, as the latter more clearly betrayed the fluctuating borders and arbitrary divisions that expose environmental determinism as political. From its basis in positivist empiricism, climate theory needed its conclusions to be rooted firmly in the soil. But the temptation to use it to account for modern national divisions was too great, and the partition of the globe into hot and cold regions becomes overlaid with the map of (most frequently) contemporary Europe. James Dunbar admitted that it was often hard to trace the causal history of what he called 'the hereditary genius of nations', but he nevertheless believed that 'consistent with national characteristics, are the essentials of a common nature and a common descent'.[25] For William Falconer, preferred examples are nations with conspicuous geographical characteristics such as Britain (an island) or Switzerland (mountainous), but he mixes peoples and nations fairly indiscriminately and is particularly fond of pointing out the failings of the modern French (not hot enough to be proud, or cold enough to be austere, they are mainly vain).

For a nation that was no longer a state, and whose borders were seen to contain more than one people, Scotland took a keen interest in the looser points of the otherwise taut network of climate. Despite Hume's antagonism to climatic causes, Montesquieu remained very popular in Scotland, and environment was widely discussed among historians and moral philosophers.[26] This is a debate, however, that tests the limits of the ability of the global to explain the local. James Dunbar explicitly argues: 'Local circumstances are so blended in their operation with a variety of other causes, that it is difficult to define them with such precision as were necessary to form an estimate of their comparative importance'.[27] Dunbar believed in a fixed geography, but he admits into it the possibility that political contingencies may give rise to the same location, producing different responses in different societies. Geography is thus determining, but not in uniform ways as societies learn to make use of their environments. This comparatively flexible model lent itself to literary texts in the post-Jacobite years, as Unionist Scots sought to identify the spatial and geographical relations of Britain and its consistent parts.

The position of Scotland can both reinforce and destabilise the north–south model of climate theory. On the one hand, Scotland is the very model of a northern nation. Rational, hardy and democratic, the Scot of climate theory has a much happier response to his or her physical situation than the starving or avaricious caricature of the Scotophobic pamphlets and cartoons which had circulated since the 1740s. James Beattie, for example, expresses the common tenet of climate theory that the poor soils of the north foster invention and hardiness: 'Want is the parent of industry. To obtain even the necessaries of life, where the climate is cold, and the soil untractable, requires continual exertion; which at once inures the mind to vigilance, and the body to labour.'[28] In Beattie's long poem *The Minstrel*, the young Scot Edwin receives a lengthy educational lecture on social and moral conduct from a hermit, culminating in this stanza:

> 'Tis he alone, whose comprehensive mind,
> From situation, temper, soil, and clime
> Explored, a nation's various powers can bind
> And various orders, in one Form sublime
> Of policy, that, midst the wrecks of time,
> Secure shall lift its head on high nor fear
> Th'assault of foreign or domestick crime,
> While publick faith, and publick love sincere
> And Industry and Law maintain their sway severe.[29]

The ideal Scot, then, learning about the geography of nations, takes environmental determinism ('situation, temper, soil, and clime') as a starting point, and from his observations synthesises an entire political system in 'one Form sublime' that characterises the nation, whether identified as Scotland or, as seems to be the case here, as Great Britain, with northern virtues of independence, industry and legal fairness. *The*

Minstrel uses a very typical north–south example to point up the specific merits of Scotland, whose barren hills foster health, frankness and liberty, in contrast to the greater natural riches of the diseased, treacherous south:

> With gold and gems if Chilian mountains glow;
> If bleak and barren Scotia's hills arise;
> There plague and poison, lust and rapine grow;
> Here peaceful are the vales, and pure the skies
> And freedom fires the soul, and sparkles in the eyes.[30]

Climate theory, then, valorises Scotland as North Britain by merging geography with politics – the most northerly part of a northern island becomes the most British part of Britain. But this identity depends on the very slightest of natural divisions, exposing the uneasy relations between environment and politics that climate theory had sought to clarify and fix. The 'natural character' of populations could be summoned up in a variety of guises to support differing political inflections. Scots could be, as in the Beattie example, peaceful, industrious northerners, whose concept of political freedom is expressed in social harmony. Alternatively, as the earlier association of the clans with the Jacobite rebellion came to be recast in terms of their participation in Scottish regiments in the British Army, Scots functioned as examples of a particular kind of warlike northerner. As the climatic north rubbed shoulders with the northern tribes of ancient Europe, both Celtic and Germanic people become identified with a warlike, fiercely patriotic constitution. Falconer describes: 'the warlike disposition of the people, who thought their blood ought not to be spilt, except sword in hand' (p. 96). In order to absorb the entirety of Scotland into the environmental politics of the nation, some shifting round might be required. In Smollett's *The Expedition of Humphry Clinker*, the Bramble family's journey through Scotland allows them to survey geographical variations as they move from Lowlands to Highlands, but although Matt Bramble uses the terms of climate theory, he reverses the usual north–south polarity: 'The Lowlanders are generally cool and circumspect, the Highlanders fiery and ferocious'.[31] Despite being creatures of their environment, the Highlanders do not wholly correspond to the image of the industrious northerner. Their poor land means that they have little to do in tending their free-roaming cattle:

Perhaps this branch of husbandry, which requires very little attendance and labour, is one of the principal causes of that idleness and want of industry, which distinguishes these mountaineers in their own country – When they come forth into the world, they become as diligent and alert as any people upon earth.[32]

Through a neat sleight-of-hand, it is only by removing the Highlanders from their natural climate, that their natural characteristics can be revealed and the clans can be reinserted into the political body of Great Britain: 'When disciplined, they cannot fail of being excellent soldiers'.[33]

Burns's interactions with global taxonomy of this sort were complex. He was not averse to importing well-worn zonal difference into a poem when it suited him. After visiting the Duchess of Gordon, he composed some lines to thank her for the invitation, seizing the opportunity to oppose the natural, northern freedom of Castle Gordon to the torrid zones and 'the ruthless Native's way, / Bent on slaughter, blood and spoil' (175, ll. 13–14). Similarly, the familiar trope of the political liberty of Scotland opposed to the tyranny of the south, which we saw in Beattie, makes a number of appearances: 'The SLAVE's spicy forests, and gold-bubbling fountains, / The brave CALEDONIAN views wi' disdain' (496, ll. 13–14). On the other hand, Burns has little truck with the climatologists' insistence that the inhabitants of southern regions, their passions aroused by the sun, were characterised by sexual incontinence, while the colder northerner sublimated desire into domesticity.[34] In a song making another contrast between the rapacious but enslaved south (in this case India) and the simple freedoms of the north, 'Winter's wind and rain' are no hindrance to Burns's sexual 'rapture' with the 'bony Lass o' Ballochmyle' (89, ll. 29–33). Most characteristically, Burns recognises the provisional applications of terms such as 'north' which can represent either a distinct global region, home of the North Wind or the Northern Lights, or a relative position as in 'I look to the North' (327, l. 1) where the compass points depend on the location of the speaker and her subjective history.

In the 'Epistle to Hugh Parker', Burns returns to the question of climatic location and its influence and links it with his own imaginative capacities:

> In this strange land, this uncouth clime,
> A land unknown to prose or rhyme;
> Where words ne'er crost the muse's heckles,
> Nor limpet in poetic shackles;
> A land that prose did never view it,
> Except when drunk he stacher't thro' it; (222, ll. 1–6)

The particular problems that Burns is experiencing in Ayrshire's 'clime' – drunkenness and literary inarticulacy – were qualities commonly ascribed to northern latitudes by the climate theory. William Falconer points to the failure of northern regions to achieve much in the way of literary distinction:

> Whilst sensibility and imagination distinguished the literary productions of warm climates, judgment, industry, and perseverance were no less remarkable in those of the northern. Hence it is easy to conceive, why poetry should be little cultivated in northern countries; and indeed I know of scarce any poems that have appeared there, that deserve that name. (p. 64)

Not only this, but excessive drinking was also a quality of cold countries: 'If we go from the Equator to the North Pole, we shall find this vice increasing together with the degree of latitude' (p. 37).[35] Drunkenness itself varied globally in its effects on the body: 'In a hot climate, a drunken man is absolutely frantic and wild; but in a cold one, it only renders him heavy and stupid' (p. 37). Cold-climate drunks evidently experience the kind of foggy hangover Burns describes in 'Hugh Parker'. But the poem slyly reminds its readers that the global reckoning upon which this localised difference depends is itself imaginary. In order to escape from his depressing environment, Burns projects a fantastic journey around the globe, wishing he really had the power to 'loup the ecliptic like a bar; / Or turn the pole like any arrow' (222, ll. 31–2). Poles and ecliptics (the apparent annual course of the sun as seen from the earth) are ideal positions that work at the level of mathematics: they are what enable global systems of location to be understood, and they produce local differences even when they themselves cannot be empirically determined. The 'ecliptic', however, is as imaginary as the right-angled triangle of 'Caledonia'; the perfect structure never to be found in nature can only be imagined as representation or inscription. And, of course, the status of Burns's imaginary journey as writing descends to the empirical places of the poem's local scale. The epistle to Parker is Burns's own little joke about poetry and topography: just as his inscriptions show that writing cannot become place, so here he demonstrates that place cannot determine writing. Even as he complains that a land which has never encountered poetry is deadening his own creative imagination, he is also writing a poem.

Burns's engagement with drinking, place and politics has its most sustained appearance in his two responses to the Acts that revised the taxation of spirits in Scotland in the 1780s. 'Scotch Drink' was written after the Wash Act of 1784 drew a distinction between Lowland whisky, which would be taxed by the quantity of 'wash' (produced at an early stage of fermentation) and Highland whisky, which continued to be taxed by the less reliable measure of still capacity. Burns launches into an energetic assertion of the irreducible Scottishness of Scotch Drink, regardless of any arbitrary legal geography. The national character of whisky-drinking is essential and somatic: the 'strong *heart's blood*' (77, l. 23). It is beer and whisky that bring together Scottish society: drink is 'the life o' public haunts' (77, l. 43), resolves legal arguments (77, ll. 73–8) and generally acts as the lubricant of commercial, cultural and convivial encounters:

> But oil'd by thee,
> The wheels o' life gae down-hill, scrievin,
> Wi' rattlin glee. (77, ll. 28–30)

This harmonious state of affairs, according to William Falconer, is the beneficial result of the northern nations' 'natural' affinity with drink. 'Drunkenness [. . .] is much less culpable in a cold climate, than in a hot one; as in the former the hospitable disposition of the people, and the necessity of the use of strong liquors to a certain degree, naturally lead to it' (p. 37). Following Falconer's line of reasoning, the 'natural' propensity of cold-climate dwellers to take alcohol is the foundation of their social cohesion and can be understood through the conjunction of physical reactions and social practices:

Fermented liquors have also the effect of opening the mind, and rendering social intercourse more free and chearful, and individuals more communicative. Thus it is observed by Tacitus, that the ancient Germans [. . .] used the time of drinking for that of public business, on account of the effect of the liquor in producing an elevation of the mind, and a freedom of debate and communication of sentiment.

Perhaps the greater use of these liquors may account, in general, for the greater openness and frankness of the northern nations; and also for the great degree of hospitality practised by them. (p. 250)

Falconer's extremely causal line of argument places liquor at the centre of the admirable democracy of the north and moves smoothly between a geographical origin and a political *telos*. But it is precisely this correspondence that Burns's next whisky poem challenges. The Wash Act had the effect of dramatically increasing legal whisky production in the Lowlands, which in turn alarmed gin producers in England. In order to stem the flow of whisky south, Parliament passed the 1786 Scotch Distillery Act, which imposed additional duty on spirits exported from Scotland to England. Burns's response was 'The Author's Earnest Cry and Prayer, to the Right Honorable and Honorable, the Scotch Representatives in the House of Commons' in which he complains about the restrictions imposed on Scottish liberty.

The poem plays with two forms of national representation: the somatic geography of climate and the contingent space of politics, neither of which seems to be doing its job very satisfactorily. Addressing himself to 'Ye IRISH LORDS, ye *knights* an' *squires*, / Wha represent our BRUGHS an' SHIRES' (81, ll. 1–2), Burns pitches into an extreme example of the absences upon which democracy rests. If there is always an institutional slippage between 'the people' constituted as a body and their representatives, then this is doubly so in the case of Scotland: Burns points to the fact that while members of the Anglo-Irish aristocracy could represent Scotland, the eldest sons of Scottish peers could not. But the poem is about the representation of Scotland in more ways than one. Arguing for the fair taxation of Scotch whisky, this is another take on Burns's recurrent musings about liberty and national identity, but a vexed and ultimately uncertain one that asks not only how can Scotland be represented in Parliament but also how any given locality can represent itself at all. Burns plays throughout with the fragility of 'place'. The term, in this poem, means parliamentary seat (the Scots representatives are warned about the vulnerability of their 'place' [81, l. 136]) and thus can only be filled by a representative. Yet, as in the derogatory eighteenth-century term 'placeman', the members' representative function is drawn not from the 'place' they represent but from the patron by whom they have been 'placed' in power. 'Scotland' herself keeps slipping from one representation to another: the members are invited to paint 'Scotland greetan owre her thrissle' (81, l. 37), but this picture changes in quick succession to an impoverished woman with her pocket picked, then an Amazonian soldier running 'red-wud / About her *Whisky*' (81, ll. 95–6).

The poem is ambivalent about the association of drink and democracy and dismisses the 'physical causes' of environmental theory that produced it:

> Sages their solemn een may steek,
> An' raise a philosophic reek,
> An' physically causes seek,
>   In *clime* an' *season*,
> But tell me *Whisky*'s name in Greek,
>   I'll tell the reason. (81, ll. 175–80)

Needless to say, things are not quite this simple. In his identification of Scotland with her national drink, Burns has already set foot in the 'philosophical reek' of eighteenth-century climate theory, extending his discussion of drink and taxation into the field of geography. Wine and whisky are not just arbitrary nation symbols but are rooted in the somatic influence of climate. Burns retraces the common argument that the people of hot nations were timid and enervated and thus easily enslaved by their rulers, whereas the bolder cold nations derive strength from fighting the elements (and each other):

> Let half-starv'd slaves in warmer skies,
> See future wines, rich-clust'ring, rise;
> Their lot auld Scotland ne'er envies,
>   But blyth an' frisky,
> She eyes her freeborn, martial boys,
>   Tak aff their Whisky. (81, ll. 145–50)

Yet, the poem's complex ironies cannot fix on any stable, causal linkage of national symbol with environment. The martial 'freedom' afforded by whisky soon turns into somatic determinism of a different kind: the courage of Scotland's alcohol-fortified regiments to die for the British state under 'royal GEORGE's will' (81, l. 165) at the same time as they are denied representation in the British parliament. As in *The Expedition of Humphry Clinker*, the politics of British military nationalism require some manipulation of environment if they are to encompass Scotland. If Montesquieu had set out to show how regional discontinuities of the law were formed by geography, then Burns, conversely, points to ways in which geography is an invention of the law.

LANGUAGE

Burns's sensitivity to the language of geography also colours his dealings with the geography of language. But Scotland's position in Enlightenment ideas about the global distribution of languages is a complicated one and will require some untangling before we can return to Burns. The geography of language took two intersecting courses in the eighteenth century. One traced the history of languages back to the original peopling of the Earth and studied the movement of peoples across the globe. The seventeenth-century obsession with tracking down the lost language of the Garden of Eden persisted into the eighteenth but now with a strongly social inflection onto the tribal population of the world, and, particularly, Europe. As Colin Kidd has rigorously documented, the 1770s – particularly Thomas Percy's *Northern Antiquities*, an English edition of Paul-Henri

Mallet's history of Denmark – witnessed a pulling apart of the Celts and the Goths, previously united in company with the Scythians under the general umbrella of Northern Tribes.[36] Distinctions began to be made between Celtic and Germanic peoples, and social and ethnic differences asserted. This became a fertile ground for battles about national identity based on etymology, a subject I shall discuss in Chapter 4. But the ancient peopling of the globe was now given a scientific basis as it became linked with the same somatic foundations and north–south divisions that had underpinned climate theory. The history of language cannot be explained by etymology alone but also by changes in regional variations in the way sound is produced by the human body. William Falconer draws language into his comprehensive survey of northern and southern difference:

> The serrated close way of speaking of the northern nations, may be owing to their reluctance to open their mouths wide in cold air, which must make their language abound in consonants. Whereas, from a contrary cause, the inhabitants of warmer climates opening their mouths wider, must form a softer language, abounding in vowels. (p. 116)

Even James Dunbar, who in general felt that the cultural sophistication of modern life was likely to smooth out geographic difference, exempts speech from this tendency: 'In periods [. . .] of equal refinement, the articulation and accents of the north, are, in our hemisphere distinguishable from the articulation and accents of the southern regions.' In the case of speech, climatic determinism, the 'direct and simple influence upon the organs' is primary.[37]

Nowadays, the classic account of the movement of languages from south to north is Rousseau's *Essay on the Origin of Languages*, and the *Essay* does provide a very useful and succinct summary of some Enlightenment assumptions about the geography of language which can guide us through the field. But Rousseau's was neither the only nor the best-known version of the subject in Britain in the second half of the eighteenth century, and a number of British accounts demonstrate not only the importance of the idea in Britain but also the variations imposed upon it by the geography of the country. Rousseau's narrative of language traces two trajectories: as languages move from south to north, so they move from interiority to exteriority. Speech moves from the interior of the body, where vowels and tones are generated, to the lips and teeth, which produce consonants and precise articulation, and with these physical changes language becomes colder, less animated. In geographical terms, there are clear 'general and characteristic differences between the tongues of the south and those of the north' caused by a social response to climate: 'In southern climes, where nature is bountiful, needs are born of passion. In cold countries, where she is miserly, passions are born of need and the languages, sad daughters of necessity, reflect their austere language origin.'[38]

British versions of this story follow the northward journey of language into secondariness and loss of an original essence. George Lemon, compiler of an etymological dictionary, writes of 'the muddy dialects, and impure branches of all the harsh, grating, Northern tongues'.[39] Lord Monboddo sees a gradual loss of both originality and affect as languages move north, each stage a paler and paler imitation of its predecessor until finally the course of speech reaches Lapland. Here the Laplanders replace the natural accent of the originary language with an artificial series of emphases: 'These, instead of the music of the human voice, the finest of all music, resemble the beating of a drum, having no other variation but that of loud and soft, quick and slow.'[40] The reliance of this global geography of language on speech, however, opens it up to the challenge of the local. Rousseau had argued that oral dialects are overtaken by the homogenising and alienating forces of writing:

Dialects tend to be distinguished by oral speech, while writing tends to assimilate and merge them; they all tend imperceptibly to correspond to a common pattern. The more a people read and learn, the more are its dialects obliterated, and finally they remain only as a form of slang among people who read little and do not write at all.[41]

Rousseau here buries one form of difference in another. In one sense, the nature of dialects is to be different each from the other. But this pattern of random variation is subsumed by another of determining difference: all dialects are alike in their warmth, affective quality and expressiveness. And as actual regional variation appears in British poetry, the same situation arises: the association of dialect with the oral means that Burns is both universally intelligible as the poet of feeling and (as most early reviews agreed) very difficult for the majority of readers to understand. In order to see what was at stake for Burns in the relation of the oral to the geographical, we can first set out two subjects of obvious importance to him: the position of Scotland and the case of song.

The geographical relations of England and Scotland offered one way of asserting the normalcy of English, with North Britain the clearer example of all the deficiencies of northern languages. Scots offers an obvious comparison with English – what the two languages have in common allows the differences to stand out, and Scots becomes a special case, often singled out in commentaries on English pronunciation to indicate where the anomalies lie. Although most pronunciation guides subscribe to the north–south theory of speech, this apparently inevitable linguistic progression can break down when it comes to Scottish speakers, whose language never seems quite to perform in the expected ways. The scientism of environmental determinism takes second place to the regional variations thrown up by political identities. Scots are often isolated for the metre of their speech or the length of their syllables. William Mitford comments: 'The Scots differ in this from all other people of whose pronunciation I have any knowledge, that their strong accent is a grave, and that they constantly acute the last syllable of every word.'[42]

James Adams, an English linguist, added to his guide to English pronunciation an appendix on the 'dialect' of Scotland. Adams declares: 'I enter the lists in Tartan dress and armour' and claims to be defending Scots from the tendency of other Britons to find them hilarious.[43] With friends like Adams, the Scots scarcely needed to turn to the more usual sources of Scotophobia. He finds it hard to reconcile the sounds of Scots with his general account of the northern movement of languages. Their speech is characterised neither by southern vowels nor northern consonants but seems to be unhealthily stuck in the middle, forming a disagreeable contrast with English: 'We suppress the harsh gutturals, or convert them into single consonants. The Scotch retain them; and when they affect to soften them, the articulation or sound resembles that of a deep asthma, or last rattling of a fatal quinsey.'[44] Despite his suspicions that there is something wrong with Scots' bodies, Adams concludes that they have deliberately adopted their peculiar habits of speech as an expression of their national independence and to distinguish themselves from the English:

It adds honour to their character, and weight to their words, for it is the received mode of speech deliberately adopted by the northern moiety of this great Isle, and is invested with right and title, title unalienable, antient right and propriety, locally invulnerable, founded in legitimate choice, and perpetuated by uncontrollable liberty.[45]

Adams's account of the development of language is, in general, very close to environmental determinism, and he implies that the 'bracing air of the North' was what allowed primitive speech to 'burst through the obstructed larynx', so it is all the more surprising that the bracing air of Scotland should not have cured the Scots of their asthmatic speech.[46]

Despite the strange logic of Adams's account, his conclusion – that Scottish speech has a political rather than a 'natural' origin – is instructive. Speaking, for many Scots, was already a political act as they sought to divest themselves of the 'Scotticisms' believed to hold back their progress in a united Britain. Speech marks out the Scot as an internal foreigner: 'the most polite of the Scots are distinguished more certainly in England by their speech, than any transmarine people.'[47] The naturalness of speech is a troublesome issue for 'polite' Scots. In Scotland's answer to Rousseau's history of primitive language, Lord Monboddo complicates the idea of a natural origin in the first place. On the one hand, Monboddo agrees that 'the first sounds articulated were the natural cries of men, by which they signified their wants and desires to one another.'[48] On the other, Monboddo also uses the complex organisation of animal society to disprove Rousseau's mysterious point of origin in which language marks an unidentifiable transition between nature and society where, Rousseau asserts, 'speech, being the first social institution, owes its form to natural causes alone.'[49] For Monboddo, nature is *already* socialised at a point of origin that, in Rousseau's social history, marks the descent into the evils of political institutions. In Monboddo's history, language is artificially invented, and its acquisition is coextensive with the formation of political structures. He concludes: 'I have endeavoured to shew, That no part of language, neither *matter* nor *form*, is natural to man, but the effect of acquired habit.'[50] Monboddo has to conceive a distinction between 'invention', which is natural, and 'art' which is not, moving his terms closer to the discourse of modern eloquence. If natural language is not entirely natural, then there is no reason why the desirable qualities of speech, its warmth and expressiveness, should not be incorporated in highly sophisticated socialised forms, exclusive to certain sections of Scottish society, namely those studying rhetoric at Scottish universities. In his *Lectures on Rhetoric and Belles Lettres*, Hugh Blair warns his audience, 'We must take care never to counterfeit warmth without feeling it'.[51]

The doubled 'naturalness' of speech is particularly apparent in the relations of Scotland to song. The most common characteristic of northern languages, according to the global theorists, was that they were unmusical. Monboddo ascribes regional variation in languages to what he calls a 'bodily faculty' that is even more subject to geography than it is to history:

There is one bodily faculty, which is found very defective among the northern nations, and which, if we were equal to the Greeks and Romans in every other respect, would render us unable to pronounce their language as they did, I mean the want of an ear and voice for music. The northern nations do not appear at any time to have been so musical a people as the antient Greeks and even Romans. But at present among us there are many who have no ear or voice at all for music, a thing which, I am told, is hardly known in Italy, and I believe far less among the Greeks, even degenerate as they are at present.[52]

If all northern languages were unmusical, none was more so than Scots. Thomas Sheridan, an Irish former actor, saw a ready market in middle-class Lowland Scots wishing to divest themselves of their accents and to avoid 'Scotticisms' in their discourse. His 1761 lectures in Edinburgh were given to packed houses, and, as Janet Sorensen observes, 'he was a role model who provided a living example that dialect speakers such as himself – whose language was practically "foreign" as he puts it – could achieve a carefully studied verbal agility and compelling eloquence that resulted in personal and civic betterment'.[53] In his later *Lectures on the Art of Reading*, Sheridan makes explicit the charge that Scots is 'unmusical'. Although, like the ancient Greeks, the Scots use accent (a term with a number of applications but meaning here variation in tone and pitch), the effect in the northern language is discordant and unmelodic:

It is indeed the use of these accents chiefly, which renders the northern speech so disagreeable to the ear: and yet it was to accents, or tones of the same nature; that the Greek owed that delightful melody, which captivated the ears of all who heard it spoken. The only difference is, that these accents or tones, being left wholly to chance among the Scots, are void of proportion and discordant; whereas the Greek accents, being regulated with the utmost pains and art, by that nation of Orators, obtained a musical proportion, which delighted the ear with accordant sounds.[54]

Sheridan here introduces a move away from Rousseau, but one bound up in the social history of speech in Scotland. The elocutionists adopt Rousseau's definition of the musicality of natural speech: 'At first there was no music but melody and no other melody than the varied sounds of speech. Accents constituted singing, quantity constituted measure, and one spoke as much by natural sounds and rhythm as by articulations and words.'[55] But they then reverse Rousseau's order of nature to make the melodic authenticity of speech a learned and performed quality. The same was true of another teacher of oral performance, Hugh Blair, for whom music is the destination of a speech perfected over time (or, by implication, through a course of lectures of rhetoric): 'For those inflexions of voice which, in the infancy of Language, were no more than harsh or dissonant cries, must, as Language gradually polishes, pass into more smooth and musical sounds: and hence is formed, what we call, the Prosody of a Language.'[56] So far from being natural to Scottish speakers, vocal music was a corrective to the kind of guttural speech that, in Adams's account, compressed their windpipe and constricted the 'tone' of the voice in the throat. According to the language teacher Anselm Bayley, the 'ready way to mend these ill habits, some perhaps may say, is to consult those who are skilled in musick, especially the vocal part'.[57]

The question of song places Scotland in a strange geographical position. On the one hand, as a northern nation, Scottish speakers did not have the physical disposition to be musical, yet, on the other, examples of Scottish music were becoming increasingly popular. Allan Ramsay's hugely successful collections of Scottish and English traditional songs were reprinted throughout the eighteenth century, and the initial publication of the *Tea-Table Miscellany* in 1724 was immediately followed up with an edition of suitable tunes for Ramsay's songs, set by Alexander Stuart. 'Scotch airs' were common in theatres and pleasure gardens and, by the end of the century, had begun to enter into literature as a sure sign of the authentic feelings of those who hear them. Edward Jerningham's long poem *The Ancient English Wake* features a visiting bard who 'gently wak'd those soft, complaining tones, / So dear to melody which Scotland owns'.[58] Many numbers entered into the repertoire of visiting Italian star singers, and William Tytler, refuting the popular myth that Scottish music had been single-handedly reformed by David Rizzio at the court of Mary Queen of Scots, argues that it was in fact Scottish song that had influenced Italian music.[59] As Leith Davis points out, ' "Scotch songs" became commodities available in shops and performed in drawing-rooms all over Britain.'[60] Throughout the century, Scottish song became a form of cultural capital in which certain distinctive qualities of Scottish language were drawn into a more generalised, polite version of labouring-class culture for middle-class consumption.

Song particularly fitted this model because it seemed to offer a kind of orality that was at once universal and localised, retaining a clear Scottish identity while simultaneously absorbing into the invention of tradition. William Tytler, for example, remarked that: 'The old Scottish songs have always been admired for the wild pathetic sweetness which distinguishes them from the music of every other country.'[61] David Herd acknowledges the theory of the climatic distribution of musicality: 'Every nation [. . .] hath its own peculiar style of musical expression, its peculiar mode of melody; modulated by the joint influence of climate and government, character and situation, as well as by the formation of the organs.'[62] This relativity sits alongside his claim that Scottish music has 'a forcible and pathetic simplicity which at once lays strong hold on the affections; so that the heart itself may be considered as an instrument'.[63] In his promotion of 'the music of the heart' as an idealised orality, Herd sidesteps the problematic construction of the physical, unmusical, northern Scottish body. Joseph Ritson defines 'national song' as an utterance whose geographical borders are blurred by natural transmission. Song may be regionally 'peculiar', but it is also 'genuine', 'natural' and conveniently removed from the social actuality of writing:

The genuine and peculiar natural song of Scotland, is to be sought [. . .] in the productions of obscure or anonymous authors, of shepherds and milk maids, who actually felt the sensations they describe; of those, in short, who were destitute of all the advantages of science and education, and perhaps incapable of committing the pure inspirations of nature to writing.[64]

Both Burns's reception as the 'heav'n-taught ploughman' of Mackenzie's review and the history of his later celebrity have tended to associate him with song, but, in fact, as David Daiches notes, Burns included rather few songs in his early editions.[65] Joseph Ritson, in the introduction to his collection of *Scotish Song*, claimed that 'Burns, a natural poet of the first eminence, does not, perhaps, appear to his usual advantage in song.'[66] Ritson does not develop this argument (other than to prefer Burns's satire), but his views on song were different from those of Burns in an important respect. Ritson expresses the view that 'the words and melody of a Scotish song should be ever inseparable'.[67] Burns, by contrast, is aware of an interesting dislocation between music and words even as he acknowledges music as the true language of nature:

As music is the language of nature: and poetry, particularly songs, are always less or more localised (if I may be allowed the verb) by some of the modifications of time and place, this is the reason why so many of our Scots airs have outlived their original, and perhaps many subsequent sets of verses.[68]

Writing here becomes provisional. Rather than being fixed in music, which authorises them as natural and sanctions them socially, words are subject to context and to 'the modifications of time and place'. Burns describes music and poetry as modes which have become disengaged from each other and which cancel out each other's origins. In one sense, music precedes words, as new words can be set to old music. Simultaneously, however, verbal language is described as the 'original' of music, but again it is an original that can go missing, leaving both music and writing deracinated. The local, so far from underpinning the universal as it does in the Currie quotation with which I started this chapter, is cut off from the language of nature by 'modifications of time and place' that introduce contexts and alterity.

The example of Burns shows how the political positioning of Scotland as a northern nation, however much it was pressed into the service of a world geography of language, tends to trouble these forms of globalised determinism. We have already seen how Burns disturbs the relations between the local and nation, expressed as a sense of place, and the same is true of his dealings with language. Burns makes clear what was already lurking in Rousseau and the north–south theory: that northern and southern languages are not functionally different. In his reading of the *Essay on the Origin of Languages*, Derrida describes the impossibility of the Enlightenment geography of language. Rousseau, as Derrida observes, believes that language has a history because the motivation for speech occurs when human beings experience a need that exceeds passion, giving rise to desire. He then maps this on the rational axis of the globe, ascribing passion to southern languages and need to northern ones. But because, as he has already argued, the relationship between passion and need is already the character of language as such, he is unable to maintain the opposition – the appearance of need in passion recurs in the constituted languages as well as in the imagined origin. Thus, the *Essay* 'shows that the opposition north/south being rational and not natural, structural and not factual, relational and not substantial, traces an axis of reference *inside* each language. No language is from the south or the north, no real element of the language has an absolute situation, only a differential one'.[69] It is not that languages of the north become increasingly the effect of need, but that need, or lack, is always necessary for language to exist. In the case of Burns, this recognition is not only of language itself but also instantiated in the impossible condition of song in Scotland.

Burns's most complex thoughts about song are not themselves songs. The two forms that I look at here – the epistle and the elegy – both depend on absence, either of the correspondent or of the subject, rather than the song's celebration of presence. Burns exposes the ideality of physical presence in Herd's idea that 'the heart itself may be considered an instrument' which omits the speaker from the relationship between song and audience. The warm, feeling body supposed to produce song is elsewhere in these poems. In the strange little 'Elegy on the Death of

Robert Ruisseaux', Burns disassembles Rousseau's narrative of authentic passion guaranteed by the speaking body. The bodily integrity of language is at once challenged by the title: over whose body is this elegy to be pronounced? 'Robert Ruisseaux' is both Rousseau and, in a translation from Scots to French, Burns. The poem foregrounds writing. It lays to rest the spontaneous generation of song (Ruisseaux will 'gabble rhyme, nor sing nae mair' [141, l. 2]) in favour of the political significance and multiplicity of writing. The poem ends: 'But tell him, he was learn'd and clark, / Ye roos'd him then!' (141, ll. 17–18). As Burns continues punning on his own name, 'Ruisseaux' turns aurally towards 'Rousseau', but with the suggestion that book-learning and writing are to be desired. 'Roos'd' stands for not only the Scots word for 'prais'd' but also the concept 'made more like Rousseau'. And this deflection of Rousseauist orality towards writing is a characteristic of Burns's own texts.

Rousseau argues that speech moves closer to the condition of writing the further north it travels. As the abundance of southern climes is replaced by northern scarcity so speakers become competitive, socialised language users. The division of labour and inequality of property depend on writing to create records and to administer ownership, moving the user of language away from their own somatic experience. But in Scotland, as we have seen, this narrative is not quite so straightforward. In order to recover the warmth and feeling of the south, language assumes a socialised orality. Hugh Blair is impeccably Rousseauist in his belief that that 'spoken Language has a great superiority over written Language, in point of energy or force' and that northern speakers 'neither regarded much the harmony of sound, nor sought to gratify the imagination by the collation of words. They studied solely to express themselves in such a manner as should exhibit their ideas to others in the most distinct and intelligible order.'[70] But he sees no necessary contradiction between this and his own reclamation of the oral for a formalised, professional rhetoric that could be taught in Scottish universities and practised in the pulpit or court of law. Burns's poems return to the idea of the impossibility of the pure, pre-social, somatic oral. His verse epistles, even as they seek to call up communal musical practices, make it impossible ever quite to pinpoint the local or press into the service of a more generalised language of feeling.

The epistles dramatise what should be interpersonal relationships inspired by the spontaneous impulses of mutual friendship, but these can never be contained within writing. In the epistle 'To James Smith', for example, Burns keeps trying unsuccessfully to escape from writing in order to go off and enjoy life with his friend Smith. Halfway through the poem he states impulsively, 'My pen I here fling to the door' (79, l. 121), which serves only to remind the reader of Burns's dependence on writing for the very existence of the poem. Letters, even if they reach their destination, may change during their delivery. Burns's epistles are often a record of the alterity that is brought about in the exchange of written texts. In the epistle 'To a Gentleman Who Had Sent Him a News-Paper', the poem/letter offers itself as an alternative version of the text sent by the Gentleman, transposed into dialect and into Burns's radically satirical interpretation of Britain's military ambitions in Europe and the Empire. The epistle ends: 'So gratefu', back your news I send you' (282, l. 37), but, of course, this cannot be the same news that was originally sent to Burns.

Much as they pursue interpersonal relations, the epistles never seem quite to catch up with their addressees. In the first epistle to John Lapraik, for example, Burns's attempt to catch up with originator of the song he has heard at a local musical gathering never succeeds. Admitting that 'I've scarce heard ought describ'd sae weel, / What gen'rous, manly bosoms feel' (57, ll. 19–20). The apparently spontaneous sensation of feeling cannot escape a prior act of description. Burns remains the '*unknown* frien' (57, l. 5) of the opening stanza, who, after describing all the occasions when he and Lapraik might meet, has to resort to a plea for 'Twa lines' from his correspondent (57, l. 129). In any case, face-to-face communication does not seem any more reliable than the written variety. In an epistle 'To Dr. Blacklock', Burns has been let down by a spoken promise to deliver a written letter, even though 'He tald mysel, by word o' mouth, / He'd tak my letter' (273, ll. 9–10). Thomas Blacklock instigated the theory that human language originated from birdsong, a possibility that had attracted Monboddo before he rejected it as too implausible.[71] The poem plays on the idea of the unreliability of the language of birds as the friend who fails to deliver the letter is called Robert Heron. The language of nature itself has here gone astray.

In the 'Epistle to Hugh Parker', Burns is even more explicit about the failure of writing accurately to transmit his feelings. He ends his letter:

> How can I write what ye can read?—
> Tarbolton, twenty-fourth o' June,
> Ye'll find me in a better tune;
> But till we meet and weet our whistle,
> Tak this excuse for nae epistle. (222, ll. 40–4)

Burns knows that what he can write is not identical with what Parker can read. And his writing is profoundly ambiguous, subverting both potential readings and the form of the written epistle itself. Does the last line mean 'take this (letter) as an excuse for my not writing earlier' or 'do not take this excuse to be a proper letter'? Apologetically, Burns gestures towards the language world of song and especially melody, but this 'better tune' remains elsewhere and in some other time, while the poem itself must remain as writing. Burns is, after all, writing *Poems Chiefly in the Scottish Dialect*, and dialect was both Rousseau's southern origin and George Lemon's 'muddy dialect of northern speech'. Taking advantage of its impossible location, Burns constructs dialect as a form of writing that is distinctively local but not tied either to the universality and self-sufficiency of idealised song or to the somatic peculiarities of northern speech.

The example of Burns demonstrates how literature is the discourse that destabilises Enlightenment spatiality, whether in the attempt to locate discrete positions or to build up global systems. The already doubled or supplementary structure of Scottish geography shows this particularly clearly. Even as it opens up the nation to metropolitan readerships, literature, in an act of ungrounding, undercuts the exemplarity that places were supposed to supply to geography. And, even as authors such as Burns, Scott or Hogg become associated with regionality, their work consistently reveals the difficulty of saying precisely where those regions lie and how one might recognise their distinctive qualities if one went there. Neither Scotland, nor the language of its inhabitants, can clearly be plotted on a global map, and, in the following chapter, we will see how these considerations emerge in narratives of border crossings.

CHAPTER 3

Great North Roads:
The geometries of the nation

In 1787, an English traveller called Henry Skrine crossed the border from England to Scotland. His reaction was one of shock and disappointment at the apparent failure of history to perform its expected task of progressive improvement:

From the length of time, and the general intercourse of the nations since the Union, I was amazed to find such a wonderful change at once in the appearance of the people and their habitations. Instead of the healthy peasant, and the neat cottage, which adorn the most remote English villages, my eyes encountered, in a cluster of mud-built sheds, a number of miserable wretches, ragged, bare-footed, and squalid, almost beyond the power of description.[1]

What is striking here is not the relatively commonplace eighteenth-century observation about Scottish working-class poverty, but Skrine's 'amazed' reaction, by the end of the century, to the apparent malfunction of progressive economic history, or what he calls the 'general intercourse of the nations since the Union'. He encounters not only the question of where to locate Scotland in terms of spatial otherness or degrees of foreignness but also how to match the geographical with the chronological. The homogenising effects of smooth temporal development are interrupted by a 'wonderful change' laid bare by geography as time and space lose their synchronicity. What should have been a gradual change in *time* (from poverty to economic growth) is not supported but contradicted by a change in *space* (from England to Scotland).

Henry Skrine's disquiet may lead us back to the pressure exerted by new forms of interest in the local and the national and their influence on Enlightenment ideas about space and time. By the end of the eighteenth century, the architectonics of the great Scottish Enlightenment formulations of history do not always prove sufficient to support the experience of travellers between South and North Britain. Stadial history – most famously articulated by Adam Smith in his four-stage version – plots human development from its earliest economic form (hunting) to its most recent (commerce). Because these stages were not globally uniform, they could all coexist within the same present, available to the gaze of the enlightened observer, though not necessarily to the pre-commercial societies themselves. Scotland seemed to offer a miniaturised version of this uneven development, a kind of historical diorama that exhibited on a small stage examples of the various stages of socio-economic history from the 'rude' Highlands to the Lowland cities of Edinburgh and Glasgow quickly expanding with the growth of trade. A journey northwards ought to be spatially predictable to the traveller familiar with the course of human society.

In such a schema, local experiences are subordinate to historical process, serving chiefly to exemplify a priori conclusions. Travel, according to Dugald Stewart, is at best illustrative of stadial history. The scattered observations of individual travellers can identify samples of the different stages in social development but are incomplete without the conjectural method of history – inferring a complete narrative of human history from instances witnessed in the present – which can make sense of otherwise fragmentary empirical details. Stewart argues that conjectural history can fill in the gaps in the 'casual observations' gathered by travellers to 'rude nations': 'In such inquiries, the detached facts which travels and voyages afford us, may frequently serve as landmarks to our speculations; and sometimes our conclusions a priori, may tend to confirm the credibility of facts, which, on a superficial view, appeared to be doubtful or incredible.'[2]

Stewart's confidence in the alliance of place and history, however, is not a full picture. Recent work on Scottish Romantic historicism – notably by James Chandler and Ian Duncan – has drawn out the fractures implicit within the Enlightenment historiographic paradigm of stadial history itself. Chandler shows how the idea of the globe as a permanent canvass upon which historical changes could be tracked is rendered impossible by the recognition not only that barbarous and developed societies can exist at the same time but also that any example of a particular stage will be characterised by the social distribution of societies at that precise moment in history. Thus, 'one could not in the same sense even speak of the "state of the globe" in relation to the barbaric state of existing polished nations. The "globe" would signify differently in different times.'[3] Duncan describes the paradoxical condition of a model that clears a position of global, ahistorical contemporaneity from which to identify its examples of historical difference, while simultaneously incorporating that disjuncture into its own conception of synchronic modernity: 'the epistemic horizon of modernity that allows a recognition of "the same" cultural stage at different times necessitates the recognition of different cultural stages – different temporalities – inhabiting, and alienating, the same "historical moment." '[4] In other words, modernity produces the position that allows us to see how different times exist in different spaces, by virtue of its own claim to be itself all one space and time. In the present chapter, I want to read this disjunction, already contained within the Enlightenment scheme that produces it, as it surfaces as a question for travel between England and Scotland.

In Smollett's *The Expedition of Humphry Clinker*, the Bramble family's journey through the kingdom is framed as a voyage of discovery for both readers and characters. Travelling with the Brambles, Clinker's journey is not yet a 'tour', with its connotations of sightseeing, but an 'expedition', implying a more dangerous or militaristic voyage. Smollett plays with geographical expectations on this hazardous journey. Anxiety about the state of Great Britain is framed partly as a question of geographical power and knowledge – Tabby Bramble is 'so little acquainted with the geography of the island, that she imagined we could not go to Scotland but by sea.'[5] In the years that followed, this geographical uncertainty was to become important for a spatial sense of the nation in history. Published tours of the 1790s and early years of the nineteenth century represent a transition between Smollett's 'expedition' and the wholesale tourism that followed in the nineteenth century, fostered, in part, by the success of Scott's poetry.[6] Aesthetic values still tended to be secondary to the questions of political economy raised most famously by the travel literature of Arthur Young, but these 1790s tours are also characterised by a wide range of expectation surrounding the idea of crossing the national border. When John Carr, who has been negatively influenced by the opinions of Johnson on Scotland, crosses into Roxburghshire, he finds himself in a state of bewilderment, caught between empirical evidence and his sense of the nation: 'I could not help exclaiming, "Is this 'Scotland?' " '[7] 'Scotland', then, is something already in quotation marks, caught between the predictions of political economy and a newer sense of the instability of the traveller's perspective.

Another traveller, the English clergyman John Lettice, further situates border-crossing as a way of addressing the emergence of modernity from the complexities and paradoxes of stadial history. Like Henry Skrine, Lettice expects progressive economic history to have wrought its inevitable effect on Scotland, but, unlike his fellow tourist, he recognises the relationship between locality and its representation in the traveller's concept of space. Lettice feels that Scotland is so far advanced in economic modernity that to comment on it at such a 'late' stage would be almost superfluous: 'a traveller from this side of the Tweed, setting forward on his journey without partiality or prejudice, and that so late as the summer of 1792, must have seen Scotland under so many circumstances of improvement and prosperity, as that his representations, if strictly just, cannot but be favourable.'[8] As far as Lettice is concerned, Scotland is already known to the traveller as a state of economic prosperity, resulting in his somewhat paradoxical assertion that true open-mindedness can draw only one conclusion. But this sense of an already-known Scotland is different from Dugald Stewart's given sense of history. For Lettice, Scotland has a kind of virtual existence; a traveller 'must have seen Scotland under so many circumstances of improvement' even though the English traveller is unlikely to have made repeated visits in person. Rather, as the eighteenth century drew to a close, Scotland had already become a represented space. In the experience of Lettice, modernity is not only the effect of history but also what makes it legible. That is to say, for the empirically minded traveller, history is not the a priori substrate of stadial theory but a process of reading in the present.

Lettice is self-consciously modern and describes himself as such. This quality, he argues, is the decentring that cosmopolitanism brings about and a reversal of the idea of the metropolis as the epitome of modernity. Where a complacent Londoner might feel out of place in Scotland, the true modern is a traveller:

If a London sybarite were suddenly dropped into Scotland from a balloon, a transient smile of surprise would find its excuse in his ignorance [. . .]. But surely we moderns, so given to boast of our moral refinements and superior philanthropy, should know to behave ourselves better.[9]

It is notable how Lettice absorbs the local and the particular into modernity. The balloon's-eye perspective afforded to the imaginary Londoner is the sign not of an enlightened overview but of frivolous drifting. Once he gets going on his travels, Lettice does not assume a stable standpoint but rather a shifting position that can adapt itself to impressions: 'I can minute on my tablet any thing I see worth notice before me; as I do, not unfrequently, the remarks of intelligent persons, whom I happen to converse with on the road.'[10] It is only this redefinition of the local that can re-establish the link between time and space in the unit common to both of them, the minute. Minuting, which Lettice does compulsively, marks the division in the later part of the eighteenth century between two forms of the local; one which establishes localities as precise points determined by their position on a fixed network, and the other which acknowledges the production of the local as a continuous process, in which localities are refashioned and produced discursively according to their immediate circumstances. Lettice reverses Dugald Stewart's contention that local observations could serve as 'landmarks' to illustrate a priori conclusions:

On quitting Gretna Green, we found ourselves not more geographically, than characteristically, in Scotland. The smallest national differences striking at first sight, which would scarcely be noticed after some familiarity, I suffered few, which presented themselves, to escape my minutes; because, on these occasions, I know you think the most trivial circumstances not without their value. To the imagination they certainly are not, although the traveller's eye must often be supposed to have fallen only on the superficies of objects: nor will judgment prize them less, where opportunity may not have been wanting to penetrate below their surface, and to investigate the causes of national character.[11]

In his rather awkward prose, Lettice is coming to terms with the idea of the local as a subject in its own right rather than as an example in a spatial/ historical schema. 'National character' is here something that inheres in transient phenomena rather than serving to illustrate a given underlying coherence. Lettice reverses Dugald Stewart's order of priority that gives rise to social regulation: the 'superficies of objects' exist in a minute-by-minute temporality that must call on the imagination to investigate their relation to issues of nationality, a point brought home by his first sentence in which the national can no longer be easily mapped onto the geo-graphical. The local cannot be predicted by the systematic and cannot be already known through the processes of history.

This chapter, then, continues the debates of Chapter 2 but looks at the problem of defining the local from a national, rather than a global, perspective. For Burns, the problem of locating the north was a matter of being there. But what about the question of going there? How was one to know through observation when one ceased being in South Britain and started being in North Britain? This is a form of geography that addresses the relation of the local to the empirical and throws up questions about modes of travel, means of transportation and the way these bear on the social and cultural production of space. Because these questions represent a problem of recognition, they put further pressure on the idea of a world divided and determined by its geographic zones. Climate theory depended on the possibility of imagining a globe divisible into its parts. Regional differences were thus predictable, the inevitability of their occurrence produced by their position in a greater structure because climate is itself produced by position. But travel within the national structures of North and South Britain interferes with this smooth continuum. John Millar frames the climate problem as a matter of 'national peculiarities' within Britain: 'How is it possible to explain those national peculiarities that have been remarked in the English, the Irish, and the Scotch, from the different temperature of the weather under which they have lived?'[12] And, as travel between North and South Britain increased in the later eighteenth century, the failure of global structures to account for the empirical observation of the local becomes pressing. As the contrasting reactions of Skrine and Lettice suggest, the national border refuses to act as an environmental divider but remains an imagined, cultural separation that demands a process of induction rather than deductions of Enlightenment historiography.

This is also a problem of chorography. As we saw in the previous chapter, climate theory assumed that space was mappable in systematic and geometrical ways – that north and south were opposites but that this opposition was made possible by the continuum of a straight line. So far from registering this as paradoxical, or even problematic, climate theory merely subdivided the continuum into a third zone allowing a middle or 'temperate' region. The term 'temperate' thus fulfils two functions in environmental determinism: on the one hand, it acts as a discrete and fixed zone, confirming the opposition between north and south by acting as a buffer between them. But, in the common sleight of hand of climate theory, 'temperate' is not in a fixed sequential series with north and south and can be freely moved to any latitudinal position depending on the writer's preference. France, for Montesquieu, was the ideal temperate zone; for William Falconer it was England. Although the temperate zone was, in the most general meaning of the term, local to these writers, it did not function as a locality, in the sense of a singular place. The local and national geographies of Great Britain in the Romantic period follow both the loosening and the adaptation of Enlightenment spatiality by throwing up more radical discontinuities and singularities than earlier structures could easily contain. Instead of plotting Britain's place on the navigable globe, the internal differences within the national structure present themselves to the attention of authors and readerships, and the position of Scotland becomes crucial in understanding the geographical inscription of the nation-state.

We can see this in two respects. First is the way in which Enlightenment paradigms of a global systematic geography are adapted to form national models. The classic example is John Sinclair's *Statistical Account of Scotland* of the 1790s. Sinclair assumes a nation whose underlying structures of natural history and political economy can be broken down into, and in turn revealed by, an inductive scrutiny of the nation. Charles W. J. Withers neatly describes this process: 'Through geography, the political and natural body that was Scotland was to be dissected and reconstituted: parish by parish, parishes into counties, counties into the nation.'[13] Or, in the words of William Thomson in 1791: 'If certain boundaries of space and time were not marked with precision, it is difficult to conceive how science could be advanced even in the smallest degree.'[14]

In a broad sense, the *Statistical Account* is a continuation of the Enlightenment practices of global division and climatic determination. Sinclair accepts the basic premises of Montesquieu, finding Hume's disagreements with climate theory 'too broad and sweeping' and agreeing that 'the character of nations must, in some measure, be affected by causes merely physical.'[15] But Sinclair modifies climate theory in that he allows not only for local variation but also for the reversal of physical determinism. Instead of a system that predicts the behaviour of human societies and culture from their physical location, Sinclair takes into consideration the effect of social practices upon climate:

the climate of Scotland, at least in the plains, must have been greatly ameliorated; for cultivation and copious population, partly by their necessary and unintended effects, partly by expedients employed for that express purpose, must have softened the rigours of the climate, and rendered the temperature of a northern atmosphere, better calculated than formerly, for the uses and benefit of the human race.[16]

Instead of place producing societies, local populations can produce place. The local remains secured within a quantifiable system, but that structure is simultaneously open to modification by local practices.

Second, we can trace the emergence of spaces that seem to lie outside systematic or mappable geographies. The cultural work of these spaces is itself twofold. On the one hand, they seem in contradistinction to the Enlightenment strategies of mapping space into discrete zones and thereby drawing space and history together in acts of mutually supportive exemplification of economic progress. But, on the other, they can be read as productions of that very process of spatial organisation – apparently empty spaces generated only to be replenished with the political content they had at first seemed to do without. This double spacing occurs at different points in the period, shaped by the contours of different political situations. First is the post-1746 response to the defeat of what was held to be militarist Scottish nationalism in its political and literary forms. One immediate consequence of the suppression of Jacobitism was the renewal of road-building in the Highlands. General Wade had already directed a substantial programme of laying out military roads in the north of Scotland following the 1715 Jacobite rising. Forfeiture of Highland estates after the 1745 rebellion transferred to Wade's successor, Major William Caulfeild, resources for a fresh phase of surveying and constructing the military roads.[17] Wade roads were long and straight and visibly super-imposed the politics of the British state over the social organisation of the Highlands. Ignoring the indigenous Highlanders' relations to land use and modes of transport (the locals objected to the damage the roads did to the unshod feet of their ponies), the military roads bridged rivers and travelled over the tops of hills. But the roads also stood for a less imme-diately visible form of social organisation. Edmund Burt, a collector of rents on forfeited Highland estates, contemplated possible objections from the Highlanders. Imagining that these would come from a tripartite social structure of Gentlemen, 'the middle order' and the lowest class, he reorganises the ancient clan system into a modern product of capitalism.[18] Burt, who is generally quite observant about the specificities of Highland society, describes a plan to found a new town in the Highlands, which would be a union of English urban planning and the 'Privileges and Immunities of a royal borough in Scotland'.[19] This model British town, although hopelessly impractical, as Burt points out, was seen as the culmination of the geographical improvement afforded by the 'Traffic' of Wade's transport revolution:

These Advantages, it was said, would invite Inhabitants to settle there, not only from the Lowlands, but even from England, and make it the principal Mart of the Highlands, by which Means the Natives would be drawn thither as to the Centre; and by accustoming themselves to Strangers, grow desirous of a more commodious Way of living than their own, and be enabled by Traffic to maintain it. And thus (it was said) they would be weaned from their barbarous Customs.[20]

The hypothetical new town is an ideal balance of geographic and economic progress with national unity. Roads unite the nation on a blueprint drawn by Adam Smith, giving it a centralised market and a commodity economy that move it from barbarism to capitalism at a stroke. Smith had established roads as the building blocks of the nation as economic state. 'Good roads, canals, and navigable rivers, by diminishing the expence of carriage, put the remote parts of a country nearly upon a level with those in the neighbourhood of the town. They are, upon that account, the greatest of all improvements.'[21] Modern Britain is brought about by the transformation of land into transportation routes: instead of their ancient function of forming natural borders, rivers are reclassified as 'navigable rivers' that carry goods through boundaries. Roads homogenise the nation, reducing the difference between centre and periphery, urban and rural; they facilitate 'carriage' and the circulation of commodities and capital in continuous motion.

For the English traveller in eighteenth-century Scotland, roads are what render alien culture legible. Samuel Johnson is famous for making the absence of trees the distinctive feature of Scottish landscapes, but in the same section of *A Journey to the Western Islands of Scotland* he also comments on roads. Despite making use of a number of military roads, and his admiration of the Highlanders' own ability to construct roads out of solid rock, Johnson is geographically unsettled by what he perceives as the lack of roads in Scotland. He finds himself in a space with 'no visible boundaries'. Unable to orientate himself by more familiar signs of the social organisation of space, he concludes: 'The roads of Scotland afford little diversion to the traveller, who seldom sees himself either encountered or overtaken, and who has nothing to contemplate but grounds that have no visible boundaries.'[22] Arriving on the island of Col, Johnson becomes anxious about its dimensions. The island seems out of kilter in terms of its political economy: too many people appear to live there for the reported size of the land to support. The matter can only be resolved in Johnson's mind by reference to road-building, and specifically English road-building:

This proportion of habitation is greater than the appearance of the country seems to admit [. . .]. I am more inclined to extend the land, of which no measure has ever been taken, than to diminish the people, who have been really numbered. Let it be supposed, that a computed mile contains a mile and a half, as was commonly found to be true in the mensuration of the English roads, and we shall then allot nearly twelve to a mile, which agrees much better with ocular observation.[23]

The imposition of English measurement (English and Scottish miles were different lengths) makes the island visible to Johnson, reinserting it into a recognisable frame of political economy and drawing it back into the nation, now once again commensurable in all its parts. For Johnson, then, space is already national and political, and his instrument for measuring this political significance is the road.

The final military roads were laid in the Highlands in the 1760s, the decade that saw the publication of James Macpherson's *Fragments of Ancient Poetry* and his epics *Fingal* and *Temora*. At first glance, Macpherson's Highlands would seem to be the opposite of the territory mapped out by the Wade roads. The locality of the *Fragments* is geographically very vague indeed.[24] It is hard to tell whether its topographical features are physical or metaphorical so seamlessly do they blend into each other. Fragment 8 starts with Ossian sitting in a wood: 'By the side of a rock on the hill, beneath the aged trees, old Oscian sat on the moss; the last of the race of Fingal.'[25] Almost immediately, however, the wood is not *where* Ossian is, but *what* he is: 'The race of Fingal stood on thy banks, like a wood in a fertile soil.' Thus, in one way, Ossian exists in a pure romance space, unbounded by the socially defining features of roads or agricultural enclosures, a north so formless that it can barely be heard let alone clearly seen: 'Dull through the leafless trees he heard the voice of the north.'[26] Yet, the shifting metaphoricity of Macpherson's writings certainly did not prevent their being received as a text for Enlightenment Scotland. For all his appeal to a Celtic imaginary, the lost, alien other of eighteenth-century Britain, with its technologies of communication and transportation, Macpherson is nevertheless writing for a British market. As a number of recent studies have pointed out, the Ossianic hero appeals to the modern British citizen whose democratic patriotism is shot through with sensibility. Warlike, yet cultured, motivated both by individual sensation and identification with a social group, the Ossianic Celt appears at a time when it had become necessary to find ways of reinscribing Scotland politically into the Union.[27] The tactful mourning of the departed Highland culture assists in its reabsorption as a cultural resource for the whole of Great Britain in the absence of any threat from Jacobitism.[28]

The political functions of the military roads and Ossianic space are then more closely interwoven than they might at first appear. If, on the one hand, the Ossian phenomenon resisted the literal redrawing of the Highlands by roads and surveys, it also cleared a space for the reappropriation of Celtic Scotland as a Romance model for the British state. Unlike stadial history, in which time and space claim to be mutually illustrative, space breaks down into different forms of temporality – a modernity produced by national systems and a romance space that draws on a form of local vagueness. But these two forms are also called into being by each other: the regulated space of modernity fictionalises its 'traditional' past into romance space, and, in turn, these imaginary spaces act both as an alternative and as a prop to modernity.

These ideas continue to congregate along the two cartographic features that come into clear cultural focus in the work of Walter Scott: the Great North Road and the border between Scotland and England. These are also two of the principal topographic figures on which the social geometries of the nation rest. The geography of Great Britain, a long, thin island, should accentuate the north–south polarity and a line drawn up or down it should be a way of understanding its internal locations. The border between Scotland and England, occurring at one of the narrowest points of the island, further emphasises a potential division between north and south as a way of geographically establishing place. In this sense, the road and the border serve the same function: to provide a visible shape to the nation. In another way, they perform different services: the border marks the distinction between England and Scotland while the Great North Road traces their union. In theory at least, the shape of Great Britain should rest on a skeletal diagram that emphasises its national divisions, and the simplest way to experience topographic difference should be to travel in a straight line along one of these axes. Of course, these two functions are not at all clearly distinct. Borders are well known to emphasise contiguity as much as difference, and that between England and Scotland, as we will see, is particularly elusive as a geographical marker.

Far from offering empirical evidence of difference, the act of crossing the border proves to be a difficult concept to place on the conceptual map of Britain. Take, for example, the title of Richard Warner's *A Tour through the Northern Counties of England, and the Borders of Scotland* of 1802. To the south of the boundary lie 'counties' – recognisable units of administration. Crossing the national division while heading north, the traveller finds that he or she is out of the boundary and into the border, or, more precisely, the Border*s*, a strangely plural place not clearly demarcated by legislative boundaries. Neither does Warner's Britain correspond to the geometries of the nation that a clear north–south division might supply. Instead of demonstrating a steady northerly progress, the south of Scotland differs more from England than does the more distant north of Scotland. The inhabitants of the Scottish Borders are 'more national in their manners, practices, and ideas than the northern counties of the kingdom; from the circumstances of *effects* being still felt in these parts, which have long faded away in the more distant divisions of the country'.[29] To be 'national' evidently here means 'different from the contiguous nation', but it is a problematic way of thinking about nationality: where does this leave the non-contiguous regions? Are they more like the country Warner has come from, England, or do they correspond to some idealised human nature devoid of national characteristics altogether?

Roads are not always the reassuring measure of national identity that they were for Samuel Johnson. Franco Moretti rightly points out that the cultural work of roads in the novel is to throw characters together, creating in the picaresque genre 'the nation as the new space of "familiarity," where human beings re-cognize each other as members of the same wide group.'[30] But the picaresque also disrupts the teleology of roads. Roads exist in time as well as space, and this trajectory opens them up to spatial hierarchies: the direction in which one travels makes a difference to the nature of the road one travels on. There were many more 'Tours' from England to Scotland than from Scotland to England.[31] Old roads tend to be called after their commercial destination – hence the number of London Roads in Lowland Scottish towns which led to the markets in the south. Yet, the eighteenth-century picaresque novel and its descendants interfere with this commercial trajectory; the road is also the scene of chance encounters, deflected journeys, robberies and kidnappings. The road is both a line between two points and an uncertain space in which travellers can appear and disappear. Roads and borders, then, are what define the geometry of the nation, while simultaneously working against any precise geometrical definition, and, in the second part of this chapter, I want to turn to their prominence in the novels of Walter Scott as he negotiates the topographic complexity of the national tale.

SCOTT AND THE GEOGRAPHIES OF THE LAW

Roads and borders had long figured in the geographical imagination of the British. When English people, especially those with a Scotophobic inclination, thought about the movement of Scots to the southern part of the kingdom, they often distilled this into the practicalities of travel itself. Most famous is Samuel Johnson's Boswell-baiting comment, 'the noblest prospect which a Scotchman ever sees, is the high road that leads him to England!'[32] The second issue of John Wilkes's *North Briton* satirically applauded the building of a new, toll-free bridge over the river Tweed for making it easier for Scots to enrich themselves by passing across it into England.[33] Scott's Rob Roy is first introduced to the reader by the figure of a border-crossing perhaps intended to recall this anti-Scottish propaganda: 'a canny North Briton as e'er cross'd Berwick Bridge'.[34] These figures represent a growing focus for Scott: in his first novel, *Waverley* (1814), Edward Waverley's journey from the south of England to Scotland is not described; one moment he is in England and the next in Scotland.[35] But, by 1817, *Rob Roy* narrates in some detail its hero's expedition up the Great North Road, and, in 1818, Scott's next novel, *The Heart of Mid-Lothian*, devotes several chapters to Jeanie Deans's travels on the same road in the opposite direction. As his novels map the nation of Great Britain, Scott becomes increasingly interested in the question of how that nation might be experienced by the travelling subject. And this attention to an empirical sense of national identity seems to be bound up in preliminary questions about the means of transportation from one part of the kingdom to another. Scott's third novel, *The Antiquary* (1816) opens at a coaching stage in a journey from the south to the north of Scotland. In *The Heart of Mid-Lothian*, Jeanie's journey is on foot one way and in a carriage provided by the Duke of Argyle in the other, and she is marked in terms of both class and region by her means of transport. She is accused by the elder Mr Staunton of being a 'stroller' and a 'vagrant'[36] because she is travelling on foot, and initially turns down his later offer of arranging a seat on a coach for her: '"A coach is not for the like of me, sir," said Jeanie; to whom the idea of a stage-coach was unknown, as indeed, they were then only used in the neighbourhood of London' (p. 309). In *Rob Roy*, the mysterious 'Mr Campbell' tells an unwanted companion that although they are travelling in the same direction, they will go at different speeds: '"We can scarce travel together," he replied, dryly. "You, sir, doubtless, are well mounted, and I for the present travel on foot, or on a Highland shelty, that does not help me much faster forward."' (p. 98).

Scott's novels, then, are increasingly busy with people travelling at various speeds up and down the nation between north and south. In fact, Scott announces at the start of *The Heart of Mid-Lothian*, it is the act of travel that constitutes history itself: 'The times have changed in nothing more [. . .] than in the rapid conveyance of intelligence and communication betwixt one part of Scotland and another' (p.13). Modernity here is an enfolding of time into space and their mutual dependence. Historical change is 'nothing more' than communication technology, but it is also what enables us to understand spatial difference. At the same time, the desire to know about different spaces, to communicate between different parts of the nation, generates history in the form of a modernisation of technology more usually associated by historians with the

later development of the railways. But what looks here like a clear statement of the homogenising effect of modern communications on the
nation becomes a more complicated affair in the fabric of the Waverley
Novels as they address the complexities inherent in Scott's bold assertion
of modernity. The seemingly atemporal perspective that gives such an
elevated spatial vantage point breaks down into its constituent parts on
the journeys of the characters, and these parts turn out to be somewhat
different from the whole modern nation united by travel.

Before looking at *Rob Roy* in more detail, we can see how Scott's
interest in the geographies of the road and the kinds of power that bring
them into being clearly stand out in *The Heart of Mid-Lothian*. Published
in 1818, the novel turns on the journey of Jeanie Deans in 1736 to seek a
British pardon at the Hanoverian Court for her sister, who has been
condemned to death in Edinburgh for infanticide. Jeanie's journey is
figured in two related ways. In one, she is 'a Scotchwoman, going to
London upon justice business' (p. 257). This journey takes a legal overview as Jeanie travels from Edinburgh to London, from the scene of mob
justice, religious intolerance and unjust laws, to an alternative metropolitan locality where public and private justice can be restored, in harmony with each other, by a centralised British monarchy. The novel's
title draws together ideas about centralised space, the law and the role of
sensibility in moral judgement. The 'Heart of Mid-Lothian' is the
Tollbooth gaol in the centre of Edinburgh. The spatial metaphor asks
simultaneously if local judgements of the heart are sufficient to settle
moral dilemmas and if regional legal practices can constitute national
justice. From this metaphor of centralisation, the novel explores the place-
boundedness, or otherwise, of subjects in motion. During the course of
Jeanie's travels, she is a witness to a different form of the law. Rather than
being centralised in the national metropolis, the law of the road is localised
by those who use it, chiefly the highwaymen and footpads whom Jeanie
falls among and who have their own laws and practices.

On the route to London, the road passes through a landscape that is
historically situated by its legal geography in the years shortly before the
systematic enclosure of common land: 'The extensive commons on the
north road, most of which are now enclosed, and in general a relaxed state
of police, exposed the traveller to a highway robbery in a degree which is
now unknown, excepting in the immediate vicinity of the metropolis'
(p. 258). The road forms here an imprecise boundary that is borne out in
the novel. On the one hand, the Great North Road is a public route to
national government and the reaffirmation of civic society, social interaction

and the common value of telling one's story: 'If she regained that public road, she imagined she must soon meet some person, or arrive at some house, where she might tell her story, and request protection' (p. 272). On the other, the road is governed by local practices and customs that lie outside official legal powers. The official public highroad is the site of contesting powers, and its legal authority is also split between a centralised national jurisdiction, which can protect Jeanie, and the vigilante justice of the Carlisle mob that murders Madge Wildfire on the dubious grounds that she 'stop[s] fo'k o' king's highway' (p. 363). The paradoxes of the road are incarnate in the person of one Dick Ostler, an employee of the Seven Stars inn and 'a queer, knowing, shambling animal, with a hatchet-face, a squint, a game-arm, and a limp' who, according to the landlady, knows 'most people and most things of o' th' road' (p. 254) and is thus able to advise on the best way to deal with highwaymen. 'Knowingness' is, here, a 'queer' property not easily visible to the eye and the province of a secretive group of insiders. Yet, it is Dick who is visibly marked by the metaphorical use of Adam Smith's national standard of 'Good roads, canals, and navigable rivers'.[37] On looking at Jeanie's pass, given to her by the thief James 'Daddie Rat' Ratcliffe, Dick 'extended his grotesque mouth from ear to ear, like a navigable canal' (p. 255). So far from being clearly demarcated by geography and the technologies of transport, the national and local, public and private, have become difficult to distinguish in the modern nation, and the novel traces fissures in the national geometries that assert a spatial communality.

The road on which Jeanie Deans travels south is also the site of Frank Osbaldistone's northward journey. *Rob Roy* asks questions about the continuous national subject. Do subjects remain English or Scottish as they move between South and North Britain, and can Britain's social geography support such a distinction in the first place? In this most uncanny of Scott's novels, how can national geographies or even topographical features constitute a way of reading political identities? Ian Duncan elegantly sums up this novel as 'devoted precisely to the intuition that modern Britain is not a "nation," in the sense of a topology of defining terms – law, sovereignty, economy, culture – converging upon a singular time and space'.[38] In this section, I want to investigate *Rob Roy* as the dissolution not only of such a topology but also of the topography of this set of terms. In particular, *Rob Roy* explores further examples of the kind of double spacing I analysed earlier in the form of the Wade roads and Ossianic space: the Great North Road from London to Edinburgh and the border between England and Scotland. In order to understand how these cultural and political geometries of Britain function in *Rob Roy*, we can set Scott's work specifically as a novelist both against his own earlier career as a collector of ballads and against the more general appearance of roads and borders in geographical discourse of the period. Janet Sorensen has written that 'while we have come to recognize that the notion of the nation as a cultural body and the idea of "the best" monolingual literary texts as a national canon emerged simultaneously, we have yet to disconnect literary studies from national paradigms.'[39] I will argue that *Rob Roy* exploits an existing culture of roads and borders and their doubled spatiality not only to uncover their reciprocity in the culture of national identities but also to suggest that their geometrical function can point to the discontinuities and heterogeneities that are inevitably left over from the fictional act of imagining the nation.

The topographic narrative of *Rob Roy* begins simply enough. Frank Osbaldistone, unwilling scion of the London commercial house of Osbaldistone and Tresham, takes his readers on a journey along the focal points of this chapter, the Great North Road and the Border, exploring their modern political significances by transporting them back to a time before the name 'North Britain' had been made a term of abuse by John Wilkes in the 1760s. The novel thus contemplates an imagined return to the possibility of a Britain of equal parts and, structured by the teleology of early nineteenth-century commercial practices, offers a kind of free-market globalisation in which local difference is subsidiary to the replicating movements of cash and credit. At first, Frank's journey seems to follow a map redrawn and homogenised by modern, commercial uniformity, the North Road a 'line' that links points of sameness rather than moving the traveller into difference:

I should have been glad to have journeyed upon a line of road better calculated to afford reasonable objects of curiosity [. . .] to the traveller. But the north road was then, and perhaps still is, singularly deficient in these respects; nor do I believe you can travel so far through Britain in any other direction without meeting more of what is worthy to engage the attention. [. . .] The characters whom I met with were of a uniform and uninteresting description. Country parsons, jogging homewards after a visitation; farmers, or graziers, returning from a distant market; clerks of traders, travelling to collect what was due to their masters, in provincial towns; with now and then an officer going down into the country upon the recruiting service, were, at this period, the persons by whom the turnpikes and tapsters were kept in exercise. Our speech, therefore, was of tithes and creeds, of beeves and grain, of commodities wet and dry, and the solvency of the retail dealers [. . .]. (pp. 86–7)

Frank is an early entry into that genre of spatial rootlessness, the hero as commercial traveller. The North Road here seems to offer an economic symbiosis of the local and the national. This is a vision of a country whose roads both support and generate a system of national capitalism: credit can be contracted and interest collected, producers can be linked to their 'distant markets', and recruiting officers can replenish the national army to fight the wars that kept the trade routes open and maintained the whole system in circulation. The uniformity of the 'line' along which Frank travels claims to do without the concept of locality. Although he describes the period of local funding of roads, his teleological narrative is also inflected with the later panoptical vision of John Louden McAdam. By the time Scott was writing the *Waverley* novels, a centralised bureaucracy was beginning to catch up with Adam Smith's vision of a nation unified by its transport systems.[40] In 1819, McAdam published his brief *Remarks on the Present System of Road Making* in which he comments, with terse frustration, on the poor condition of Britain's highways. Road maintenance was in the main financed through tolls collected at turnpikes, a relatively ad-hoc system which was subject to corruption and hindered the expansion of road-planning beyond local control. Local landowners were apt to have planned roads rerouted in order to maintain their domestic privacy or to facilitate the transportation of their agricultural produce. A General Turnpike Act was passed in 1773, to apply to all present and future roads, but this had the effect of strengthening the control of local interests and was burdened with clauses allowing for exemptions, multiple categories of tolls and special cases.[41] A successful national post road, like the Great North Road, was a triumph of centralised control over an intractable local agency – what McAdam calls 'superintending and controuling power' – and an important part of national homogeneity.[42] Sinclair's *Statistical Report* proposes the Great North Road as a marker not only of links between Scotland and South Britain but also of Scottish modernity. Local maintenance has proved ineffective, and 'a new turn-pike act was thought necessary, for completing and upholding the repairs of that great road.'[43] The Turnpike Act has made improvements so that 'this part of the post-road, through Berwickshire, which was formerly the worst and most dangerous part of it, between Edinburgh and London, is now in perfect good repair; and the increase of travellers, especially in carriages, far exceeds all expectation.'[44]

Looking back over his account in the *Analysis*, Sinclair places roads in a direct causal relationship with agricultural improvement and the future of the nation: 'The want of roads, and wheel-carriages, was a further

obstruction to improving the soil.'[45] McAdam, too, saw roads as a form
of modernity and expressed this in terms of the centralisation of power.
The responsibility for enacting the policies of the Commissioners for
Roads had thus far fallen to poorly organised local surveyors, and McAdam
calls for an office to oversee them. His ideal is a kind of panopticon of
the roads; the centralisation of an unseen administration would guarantee
the industrious performance of the road-building itself: 'A vigilant and
unremitting superintendence is wanting to ensure an economical and
effectual execution.'[46]

The road Frank travels on is similarly an economic function, a line
linking points of similar commercial and social value. Mapped for him by
a series of empirical encounters, he nevertheless translates these with ease
into the discourse of political economy, of the nation-state defined not
only, or even primarily, by its territorial borders or acquisitions but by the
wealth and economic functions of its inhabitants. Later in the novel, such
a discourse is replicated and expanded by the Glasgow merchant and
magistrate Baillie Nicol Jarvie in whose commercial reckoning the 'north'
becomes a manufacturing space consisting of the industrialising towns of
Lowland Scotland and the north of England: Stirling, Musselburgh and
Edinburgh compete to produce goods as cheaply as Manchester, Sheffield
and Newcastle. Looking forward towards the north–south divisions of the
novels of Dickens and Gaskell, the north becomes a modern urban space
produced by manufacture. In this modern world, historical boundaries
are subject to erasure. The old political border separating North and
South Britain becomes diminished in a general principle of circulation,
and Frank himself observes that the old north-south division *separating*
the two countries is now less important than a new *unity* in which both
countries anticipate trade with the West. Frank looks forward not only
to his own writing present (the 1760s) but also, implicitly, to the time of
the novel's publication when Glasgow had grown rich on the sugar and
cotton trades.

Glasgow lay on the wrong side of the island for participating in the east country
or continental trade, by which the trifling commerce as yet possessed by Scotland
chiefly supported itself. Yet, though she then gave small promise of the
commercial eminence to which, I am informed, she seems likely one day to
attain, Glasgow, as the principal central town of the western district of Scotland,
was a place of considerable rank and importance. (pp. 236–7)

Frank's journey up the Great North Road, however, exposes him to more
than the commercial advantages of the Union. Frank naïvely thinks that

highway robbery is a phenomenon that pre-dates the modern capitalist economy:

A man in those days might have all the external appearance of a gentleman, and yet turn out to be a highwayman. For the division of labour in every department not having then taken place so fully as since that period, the profession of the polite and accomplished adventurer [. . .] was often united with that of the professed ruffian. (pp. 88–9)

More specifically, he sees the situation in spatial terms: highwaymen can go about their business because of 'the number of unenclosed and extensive heaths in the vicinity of the metropolis' (p. 89). The highway robbery that goes on in *Rob Roy*, however, is entirely bound up in the mercantile economy of Frank's origins. Rob, the ostensible outlaw and footpad, is perfectly adept in the world of commercial negotiations. A conversation between Rob (as 'Mr Campbell') and the landlord of the Durham inn at which he and Frank are staying underlines the parallel between the new commercial system and apparently older, primitive Scottish practices. The landlord applauds the lack of Scottish highwaymen, ascribing it to the poverty of that nation, only to be told (by a Scot implicated in highway robbery) that the real cause can be expressed as a modern notion of commercial practice:

'That's because they have nothing to lose,' said mine host, with the chuckle of a self-applauding wit.
  'No, no, landlord,' answered a strong deep voice behind him, 'it's e'en because your English gaugers and supervisors, that you have sent down benorth the Tweed, have taen up the trade of thievery over the heads of the native professors.' (p. 93)

Highwaymen stand in a double relation to the law. Peter Linebaugh's study of crime in the eighteenth century shows how they were both outside the laws of the capitalist economy and emblematic of its driving force. Rob's speech above is a good example of Linebaugh's observation that the 'ironic parallel between criminal thievery and mercantile deceiving was thus more than a device of the polemicist's imagination',[47] or, as Ian Duncan remarks of Rob, 'who better than a freebooter should thrive in the new economy?'[48] The highwayman then represents a hinge about which the spatial and economic meanings of the Great North Road turn. On the one hand, highwaymen defy the linear temporal logic of the road as a line of uninterrupted commercial travel; they occupy the non-quantifiable romance mode and are given, like Rob, to turning up unpredictably and in unexpected places. On the other hand, they are the very embodiment of the economic modernity they seem to challenge.

This kind of spatiality is double both internally and in terms of an apparent opposition between spaces, as we saw in the case of Ossian and the Wade Roads.[49] The Great North Road sits both together with and across another space encountered by Frank Osbaldistone. Shortly after telling us about his everyday encounters, Frank includes details of a pub conversation with some other travellers in which they scare each other with stories of footpads and highwaymen, a glimpse of the romance world of mysterious foes met by the roadside into which Frank is about to fall. The commercial world is haunted by stories which, while 'familiar in our mouths as household words' (p. 87) will nonetheless take on a distinctly *unheimlich* or uncanny character as the narrative progresses. Intermeshed with the calculable geography of modern Britain are places less easily systematised and less readily visible in statistical accounts.

The same sense of an uncanny familiarity lurks in Frank's own sense of a certain 'north', which, despite never having been there, he calls 'my native north' (p. 100) as if the very term 'native' were available only from an external perspective. The same sense of a displaced home works against an easy distinction between England and Scotland, if both can be said to be northern nations. Prior to the trip that forms the start of the narrative, Frank's knowledge of Scotland is formed from his Northumbrian nurse whom he chiefly remembers from her vitriolic account of an 'opposite frontier' inhabited by ogres and giants, an early education which has left her charge looking upon the Scots 'as a race hostile by nature to the more southern inhabitants of this realm' (p. 95). Yet, what sticks in Frank's mind is the refrain of a ballad which was his nurse's favourite and which conjures up the mythic space of 'the north country': 'Oh, the oak, the ash and the bonny ivy tree, / They flourish best at home in the North Country!' (p. 95) The song, supposedly marking the north of England as 'home' was popular on both sides of the supposed 'frontier' and, in fact, is noted as traditional in Chambers' *Popular Rhymes of Scotland*. The 'north country' is both the 'opposite frontier' of national geography and a portable locality, which can recur in other places to signify the movement of displaced origins. The 'North Country' is the space where we want to be but never are. The speaker of 'The oak, the ash and the bonny ivy tree' is in London. More exotically, Act II of Joanna Baillie's 1810 musical tragedy *The Beacon*, set on a Mediterranean island, opens with a fisherman singing a ballad about a lady in love with a knight of 'the north countree'.

A man dressed as a palmer accosts her, and she asks him 'Art thou from the north countree?' as if people from the north country might spring up anywhere at any time to signify an uncanny or displaced home which one can never attain as it is only imaginable by dint of *not* being there.[50]

The 'North Country', then, is where ballads take place, a space that occupies both northern England and southern Scotland without conforming to the specific characteristics of either nation. Thomas Percy commented in 1765: 'There is hardly an ancient Ballad or Romance, wherein a Minstrel or Harper appears, but he is characterized by way of eminence to have been "OF THE NORTH COUNTREYE."'[51] John Pinkerton concurred in *Ancient Scotish Poetry* that ancient bards are 'all of the *north countrie*'.[52] Ballad-collectors empathise its geographical imprecision. When the antiquarian George Ellis wrote to Scott suggesting that a map might be a helpful accompaniment to the *Minstrelsy of the Scottish Border*, Scott replied: 'you are to know that I am an utter a stranger to geometry, surveying, and all such *inflammatory* branches of study, as Mrs Malaprop calls them. [. . .] Hence my geographical knowledge is merely practical.'[53] Allan Cunningham, whose collection of *The Songs of Scotland* appeared in 1825, is even less explicit about the spatial delineation of the Borders. Lamenting the decline of the Lowland Scots as 'a poetical and imaginative people', Cunningham contrasts *The Odyssey*'s ancient lack of geographical specificity with the modern mathematisation of space, governed by the tools of global navigation and opposed to the free spatiality of the ballad world:

When the King of Ithaca was storm-bound and spell-bound by the ancient poet, maritime discovery had not laid down her charts, settled the longitude and latitude of the isles of the ocean, and given the inhabitants and productions a place in history; he was therefore at liberty to find land where he listed, and to people it with enchantresses and winged fiends, since the critics could not turn to the last map and the latest voyage and cry, 'This man confounds navigation, and pulls history by the nose'. Our steps are regulated by the compass, and our motions by the quadrant [. . .].[54]

To underscore its geographical fluidity and indeterminate antiquity, the north country comes with a variety of deliberately anachronistic spellings: *countree, countrie* and *countreye* are all used in modern printings. This is an archaism produced to underscore a sense of national modernity; the 'North Country' is a modern, mythic space born of the antiquarian imagination, and many commentators have noted how English and

Scottish ballad-collectors use it to blur national boundaries and to present a cultural Britishness. As in the case of Macpherson, geographic generalities can have specific political goals. Susan Stewart remarks: 'For Percy, this task of antiquing the region is tantamount to an erasure of the border as separation and hence the melding of a "national" (i.e. "British") tradition.'[55] The borders remain an imaginary locality, different from either England or Scotland but representing an ideal, romance space in which national difference itself seems unimportant. Leith Davis comments of Scott's *Minstrelsy:* 'Not only do the Borders represent an alternative culture to that found in the rest of Britain, they also represent an alternative politics, an ideal mixture of unity with diversity.'[56] This is undoubtedly the case: the fluidity of the North Country allowed Scott to 'contribute somewhat to the history of [his] native country'[57] without asserting a specifically Scottish identity, and he made a considerable amount of money by converting it into cultural capital for the British readership of the *Minstrelsy*. In *Marmion*, his 1808 narrative poem set largely on the Northumbrian side of the Border, Scott is even more openly patriotic, invoking the Border Minstrel from an unspecified 'northern clime' to eulogise the British dead of the war with France:

> Though not unmark'd, from northern clime,
> Ye heard the Border Minstrel's rhyme:
> His Gothic harp has o'er you rung;
> The Bard you deign'd to praise, your deathless names has sung.[58]

British patriotism of this kind emerges as if naturally from the ancient, warlike regions of northern climes. But the doubled space of the Borders also had a much more specific political resonance. Coexisting with the 'North Country' as an indeterminate, archaic ballad space are the Borders as a highly regulated legal territory whose prominent and detailed geographical mapping was entirely the product of legal enforcement and marked the national frontier very clearly. The land either side of the national border, from 1297 to 1603, was divided into mirroring sets of East, Middle and West Marches, each supervised by an English or Scottish warden respectively, whose duties, described here by Scott in his introductory essay to his *Border Antiquities*, were 'preventing and punishing all disorders committed by the lawless on either territory' as well as holding 'days of truce [. . .] in which, with great solemnity, they enquired into and remedied the offences complained of by the subjects of either realm.'[59] In fact, Scott, with an anthropological eye, sees a prominent and diverse legal system of 'strict regulations' so entrenched in Borders society that it seems to arise naturally from it:

A natural intercourse took place between the English and Scottish marchers, at border meetings, and during the short intervals of peace. They met frequently at parties of the chace and football; and it required many and strict regulations, on both sides, to prevent them from forming intermarriages, and from cultivating too close a degree of intimacy.[60]

So far from the incommensurable non-space of the 'north countree', Scott's border is carefully measured, and he particularly admires the modern communications technology of one warden for having 'established a line of communication along the whole line of the Border'.[61]

The border between England and Scotland, then, is simultaneously both the most, and least, geographically determined space in the country, both the malleable space of the North Country and the closely regulated legal border of the Marches. Scott emphasises this highly visible legal geography in much of his writing about the Borders, and this takes us back to the way the supposed antiquity and geographical fluidity of the North Country are also in the service of modern, political legislation. As the same time as Scott was conducting his preliminary fieldwork for the *Minstrelsy of the Scottish Border*, that very Scottish Border was witnessing contemporaneous political disturbance. The summer of 1797 saw the outbreak of popular opposition to the Scottish Militia Act, passed in July of that year, which inaugurated in Scotland a similar system of conscription to that current in England, in order to raise further troops for the war with France. Following the Militia Act, county authorities in Scotland would now be able to conscript men by ballot. Hostility to the Act soon started in the Border village of Eccles, a few miles north of Jedburgh. Protests followed in Selkirk and in Jedburgh itself, where the crowd was dispersed by the local yeomanry.[62] The Duke of Buccleuch, under whose patronage Scott was shortly to become Sheriff-Depute of Selkirkshire, published an *Address to the Inhabitants of the County of Mid-Lothian* in an effort to restore order by pointing out to the local people the merits of the Act. Some of those taking part in the original Eccles demonstration were tried at the Edinburgh High Court, where Lord Braxfield handed down sentences of transportation, commenting that the opposition to the Militia Act had been 'an attack on the law itself and had a tendency to break the bonds of society, and to affect the dissolution of the state'.[63] Subsequent sentencing was less severe, but two men involved in the Jedburgh incident were each given two years' imprisonment.

The prominence of Selkirk and Jedburgh in the hostility to the Militia Act resonates with the Middle March of the *Minstrelsy*. In the sixteenth century, Jedburgh had been the principal centre for trying offences on the eastern border, and Scott was particularly fond of referring to 'Jeddart Justice', an early form of shooting first and asking questions after, or, as Scott describes it: 'trial after execution.'[64] Scott's whole contribution to ballad-collecting is distinctive in part because he sees the ballads as authentic examples of local history with precise details of localities and events. In particular, the Border of the *Minstrelsy* is one closely articulated by the law. Scott's explanatory notes are full of details of regional jurisdiction, forms of punishment, articles of the Border Laws and attempts to establish truces. In his notes to 'Lord Maxwell's Goodnight', Scott offers a note of some length explaining the 'Bond of Manrent', a bond of allegiance in which a lesser clan promised loyalty to a more powerful one. The bond was for life, but Scott stresses its importance in violent inter-family quarrels with the effect of 'maintaining unanimity and good order' in dangerous times, a form of recruitment that resonates with the Militia Act.[65] Thus, the legal geography of the borders works in two ways. First, the indistinct contours of the 'North Country' allow the cross-border violence to evaporate into an archaic past, performing the same function as the warlike Celts of Ossian had done for Jacobite nationalism. But the empty spaces of the borders are simultaneously overlaid with their modern geography, reminding a fractious peasantry of the benefits of national conscription and the contemporary jurisdiction of the Duke of Buccleuch. The county, as legal administrative unit, modernises the old space of the March and regulates its martial character within systematic, national patriotism.

A number of Scott's novels go over this divided ground. In 1820, *The Monastery*, a novel about the changes in juridical power in the region during the Scottish Reformation, sees both the archaic religious jurisdiction of the Catholic Church and regional in-fighting between unruly borderers supplanted by the modern bureaucratic talents of the Earl of Moray. But *The Monastery* ends inconclusively, its regional peace unassured and its characters disillusioned. The only one of Scott's novels to have a sequel, *The Monastery* looks forward to *The Abbot* in which Moray finds himself caught up in even greater national tensions between Mary Queen of Scots and Elizabeth I. In *The Monastery* itself, Moray's claim to restore the national balance of power by regulating the border is set against a local geography governed by superstition and magic in which the resident spirit of the House of Avenel is able to transport books and people from place to place with no apparent reference to the spatial laws of physics. Scott's novels bring together different constructions of the national and the local – both different from each other and with internal differences within each term – and investigate the impossibility of completely mapping the local onto a culturally coherent national geography.

Like *The Monastery*, *Rob Roy* works against too easy an identification of the novel genre with national unity. As is the case with most of Scott's novels, *Rob Roy* is not a good example of the notion of the novel as a national commodity which brings readers together in a shared national consciousness, expressed in Benedict Anderson's comment that 'fiction seeps quietly and continuously into reality, creating that remarkable confidence of community in anonymity which is the hallmark of modern nations.'[66] *Rob Roy* announces the idea of a political border as something difficult to place geographically and which may be out of kilter with the experience of those who come up against it. On a ride with Frank, his Northumberland cousin Diana Vernon points to a 'whitish speck' which she tells him is a crag in Scotland. Frank is surprised that they are so close to the border and denies that he could ride there, as Die asserts, within two hours. When she insists, he replies: 'I have so little desire to be there, that if my horse's head were over the Border, I would not give his tail the trouble of following. What should I do in Scotland?' (p. 124) The national border is, here, a matter not of given space but of perspective, its topography rendered by the absurd image of Frank's horse, frozen in motion, with its back end unable to follow the front.

Rob Roy is particularly interested in the relations of geography and the law, and in the failure of each to define the other. The novel further explores ideas about localisation as Scott traces the shift from the interdependence of space and law to the non-inevitability of law itself – the sense that laws must be produced locally and will have a determining effect on the social production of space. As Nicholas Blomley observes, there is a long tradition of using geography to map the spatial discontinuities of the law:

One important – and long-lived – way in which law has been geographically conceived is as discontinuous and regionalized. In what can be termed a regional approach, the spatial diversity of law and legal systems is mapped out and then analyzed in terms of the "underlying geography" of the physical and human environment.[67]

But the post-Montesquieu tradition of arguing that laws develop in accordance with regional difference is simultaneously dependent on the single law of climatic theory – the idea that the globe can be mapped according to a coherent and predictable structure. Northern and southern laws are different from each other, but both must correspond to a fundamental principle of global determinism expressed as a system of comparative geography. Although there can be no manifestation of a transcendental law that governs all human societies, there remains nevertheless the possibility of predicting any form of law or government from its location in a structure.

For Montesquieu, laws could be both essential and relational at the same time: 'Laws, taken in their broadest meaning, are the necessary relations deriving from the nature of things.'[68] But travellers in the 1790s, as we have seen, recognised that laws could produce the nature of things on a local scale as well as, or instead of, being derived from them in general. In Northumberland, John Lettice praises the improvements made by local landowner (a Dr Graham) which have altered 'a region of borderers, characterised by wildness and barbarity' by introducing local justice: 'a regular, active, and summary administration of justice, dispensed, at the smallest cost, in the different manor-courts instituted throughout the domain, have altogether wrought a wonderful change in the manners, habits, and welfare of a numerous and increasing race of peasantry.'[69] Law becomes written onto the landscape in a physical discourse of property rights, again incorporating the local into the national system of 'improvement'. For James Plumptre, crossing the eastern border in 1799 by the 'Union Bridge' over the Tweed, this codependence of local regulation and national improvement could easily be translated into conceivable geographical objects:

I now found myself in the neighbourhood of Scotland in seeing two women digging in a plantation, and arriving at the Union Bridge, a very handsome structure, crossed the Tweed and entered Scotland. The banks of the river are very pleasant particularly a gentleman's seat, Mr Marjoribanks, a little farther up.[70]

Rob Roy unpicks the seams of a nation held together by a national economy and property rights and the legal geography that reifies these into Union Bridges and gentleman's seats. When Frank asks his cousin for 'some lights on the geography of the unknown lands' of Northumbria, Rashleigh replies:

It is not worth while; it is no Isle of Calypso, umbrageous with shade and intricate with silvan labyrinth – but a bare ragged Northumbrian moor, with as little to interest curiosity as to delight the eye – you may descry it in all its nakedness in half an hour's survey, as well as if I were to lay it down before you by line and compass. (p. 169)

The novel form affords Scott much more ironic potential than had the *Minstrelsy of the Scottish Border:* Rashleigh's apparent offer of openness about the 'bare' landscape disguises the fact that he is already plotting to ruin Frank's side of the family and start a Jacobite rebellion. The improbable suggestion that he might 'lay it down before you by line and compass' hints to the reader of the failure of national surveys to reveal the entirety of what happens in any particular locality. And this is attested in the novel's representation of local justice. The legal system in Northumberland is corrupt and haphazard – the local magistrate is a Jacobite sympathiser, simultaneously in the pay of the neighbourhood English gentry, whose attempt to imprison Frank is prevented only by the arrival of Die Vernon pretending to be on a social call.

In these ways, the novel uses its own geography to suggest that property is not a reliable guide to legality and that the division of the nation into locally governed parts cannot be put back together into the coherent political and commercial whole represented by works such as the *Statistical Account.* Frank's own border-crossing is a deflection from his progress up the Great North Road, reminding us that he does not take it all the way to its national *telos* of Edinburgh. Guided by the gardener Andrew Fairservice, to whom the route is familiar from his smuggling days, and who has appropriated his employer's horse, Frank steals across the border at night on a 'broken track':

Extricating ourselves by short cuts, known to Andrew, from the numerous stony lanes and by-paths which intersected each other in the vicinity of the Hall, we reached the open heath; and riding swiftly across it, took our course among the barren hills which divide England from Scotland on what are called the Middle Marches. The way, or rather the broken track which we occupied, was a happy interchange of bog and shingles [. . .]. (pp. 229–30)

In one sense, we are in the indeterminate North Country of unmapped spaces and unofficial routes. But this doubled space, Scott reminds us in the above quotation, is also the legally determined Middle Marches of the old Border Laws. The borders are both opposed to the commercial geography of the road and its doppelgänger, scene of an alternative yet homologous economy. William Thomson, crossing the border in 1791, makes the connection quite explicit:

This smuggling trade nourished on the borders a degree of wealth and population that has not, since this period, been nearly equalled: and, to shew the intimate connection between the monied and landed interest, the price of Land,

and the rent of Farms in the parish of Jedburgh, and other places near the English border, was almost as high as it is at present.[71]

Rob Roy not only fictionalises the geography of the nation but it also reveals the ways in which geography is itself performed rather than static or given. Demarcations are fluid and dynamic and are rhetorically produced rather than being anchored in the land or on maps. Borders are not physically determining but ideal and imitative, and the narrative of *Rob Roy* invokes not one border but two. The border between England and Scotland divides the country in national terms, but the Highland Line complicates that division, turning a bipartite structure into a tripartite one. A key moment in the novel's topographical debate articulates this spatial dislocation of national identities. Once in the Highlands, Baillie Nicol Jarvie, Glasgow merchant and magistrate, and Owen, Head Clerk of the Osbaldistone firm, 'delightedly' compute the population of the Highlands in relation to the land, much in the same way as Samuel Johnson had on Col. Jarvie positions the region as a pre-modern economy whose 'uncivilised people' are too backward and lazy to sustain the agricultural improvements of the rest of the country:

Now, sir, it's a sad and awfu' truth, that there is neither wark, nor the very fashion nor appearance of wark, for the tae half of thae puir creatures; that is to say, that the agriculture, the pasturage, the fisheries, and every species of honest industry about the country, cannot employ the one moiety of the population, let them work as lazily as they like, and they do work as if a pleugh or a spade burnt their fingers. (p. 300)

A shocked Frank replies, 'But is it possible [. . .] that this can be a just picture of so large a portion of the island of Britain?' (p. 301), suggesting that it is *not* in fact possible to give an accurate picture of either a portion of the island or its totality. Jarvie goes on to claim that 'mony hundreds o' them come down to the borders of the low country, where there's gear to grip, and live by stealing, reiving, lifting cows, and the like depredations!' (p. 301). Jarvie's distinction between his own commercial, profitable, lowland Scotland and the primitive Highlands fails at the very point of articulation, as the borderline between legal and extralegal practices has already been repeatedly obliterated during the course of the novel. Highway robbery in England, smuggling in the Borders, and blackmail in the Highlands are all border activities that work against the idea of a nation divisible by legal geographies and mappable into regions that can be identified by economic practices.

Rob Roy is a novel in which linear or systematic space comes up against the idea of space as something delineated not by the way in which it is mapped but by the way it is used. Far from being fixed by their zonal or cartographic location, places can remain in the same physical position but change their nature according to their social significance. At Osbaldistone Hall, Frank realises that he must conduct his lessons with his cousin Diana Vernon in the mornings only as in the evenings she uses the library as a personal, female space: 'in the mornings the library was a sort of public room, where man and woman might meet as on neutral ground. In the evening it was very different' (p. 198). The same place can be two very different localities. This example of the domestic use of space is given other political resonances as Frank continues his journey into Scotland. He discovers that space itself is culturally variable and that his accustomed signifiers of public and private no longer operate in the Highlands. Travelling with Jarvie and Andrew Fairservice, Frank finds an inn in a deserted spot and persuades the landlady, against her better judgement, to let them in. A Highlander remarks in ironic tones that Frank appears to have made himself at home:

'I usually do so,' I replied, 'when I come into a house of public entertainment.'
    'And did she na see,' said the taller man, 'by the white wand at the door, that gentlemans had taken up the public-house on their ain business?'
    'I do not pretend to understand the customs of this country; but I am yet to learn,' I replied, 'how three persons should be entitled to exclude all other travellers from the only place of shelter and refreshment for miles round.' (p. 324)

The novel sets up here something like the difference between Henri Lefebvre's distinction between 'representations of space' and 'representational spaces'.[72] The former Lefebvre characterises as dominant social formations that form institutional spaces, in this case Frank's distinguishing of apparently universal public space signified by the inn. But the local signifier of the white wand to denote the inn's usage points to a 'representational space' under the control of what Lefebvre calls its 'users' – what the Highlander thinks of as people going about 'their ain business' of local social relations as opposed to the assumed uniform 'business' of national commercial practices. To the locals, Frank's party are 'Glasgow tradesfolks' whose propensity 'to gang frae the tae end o' the west o' Scotland to the ither' (p. 328) interrupts the business of the Highlanders. Like the High Road and the Border, the Inn is both a romance space, where picaresque characters mingle, and one made legible by its commercial or political regulation.

Rob Roy, then, is a novel about the incommensurability of the nation. If spaces can be generated through temporary practices, like the displaying of the white wand, then they cannot be brought under the permanent regulating power of surveys or statistical accounts. National geographies of roads and borders are an indication of how the nation was imagined and geographically constituted, but they also reveal the extent to which the inscription of place resists totalising systems. The novel, at all points, works to qualify Sir Hildebrand Osbaldistone's optimistic assertion of geographical liberality that 'the king's road is free to all men, be they Whigs, be they Tories' (p. 164), not only because roads are always politically charged but also because the appropriation of spatiality by any interest will divide and double that space.

CHAPTER 4

Antiquarianism and the inscription
of the nation

Scott's third novel, *The Antiquary* (1816), is a story that takes place in an impossible location and one that seems to confound the geometries of Great Britain discussed in the previous chapter. Its titular antiquarian obsesses fruitlessly about the location of the last battle between the Romans and the British. Fairport, where most of the action happens, is described in ways that situate it both on the north and the east coasts of Scotland.[1] Yet, these puzzling localities are the scene of important debates about the nation and its geography. Like *Waverley* and *Rob Roy*, this novel features a young man journeying north, the paradigm of the national tale in which a traveller from the national 'centre' visits the supposed peripheries of the country in order to investigate their differences and to reabsorb them into a United Kingdom. In an even more down-to-earth way, the novel is interested in its own topography: where things can be found and what places are 'really' called. The very title introduces a tension between these two ideas about place: the nation as modern state or geographical area can be conceived only in overview and understood only as a general concept, while antiquarianism produces its effects from the individual or the atypical. A number of recent commentators remark on this tension. Mike Goode shows how, in contrast to philosophical history, antiquarianism works 'by privileging the particular over the general, the rare over the representative, and the empirical over the theoretical'.[2] Katie Trumpener writes about the contrast between English nationalist poetry as 'a dislocated art, standing apart from and transcending its particular time and place' and late-eighteenth-century bardic poetry which 'gives new emphasis to the social rootedness and political function of literature'.[3] Yet, antiquarianism and nationalism are inextricably linked at the point of antiquaries' interest in origins of British peoples. For the practice of antiquarianism, the challenge is to position the unsystematic 'finds' of antiquarian inquiry in such a way as they can evoke continuities with the past. What seems random, or even absurd, in the present, can call on nationalist histories in order to become reabsorbed into the narrative of cultural unity. Or, in spatial terms, what is discovered locally can be synecdochal for the national. In order to understand, therefore, what was at stake in Scott's critique of antiquarianism in relation to national historical geographies, I will explore some of the contexts invoked by the novel, as they seek to construct a sense of the nation from the specific or the local.

This chapter argues for a revaluation of antiquarianism when its focus is moved from the study of objects to that of language and from object-based antiquarianism to the genealogies of toponymy. In a seminal essay, Arnoldo Momigliano calls antiquarianism 'static'. As Susan Manning has shown, it was deemed childish in the Scottish Enlightenment through its association with things rather than words and was therefore thought to be unable to deal with the sequential development of history.[4] Ina Ferris points out how antiquarianism is at odds with narrative itself: 'To inhabit antiquarian discourse [is] to live in the detail, in the peculiar – is to linger in an incremental non-narrative form.'[5] Scott's antiquarian, Jonathan Oldbuck, is indeed afflicted by such fragmentary stasis, surrounding himself with 'a profusion of papers, parchments, books, and nondescript trinkets and gewgaws' (p. 22), but his conversations return obsessively to the derivation of words from the ancient languages of Scotland. Through *The Antiquary*, we can reassess the association of antiquarianism with the non-linguistic. If we think about antiquarian interest in inscription – both the inscriptions on ancient objects and the inscription of names on the landscape – then it will no longer be possible to make a clear distinction between objects and writing.

'PROPER SCOTLAND': GEORGE CHALMERS' *CALEDONIA*

An extended joke in *The Antiquary* is the impossibility of resolving the interminable argument among antiquarians about the identity of the Picts, a people who acted as a kind of linguistic football over which rival parties fought for possession. Scott's feuding antiquarians, Jonathan Oldbuck and Arthur Wardour, are fond of this subject and turn for support to the work of two rival historians of ancient Scotland, George Chalmers and John Pinkerton, who diverged on the question of whether the Picts were a Celtic or a Gothic people.[6] Pinkerton's anti-Celticism led to some virulent diatribes on modern Highlanders who were, in his view, no better than their barbaric ancestors and 'incapable of industry or civilization'.[7] Chalmers, by contrast, was not especially concerned with the racial characteristics of Celts, ancient or modern. His interest was primarily linguistic and nationalistic; in short, Chalmers wanted to write the history of Great Britain with Celtic languages providing both an originary and a common point of reference. In the early nineteenth century, when Chalmers was preparing for publication the first volume of his mighty *Caledonia*, this was not a very promising task. Celts were thought either to be ethnically other from a homogenising sense of Anglo-Saxon or Teutonic Britons or part of a national identity which, although expressive of a certain ancient Britishness, was now lost. Particularly, Celtic cultures were associated with the oral and the impermanent, whether in Bardic lamentations for a vanished past or in Samuel Johnson's belief that Gaelic 'merely floated in the breath of the people, and could therefore receive little improvement'.[8] Pinkerton went so far as to claim that the traces of ancient Celtic languages had disappeared altogether: 'Celtic etymology is mere delusion; for we do not only know nothing of the reason of the name, but we know not even the Celtic tongue.' This, Pinkerton argued, is 'because the language is hardly a written one, and its orthography, on which etymology depends, is quite various and lax'.[9]

The challenge for antiquarians, then, was to promote the language of ancient Scotland to the status of writing and, by implication, to forge a link between ancient national languages and the modern, literate state. The idea that etymology depends on writing gives a very different trajectory from the oral origins of national languages or the voice of the bard that merges with natural landscapes. Linguistic antiquarians, whether they believe in Gothic or Celtic toponymy, have a clear sense of naming as a form of inscription, an originary language already at Rousseau's stage of writing in that it defines, clarifies and makes distinctions and expresses ideas rather than feelings. Topography, for Chalmers, is an intellectual concept, the 'rational notion of the original colonization of North-Britain' (vol. I, p. 30).[10]

We can read this notion of primitive local inscription as a form of national history. Earlier accounts of the origin of languages are, at the start of the nineteenth century, given a new nationalist inflection to answer emergent questions about the ethnographic origin of peoples and their role in the production of new concepts of the nation. The quest for a universal oral language expressive of pre-social passion now competes with specific social origins as a form of inscription. The originary is not a pure concept of human nature but now includes acts of differentiation, division and peculiarity. Of course, 'natural' origins do not disappear. On the contrary, acts of national distinction are seen to be underpinned by the universal act of naming itself. Toponymy had long been recognised as a reliable source of knowledge about the ancient past. Leibniz believed place-names to be a window on pre-historical nature: 'Since the distant origins of nations transcend history, languages take for us the place of old documents. The most ancient vestiges of languages remain in the names of rivers and forests, which very often survive the changes of populations.'[11] More recently, Lord Monboddo had asserted that '[a]s language therefore is the most lasting of all the memorials of men, so, of language itself, the names of places are what last the longest.'[12] William Thomson, in his tour of Scotland (written under the pseudonym 'Thomas Newte'), managed to blend stadial historiography, which argues that cultures are geographical and historically variable, with Adamic language theory, which asserts that language was delivered all at once in the Garden of Eden. Thomson's argument implies that had primitive peoples not named the topographical features they encountered, their modern successors would not now be able to grasp what these features actually were:

It is in the first of these stages that men are qualified to give names to regions, districts, and towns, descriptive of their nature. Who but a hunter and warrior, accustomed to traverse valley beyond valley, and mountain beyond mountain, could have discovered that vast plain that intersects Scotland had nothing equal to it in all the land; and that it might, therefore, by way of eminence, be fitly denominated Strathmore?

For Thomson, the very possibility of environmental knowledge is dependent on this primitive act of naming, without which 'the natural divisions of the country would not have been marked by proper names. Through the want of these the greatest confusion would have reigned in civil affairs, and the most formidable impediments have been opposed to the progress of knowledge.'[13] The original landscape is already divided in acts of naming, allowing it to be legible after the advent of 'civil affairs'. Thomson's primitive people know what things are really called and thus inaugurate a smooth, incremental history of social and intellectual progress.

  In locating the field of battle in the etymology of place-names, Pinkerton and Chalmers, both Unionist Scots, are aware of their strategic importance in discussions of the origins of national history. But the specific place of the nation of Scotland within the state of Great Britain gives a particular complexity to their arguments. The naming of places is important for Romanticism in general but not uniformly so across all parts of the kingdom. For Wordsworth and Clare, place-names are psychological and individual; they presuppose the centrality of the subject and assume his or her experiences as an organising principle. In the advertisement to his *Poems on the Naming of Places*, Wordsworth can conceive of places as organic and communal; they come into being in a private act of naming, restricted to 'the Author and some of his Friends':

> By Persons resident in the country and attached to rural objects, many places will be found unnamed or of unknown names, where little Incidents will have occurred, or feelings been experienced, which will have given to such places a private and peculiar Interest. From a wish to give some sort of record to such Incidents or renew the gratification of such Feelings, Names have been given to Places by the Author and some of his Friends–and the following Poems written in consequence.[14]

Wordsworth, then, is confident in a sense of the singularity of location and the possibility of its being generated empirically. Discrete places emerge from, and supersede, their surrounding space by the agency of human experience and the stories told about them. There is no boundary between this creation of a private space through naming and a sense of the nation, because patriotism is – or should be – rooted in the kind of organic community Wordsworth is describing. But the *Poems on the Naming of Places* are not quite without a nervous apprehension that British history might throw up rival systems of naming. Writing on 'To Joanna', Hilary A. Zaid comments that 'Wordsworth often fears that public exposure will bleach texts of their private meanings, and he frequently attempts to combat this slippage by associating words with a specific place at which the meaning is believed to inhere.'[15] Lurking at the edges of private naming is the sense that the landscape has already been inscribed by contesting historiographies. Wordsworth footnotes his own act of engraving Joanna's name like a 'Runic priest' on the rock with the observation that '[i]n Cumberland and Westmoreland are several Inscriptions upon the native rock, which from the wasting of Time and the rudeness of the Work-manship had been mistaken for Runic. They are without doubt Roman.'[16]

What for Wordsworth, constructing his acts of communal naming in the autonomous, organic space of Grasmere, is a footnote becomes, by contrast, a question of important national identity for Scottish writers for whom the difference between Roman and Runic inscription could mean a great deal. For a nation in which the local was already pressed into the service of the political economy of 'improvement', place-names had a clear national character. And for Tory, Unionist antiquarians, the nature of primitive inscriptions was key to the study of place-names.

The first challenge was the name of the nation itself. Chalmers uses a set of overlapping identities which, even as he insists on the correct and specific use of names, allows him to put together a complex sense of the place of the nation in space and time. 'Caledonia', the book's title, is an overarching term that secures Scotland's primitive origins with those of the civic state and guarantees both with the authenticity of the natural. 'Caledonia' is at once a specific tribe, a natural feature (meaning 'of the woods'), a Latin appellation for the whole nation, and the neoclassical title of Chalmers' intellectual labours. 'North-Britain', by far Chalmers' most frequently used term, is a structural tool that establishes a geographical equivalence between England and Scotland and unites the nation in ancient and modern uses of the term. In an example of how geography was used to neutralise the potential Scotophobia of the designation 'North Britain', Chalmers uses the term to collapse two temporal identities into each other. 'North Britain' is Enlightenment Scotland, recognised by 'the intelligent world': 'Ages elapsed [. . .] before the British Island, as it came to be sub-divided into parts, was known to the intelligent world by the geographical appellations of South and North Britain' (vol. 2, p. 4). Yet, Chalmers repeatedly uses the term to describe the north of Britain, before any modern borders were established, allowing 'North Britain' to hover between a geographical and a political space. Chalmers also has a third term whose meaning is not always precise. 'Proper Scotland' is a space that is both ethnically and geographically determined. Chalmers uses it to refer to the land of the Scots, excluding the northern islands and Caithness and denoting land not settled by Scandinavian invaders. But, in another sense, 'Proper Scotland' is also one and the same as the whole project of *Caledonia*. Place-names are 'proper' because they are real and self-present, as in William Thomson's argument that we can only understand landscape because of the 'proper names' bestowed on it by original peoples. 'Proper Scotland' carries both meanings of the term: Scotland itself and Scotland properly named. Explaining the origins of 'Caledonia', Chalmers tells us that the 'proper *Caledonii*' are those who 'inhabited a great portion of the forest, *Celyddon*' (vol. I, pp. 64–5). The Caledonians' language comes from the land and bestows names back onto it. 'Proper Scotland' is a pure line of linguistic descent inscribed onto the spatial contours of the country. Chalmers will argue that its names are not local to Scotland but a substrate of Britain as a whole. Place-names are what give Scotland its real identity and render it not supplementary to England but originary for Great Britain. 'Proper Scotland' is the link between geography, language and national identity that offers continuity where mere objects might remain fragmentary.

To understand how Chalmers sought to make ancient Scotland pan-British and to grasp the ambition and comprehensive scope of his project, we can explore the ways in which an older tradition of the study of language origins is becoming deflected into a newer, and at first contradictory, tradition of antiquarianism. A striking example is another book on Celtic etymology from the same period as Chalmers' work: Gilbert Dyer's *Vulgar Errors, Ancient and Modern.* Like Chalmers, Dyer thinks that local place-names are part of the general language of proper names, which can, in turn, constitute national history. To move place-names to the fore as signs of national importance marked a significant departure from the course of language theory. Eighteenth-century philology had a strong class basis that privileged 'abstract' modes of language over particular utterances and posited words as carriers of universal, permanent ideas rather than specific applications. Hugh Blair makes what he sees as an abstract mode of language an indicator of national progress: 'The more any nation is improved by science, and the more perfect their Language becomes, we may naturally expect, that it will abound the more with connective particles; expressing relations of things, and transitions of thought, which had escaped a grosser view.'[17] Particles (by which Blair means connective parts of speech such as prepositions and conjunctions) have a transcendental function in that they appear to be universal and not tied to the specific functions of nouns and verbs. Olivia Smith notes: 'The concept of pure reason depended largely on the definition of the particles, for it was their existence which proved that the mind could act without referring to either time or place.'[18] Antiquarianism, by contrast, is all about the specificity of time and place. Particularly, if it is thought of primarily as the recovery of objects, then, as Yoon Sun Lee remarks, 'the existence of the antiquarian object is contingent on processes of obsolescence and fragmentation, as these afflict cultures, institutions, and nations.'[19]

Place-names are, self-evidently, attached to individual locations. The tours and surveys of Pennant and Sinclair, for all their goal of rationalising and systematising topography, were obliged to ask local people what places were called. Pennant's preliminary question was: 'What is the ancient and modern name of the parish, and its etymology?'[20] Dyer gets round the specificity of local names by some deft, if fantastical moves. *Vulgar Errors* is a late flowering of Adamic language theories grafted onto the study of place-names. At the very start of his study, he reaches back to theories of Hebrew as the origin of language itself, when names, things and concepts were inseparable: 'every Hebrew word must at once be a name, and a definition of the subject.'[21] For Dyer, original language springs directly from the Earth. His examples, he claims, 'prove that the features of nature gave names to men and to trees, prove not that either men or trees gave denominations to these features, or to letters' (p. i).

Functioning in the same way as Hebrew is a proto-language that Dyer usually refers to as 'Celtic'. Celtic gives clues to the universal philological principles upon which the work rests. The correct understanding of local place-names, Dyer argues, can lead to an understanding of global geography: 'Our ignorance of the significations of old names has doubtless been a great impediment in [. . .] the adjustment of the ancient topography and geography of the earth' (p. xxii). His examples promote Celtic both as a world language and as a system of naming that contains its own connective grammar. Paradoxically, the very act of naming specific places depends upon that particle-laden language that indicates abstraction. The study of place-names works like a microscope: apparently simple words are revealed to be complex and interdependent, their meanings arising from the relations of prepositions, articles and adjectives. Even the smallest of seemingly unitary morphemes blossom under Dyer's scrutiny: 'The old monosyllabic words of the world still existing in languages, contain certain roots, prefixes, and postfixes' which 'refer directly to the ancient names of Asia, of Africa, and of Europe' (p. ii).

In Dyer's work, then, place-names become the key to unlocking the history of world culture and resolving the problem of how local names can also be abstract. Dyer squares the circles of competing forms of authenticity: although place-names can be ascertained by asking the people who live in those specific places, they are also the signs of world civilisation. They are both rooted in natural phenomena and touched with the perfect abstraction of eighteenth-century language theories. This also has national implications. In the imaginary world of Dyer's Celtic, the 'native' language forms a secure substrate that obviates the problems Johnson encountered in isolating purely 'English' words.[22]

The relevance of such linguistic harmony for Scottish topography is suggested by the dedication of Dyer's work. *Vulgar Errors* was dedicated to the United Highland Societies of London and Edinburgh, and we can see it as part of a reappropriation of the Highlands as a pan-British space made respectable by antiquarian inquiry. Though neither London nor Edinburgh is in the Highlands, their south–north correspondence gives the impression of a structural equivalence that glides over the unevenness the geographical Highlands would produce. The Highlands become

'United' with the rest of the Kingdom by their absorption in the apparently national reach of a scholarly community. Dyer's work introduces for us what was at stake for George Chalmers' much more widely read *Caledonia* and the potential for constructing ideas about history and national identities out of the powerful tool that place-names had become. Both concrete and abstract, both local and national, place-names offered a way of moving the peripheries of Great Britain to the linguistic centre.

For Chalmers, the 'topography' of Scotland is not its landscape but the record of its naming. *Caledonia* has a very specific aim: to produce a picture of the whole of Great Britain, showing both the homogeneity of the nation and its specific roots in ancient Celtic history. Chalmers has a finely calibrated idea of the disciplinarity of his work as he situates himself in the shifting relationship of space and time, history and geography. Throughout *Caledonia*, he insists that geography, not history, is the best record of the earliest period of the nation. He thinks of topography and speculative history as two different forms of language. Topography is inductive, constructing its national genealogy from actual place-names, whereas the deductive powers of history are obliged to invent local details to suit grand historical narratives. Topography is therefore rational, factual language, whereas history, typified by Pinkerton and the Gothicists, is absurd logomachy, a futile argument about language:

> If language be the genealogy of nations; if the topography of Scotland exhibit to the eye, and show to the understanding, the several tongues of the successive settlers; it follows, from those circumstances, that topography must furnish proofs, the most satisfactory, of the nature of the people who gave the existing names to the ancient settlements. This argument has been found so oppressive to those theorists, who substitute conceit for knowledge, and assertions for facts, that they have endeavoured to free themselves from the weight of reasoning, which they could not support, by transforming the Gaelic names into Gothic, and by metamorphosing the language of the Maps; so as to substitute fiction for fact, and to establish the absurdities of error, for the consistencies of truth. Those theorists seem not to have been aware, when they thus endeavoured, by a stroke of perversion, to convert the *Celtic* topography of North-Britain into Gothic logomachy. (vol. I, pp. 490–1)

Chalmers is constructing that sophisticated, modern version of Adamic language that William Thomson described and making it political. The nation becomes visible in acts of social naming, and if places *are* what they are called, then topography is the ground that verifies and authenticates any political position. Chalmers uses this technique in order to build up his structure of the modern British state in which Scotland, so far from occupying a secondary position, acts as the model for the whole.

First, Chalmers uses the 'truth' of place-names to assemble a visible, structural form of Great Britain, in which names are not politically contingent. The work opens with Chalmers' extensive 'Dictionary of Places, Chorographical and Philological', a view of Britain laid out diagrammatically to reveal the structural equality of place-names. Rivers and other geographical features are entered into parallel columns headed 'South Britain' and 'North Britain', while footnotes give further examples from the whole nation and their derivation, occasionally from Welsh or Cornish but usually from an unspecific Celtic language that Chalmers calls 'British' (a source of several inaccurate claims). For example: the Ken (actually 'Kent') in Westmorland, England, appears alongside the Ken in Galloway, Scotland, while a footnote informs the reader that '*Cain* (Brit.) signifies *white, clear*, or beautiful' (vol. I, p. 45 n.). No longer in a vertical order of priority, England and Scotland appear side by side, underpinned by the genealogy of what is now only a Scottish language. In rendering Celts as topographical signifiers, their specifically Scottish connotations become absorbed into a structural Britishness expressed as a form of location. We see 'in the names of mountains, and waters, the real precedence of the British people' (vol. II, p. 79). In evacuating the political content from ancient tribes and turning them into the signifiers of place, Chalmers inscribes a national geography where cognate names of places and rivers act isotopically to map a united kingdom in a manner at once 'historical and topographical'. Political divisions in the kingdom may be ironed out by ancient continuities of naming, and the prominence of rivers in Chalmers' tables underscores the idea of a whole nation. As Jonathan Bate points out, rivers, since Drayton's *Poly-Olbion*, had been seen as threads that laced up the nation.[23] The idea of rivers as national continuity, rather than the natural border of the Tweed which had formed a focus for anti-Scottish propaganda in the eighteenth century, advances Chalmers' plan of mapping Britain by naming Scotland.

Chalmers develops his theory of topographic language as a conjunction of his ancient Britons with modern Scottish intellectuals. At first, he seems to confirm the general opinion that primitive peoples do not construct complex civil societies: 'The Aborigines of North-Britain, like other rude people, in the most early stages of society, were probably less governed by law, than by religion' (vol. I, p. 69). Yet, immediately afterwards, he has organised his aboriginal North British into something strikingly like the professional middle classes of modern Edinburgh, centre of literature, science and the law:

Among the priests of *Druidism*, there appear to have been three orders; the Druids, the Vates; and the Bards, who severally performed very different functions: the *Bards* sung, in heroic verse, the brave actions of eminent men; the *Vates* studied continually, and explained nature, the productions of nature, and the laws; and the Druids, who were of a higher order [. . .] directed the education of youth, officiated in the affairs of religion, and presided in the administration of justice. (vol. I, p. 70)

In modernising his ur-Scots in this way, Chalmers circumvents the 'problem' of their association with the oral and inscribes them into the institutions of writing. And, thus, he absorbs the idea of nationality as an ethnic origin – a problematic question for Scots both in terms of anti-quarian disputes and modern divisions in the country – into the more homogenous idea of nationality as a set of civic and social relations.[24] The classification of peoples as Celtic or Teutonic was, in the early nineteenth century, taking on the characteristics that would continue to identify British history and politics as fundamentally Anglo-Saxon and to mark the Celt, particularly the growing numbers of Irish immigrants, as back-ward or racially other.[25] But Chalmers is comparatively uninterested in Celts as ethnic subjects, having already transmuted them into structural signifiers to be plotted on the cultural networks of civic society. For him, these ethnicities can only be understood through the emergence of modern cultural institutions: the establishing of new chairs in Scottish universities and the foundation of the Society of Antiquaries.

The history of North Britain, then, is really the *telos* of its status as a modern commercial nation, in the process of establishing forms of institutional public and professional knowledge, and Chalmers is clear about this in his preface. He regrets that the Society of Edinburgh for the Encouragement of Arts, Sciences, and Manufactures was unable to award a gold medal in 1756 for the best history of early Scotland, or a subsequent medal for a history of the 'rise and progress of commerce, arts, and manufactures' (vol. I, p. vii). Chalmers is belatedly offering *Caledonia* to fill this intellectual void and, substituting 'origin' for 'rise and progress', splices the two histories together. In the modern nation, only the spe-cialisation and institutionalisation of knowledge, typified by contem-porary Edinburgh, can grasp and analyse that history. One of Chalmers' many pronouncements on the superiority of geography over history reads: 'The topography of North-Britain, rather than her history, supplies that demonstration. This truth will appear, whether we look, for local language, into her charters, her tax-rolls, or her maps' (vol. I, p. 481). Chalmers here elides the idea of a 'local language' with the very instruments of state bureaucracy that produce the nation as a civic society rather than as a consolidation of ethnicities. Original local names may be discovered on these documents, but it is the statewide measures of taxation and legalisation that precede their discovery and make them legible, just as Chalmers' 'discovery' of the Caledonians is preceded by the intellectual demands of the Society of Antiquaries, to which he had been elected in 1791.

Chalmers' enfolding of ancient and modern bureaucracies into each other constitutes a referential resource that he and other Scottish antiquarians were to insert as a prominent stage in their national history: the Roman invasion of Scotland. Both the Republic and the Empire had been important to the development of ideas about history and civic society in the Scottish Enlightenment, but, outside the study of antiquarian monuments, comparatively little had been written about the Roman period of Britain. For Hume and Ferguson, Roman civilisation had been metaphoric or paradigmatic, indicative of the ways in which the arts or national defence function in different forms and stages of powerful government. Chalmers is uninterested in social parallels and neoclassical models, and the Romans, like the Celts, are absorbed into his geometric model of Britain to function metonymically within the structure of antiquarian history. The Romans are not parallels for neoclassical society but – however remotely – contiguous. And this contiguity is provided by Scotland. An example is his invoking of Roman law, the basis for Scottish, but not English law. In identifying the law as the source for topography, and topography as a better account of national origins than history, Chalmers introduces a structural model that will inform the whole of *Caledonia* and will help him construct the geometry of Great Britain so that Scotland can stand for the whole island. Scottish law is an important source for tracing the origins of modernity in a Celtic past as many Scottish legal terms 'owe their origin to the Celtic language' (vol. I, p. 446). From here, Chalmers proposes Roman Britain as an originary period which was at once Celtic, British, and juridical as laws in North and South Britain had the same foundation: 'During the Roman period, the same laws continued common to both' (vol. I, n. 446).[26]

Roman Britain allows Chalmers to make use of the supplementarity of the north. John Lucas writes that bards and druids, the assumed builders of antiquarian sites, emerge in the eighteenth century as part of 'a "new" history, in which a distinctively northern tradition of "British" emerges in opposition to the Roman'.[27] But this was not the complete case for Chalmers who draws the Romans into Scottish-British identity. He writes: 'At the epoch of Agricola's invasion, North-Britain may be viewed as a mirror, that reflects back the condition, in which was South-Britain, at the more distant era, when Julius Caesar first invaded the shores of our island' (vol. I, p. 57). This is an interesting piece of geographical sleight of hand, not least because the more usual narrative of the Romans in Scotland was to play up Celtic resistance. But again, Chalmers' Celts are strategic rather than historical: on the one hand, North Britain and South Britain are structurally identical: equal geographical parts, equally colonising and colonised, and a very different model from the internal colonisation of Scotland by England. But, just as Scotland is the northern part of an already northern nation, so its history acts as a mirror for the history of South Britain. Or, more precisely, in Chalmers' phrase, Scotland acts a mirror for 'our island' as a whole. In short, then, Chalmers announces that the topography of *Scotland* is a way of knowing about the origins of *Britain*. His move to counter Scotland's status as secondary or supplementary to England is subject to the general logic of supplementarity itself. The Romans are the point at which Chalmers' quest for the purity of national origins breaks down. Instead of the Adamic naming of places at a point of natural origin, national ancient history must be accessed through law and bureaucracy. And, instead of the 'native' Caledonians of Proper Scotland, who merge seamlessly with their topography, our understanding of national history can only be grasped at a point of colonisation. This deconstruction of the pure national origin takes us back to another text very interested in Roman Scotland, *The Antiquary*.

'THE CREDIT OF SCOTTISH HISTORY': INSCRIPTION IN SCOTT'S *THE ANTIQUARY*

The Antiquary seems, at first glance, to be a text about the position of the local at a time of heightened national awareness. Set in and around a small Scottish town in 1794, the novel is permeated by a threatened invasion by the French. If, as Linda Colley argues, Britain's wars with France were principally responsible for the constitution of forms of national identity, then this novel about antiquarians, published just after the end of the Napoleonic wars, might be taken as an exploration of forms of Britishness as a cultural category.[28] Yet, the novel is very resistant to this model. Not least, for a novel that is so much about historiography,

The Antiquary is curiously reticent about the representation of history. The feared invasion forms the novel's historical 'event', but not much is heard of it until the end when it seems like a device to consolidate Lovel as the straightforwardly British hero the novel has decidedly not promised. In terms of the novel's Gothic family plot, Fiona Robertson astutely observes that the problematic past can only be resolved by one of the few characters who has *not* engaged in historical research: 'The Glenallans [. . .] must be reconciled to the present day by way of a hero brought up in ignorance of his identity and inheritance, a legitimate representative but an ideological opponent of the dead past which he alone can revitalise.'[29] But, as its title suggests, the space cleared by the absence of events can be filled – or so it seems at first – with the interests of antiquarians: ruins, objects and, especially, languages. The novel's frequent references to Chalmers, Pinkerton and the controversy over Scotland's original languages, foregrounds the functions of language itself, and Scott explores how modernity generates its own myths of customs or origins and how these function not as the recovery of the past, or even the reinvention of homologous traditions or objects, but as a continuous process of circulation, fed by different social contexts.

The Antiquary looks at the relations of language and history, linked through the metaphor of currency, both in its financial sense and in the idea of what is current. Money, in *The Antiquary*, takes the form both of the collector's pieces, or 'medals' beloved by the antiquarian, and of cash and credit. The novel considers money as object – the material witness of the past – and as a system of exchange and renewal that functions in the present and, thus, works against the idea of a layered, static history that can be excavated by the antiquarian. If Monboddo had insisted that place-names were the most enduring memorials of man, he further adds that language is 'not only most permanent and durable, but it is one of those arts which men easily carry about with them',[30] and it is just this fluidity and circulation of language that Scott explores as the novel sets the possibility of a rooted place, known through its objects or place-names, against the virtual space of a modern economy.

The Antiquary is usually read as a satire on antiquarian excess, but it also takes a serious look at the claims of antiquarianism both to reveal the past and to shore up present ideas about class, ownership and cultural capital. In this novel, etymology is the site of disputed cases for legitimacy and cultural authority; names, places and coins are subject to forgery. Language breaks down as the key to ethnic origins, ancient history and property rights. *The Antiquary* is interested in names: how places acquire their names and how the names of people determine or influence their behaviour. People are named after places – Oldbuck is known locally as Monkbarns from the land he owns – but the novel is also about rootlessness and the problem of naming. Significantly, the original Oldenbuck claimed by the family as an ancestor was a Protestant printer obliged to leave Germany in the sixteenth century; the source of the name is one of inscription and displaced origins. *The Antiquary* rejects the direct and observable lines of descent promised by Chalmers. Topography is not a useful form of cultural capital in the novel, which renders the nation a far more fluid and diffuse place. As Yoon Sun Lee puts it, 'this novel celebrates the moral coherence and historical continuity of the British nation as an improbable but highly profitable fiction.'[31] National identity turns on a question of location: is the nation a hypothetical place, existing in the continually changing present of a credit-based economy, or can the nation be experienced locally, in the artefacts, customs and names of its inhabitants across time?

Despite the novel's references to the place-name arguments between Chalmers and Pinkerton, its contribution to the fictions of Scottish geography is to break down the relationship between locality and nation and to disrupt the lines of topographic continuity that the antiquarians had proposed. *The Antiquary* opens by lulling the reader into a false sense of security on the matter of place-names. We are introduced to the as-yet-unnamed hero by means of his location. Travelling 'towards the northeast of Scotland', he has bought a ticket for 'one of those public carriages which travel between Edinburgh and the Queensferry, at which place, as the name implies, and is well known to all my northern readers, there is a passage-boat for crossing the Firth of Forth' (p. 5). Naming here seems to be the least problematic of activities: Queensferry is knowable both because its identity is directly communicated by its name and because its name is known within the language-community of Scotland in any case. Queensferry is clearly in Chalmers' 'proper Scotland' in both senses of that term. Needless to say, this does not remain the case for long and, in fact, is not even the case at the start of the novel as the here-unnamed hero will go through a differential series of proper names, determined by the changing social contexts that define him: Mr Lovel, Major Neville and, eventually, Lord Geraldin. Fairport, where the action takes place, is not the 'real' name of the place but merely so dominated, Scott says mysteriously, 'for various reasons' (p. 13).

Such indeterminate locations point to a loosening of the relationship between antiquarianism and the nation imagined as a whole. So far from

Chalmers' harmonious picture of an ancient national lineage that unites local speakers with institutional scholars, Oldbuck's vision is class-based. Visiting the ruined library at St Ruth's priory, he laments the loss of historical documents which would have contributed to national history. Historiography is the master discourse of the nation – Oldbuck would be happy if the ancient scholastic works of the church 'had leapt out of our libraries, for the accommodation of grocers, candle-makers, soap-sellers, and other worldly occupiers', but historical texts are a different matter: 'to put our ancient chronicles, our noble histories, our learned commentaries, and national muniments, to such offices of contempt and subjection, has greatly degraded our nation, and shewed ourselves dishonoured in the eyes of posterity to the utmost stretch of time – O negligence, most unfriendly to our land!' (p. 131). Oldbuck's inclusive 'our' glosses over the fact that he sees tradespeople as unworthy custodians of national learning. His confident sense of historical continuity remains at surface level; much less certain is the way in which the nation is to be constituted in terms of class, gender and party. We are, here, a long way from Chalmers' assumption of a general Britishness consolidated in its institutions and confirmed by local contributions to statistical surveys, maps and legal documents.

The naming of places raises questions about the continuities and communalities that antiquarian linguists had sought to establish and addresses the unavoidability, or even the usefulness, of Chalmers' fear that discussions of naming will descend into 'absurd logomachy'. The arguments between Oldbuck and Wardour reveal the complexity of social naming and the political nature of writing. In one typical exchange, Oldbuck asserts his printing ancestry to score a point (as Wardour takes it) over Wardour's illiterate aristocratic forebears: 'not one of whom [. . .] could write their own name' (p. 50). Wardour objects to this slur, claiming that the name of his ancestor, one Gamelyn de Guardover, is 'written fairly with his own hand in the earliest copy of the Ragman-roll' (p. 50). But the mention of this document, signed by the Scottish nobles who paid homage, initially in 1291, to the English king Edward I, allows Oldbuck to come back with the assertion that it 'only serves to shew that he was one of the earliest who set the mean example of submitting to Edward I' (p. 50). The signature, that most proper of proper names, is divided at the point of inscription. Oldbuck uses the oxymoronic term 'earliest copy', reminding us of the necessary iterability of signatures. Edward did produce a second document with further signatures to it in 1296, but, as Oldbuck's response indicates, Wardour is referring to the first document, which cannot, in the literal sense, be said to be a copy. Legal and political documents, for Chalmers one of the best witnesses of national continuity, are here revealed to be very poor sources of originary evidence. The paradoxical status of the 'earliest copy' reminds us of Jacques Derrida's argument that the personal signature, the sign that claims to guarantee the continuity and preservation of the unique subject in every future context, is in fact dependent on its iterability – its capacity for being imitated and repeated in ways that undermine the apparent originality and uniqueness of its first inscription.

The novel explodes models of history that imagine original states of being. Oldbuck's dismissal of Wardour's ancestor as a political lackey also invokes the Rousseauist argument that writing moves the subject away from originality and self-identity and into the conventional world of the political in which self-determining individuals are turned into political subjects. But where Rousseau mourns this loss of original language, Scott's novel accepts, even embraces, the generative force of social and political discourse. Language, as befits the historical novel, is performative rather than documentary, and efforts to trace linguistic origins will produce not the origin itself but more and more discussion about it. *The Antiquary* holds this debate in relation to the problem of etymology, and particularly of toponymy. If, as the novel seems to posit by example, names cannot be traced back through genealogy, and there are no documents which give a privileged access to original meanings, then the national coherence that Chalmers sought to demonstrate cannot be shown to inhere in naming.

In one of the novel's most famous scenes, Lovel and Oldbuck take a turn through Oldbuck's property. As a sign of things to come, Oldbuck points to an apple tree whose fruit used to be collected by the wife of a neighbouring baron: 'Her husband [. . .] suspected that a taste so nearly resembling that of Mother Eve prognosticated a similar fall' (p. 27). We are already in the territory not so much of original sin (although the novel is in part about legitimacy) but of that long-standing interest in the history of language in the postlapsarian world and the loss of an authentic relation between words and things. As the scene progresses into this world of linguistic confusion, systems of naming become multiple and con-textual, inhabiting different forms and traditions. Oldbuck first tries to assert a local authority whose singularity has not been absorbed into the greater nationalist scheme of the *Statistical Account*. He identifies the ruin of a pre-Reformation *hospitium*: 'I know our minister has said, in the Statistical Account, that the *hospitium* was situated either on the lands of

Haltweary, or upon those of Halfstarvet; but he is incorrect, Mr. Lovel – that is the gate called still the Palmer's Port' (p. 27). But Oldbuck's readiness to naturalise place-names into a kind of local functionalism turns out to be as much of a fantasy as Scott's naming of his own house, Abbotsford, along the same lines as the Palmer's Port, or, indeed, as Monkbarns' own name, which follows the same pattern of monastic localities.

Neither does Oldbuck's attempt to identify a nearby mound as a Roman fort fare any better. The Romans, sign of the heterogeneity of national origins, interfere with Oldbuck's confident etymologies. He appeals first to the Wordsworthian idea of place-names being generated through the memory of local inhabitants: 'Why, the very common people, the very least boy that can herd a cow, calls it the Kaim of Kinprunes' (p. 28). Then he rationalises this with an appeal to philo-logical toponymy – the entirely circular argument that because he believes Romans to have been present in the area, their presence is indicated by the Latin origin of place-names. He derives 'Kinprunes' from the Latin 'pruina', hoarfrost, and backs this up with the observation that this must be correct because there are a great deal of hoarfrosts on the north-eastern coast of Scotland. Oldbuck's trump card is the same as Chalmers' appeal to a topographical autochthony – the idea that place-names grow out of the natural features of the land and can therefore be taken to be the best record of the foundations of the nation: 'The names, which the original planters imposed on the great objects of nature, and which have con-tinued, for the information of every age, exhibit [. . .] the real lineage of the tribes, who occupied the British world' (vol. II, p. 1). But *The Antiquary* continually refuses these lineages. The mound turns out to be a temporary shelter for a wedding held a few years ago and not called anything very much, as we are informed by local character Edie Ochiltree.

Names, like so much in the novel, are provisional or contingent and their derivations fluid or hybrid. So far from denoting the great historical sweep from 'the foundations of the nation' to the present, names are functional and transitory. Edie is not the privileged bearer of folk-names designated as any more 'real' than Oldbuck's fanciful Roman derivation. All either of them have to go on as typographic evidence are the letters 'A. D. L. L'. carved on a stone, which Edie claims stands for 'Aiken Drum's Lang Ladle' (p. 31) and commemorates the wedding feast, while Oldbuck supports his Roman theory with '*Agricola Dicavit Libens Lubeds* [Agricola willingly and happily dedicated this]' (p. 29). Judith Wilt and

David Hewitt have untangled the various parodic and associative meanings suggested by these interpretations, uncovering a complex web of contexts for the novel, a form of history that is reticular rather than linear.[32] And this, in turn, suggests a more serious note to the novel's antiquarian comedy. The construction of elaborate theories from single letters was a common joke on antiquarians. Lovel is reminded of a similar example, and Smollett's *Peregrine Pickle* tells the story of an antiquarian who, on scrutinising a worn farthing, concludes that it is a Roman medal on the grounds that the surviving letters N and I of the inscription 'Britannia' prove that it 'was struck by Severus, in honour of the victory he obtained over his rival Niger'.[33] The evident frequency of the figure in popular culture underlines not only its comic potential but also the way it becomes a function of language itself, not least in the form of the novel with its own history of generic variegation and discursive heterogeneity.

The Antiquary is full of examples of the inevitable hybridity of language. Pictish, the novel's chief bone of contention between its warring antiquaries, becomes a synecdoche for language in general and a sign of the impossibility of understanding it through the genealogies of antiquarianism. Pictish is the antiquarians' Holy Grail, the lost language that promises to guarantee the purity of their linguistic lines of descent even as it recedes further from their grasp. In Wardour's and Oldbuck's interminable argument about the alleged Pictish place-name 'Penval', each claims one syllable to support the countering arguments that the Picts spoke a Celtic or Gothic dialect. Wardour maintains that *pen* is the same as *ben* or mountain, while Oldbuck insists that *val* is the Gothic form of modern English w*all*. As Lovel points out, the mythic language of the Picts seems to consist only of two syllables and that Wardour and Oldbuck 'have been confessedly obliged to borrow one of them from another language [. . .]. Each of you claim one-half of the word and seem to resign the other' (p. 49). Primitive language, so far from indicating a pure or true line of descent, in fact reveals difference at the supposed origin. The well-known hybridity of the British as a 'race' is here seen as a quality of language – unable to produce any single source, the antiquarians become locked in an argument that supports only the endless differential process of their own etymology.

What is most striking about Oldbuck's dialogue is the sheer abundance of relations that it generates. Teetering between sober etymology and a wild Shandean association of ideas, he spawns an incessant stream of connections between words. Oldbuck has been the butt of much criticism for this habit, and, given the length of his forays into dubious etymology, readers may agree. But if antiquarian language fails as archaeology, it does not mean that Oldbuck's discourse is wholly without relevance in Scott's unhistorical historical novel. Scott suggests that one reason why language may not be a good recorder of history is that it is so functional and adaptable in the present. Synchronicity in language is a matter of usage and context. Oldbuck's sister volunteers to try a spell for deterring witchcraft from one of her brother's books. She recalls that the ingredients were vervain, dill and 'pepper-corn', instigating a tirade from Old-buck: 'Hypericon, thou foolish woman! [. . .] d'ye suppose you're making a haggis – or do you think that a spirit, though he be formed of air, can be expelled by a receipt against wind?' (p. 83). The joke here is that even in his tirade against his sister, Oldbuck cannot quite dismiss the kind of etymology – functional and associative – that she uses. It is, after all, highly probable in world of spells that, according to the system of what J. G. Frazer was to call 'homoeopathic magic', the metonymic air–wind association would work quite well. In any case, Oldbuck invents his own etymology of this kind in his wholly made-up descent of the word 'shathmont' (a unit of measurement) from an old form of 'salmon' on the grounds that there was a medieval legal requirement to leave a particular space for water (presumably containing salmon) to pass through a dam and that the two words sound quite similar anyway (p. 66). There can be no transcendent language. Even the particle, Enlightenment language theory's universal part of speech, is subject to the specificities of context in Olbuck's comic personification and particularisation of the word 'but': '*But* is a sneaking, evasive, half-bred, exceptious sort of a conjunction, which comes to pull away the cup just when it is at your lips' (p. 83).

'Property', in this novel, is not a quality of the proper in Chalmers' sense. Instead of land marked out by the proper names bestowed on it by aboriginal inhabitants, Scotland is inscribed by the legal discourse of property. Grizel Oldbuck tells the story of a local lawyer, Rab Tull, who meets up with a Latin-speaking ghost. Rab's Latin is not good, but, being a lawyer, he does manage to recognise the word 'carta', a term which Grizel replaces with the more familiar 'carter', only to incur another stream of her brother's wrath. Undeterred, she carries on with the story: 'Weel, weel, *carta* be it then, but they ca'd it *carter* that tell'd me the story. It cried aye *carta*, if sae be that it was *carta*' (p. 72). In contradistinction to Chalmers' etymologies, language has no natural genealogies that preserve meaning. The difference between 'carter' and 'carta' has to do with the context of narration, not the meaning of the word itself. And this turns out to be at least as reliable a source of toponymy as Oldbuck's: the 'carta' in question turns out to be the charter of ownership of the original lands of Monkbarns. Such a discovery marks a radical departure from the reliance of place-name theorists on a form of historical translatability, the idea that all modern names are legible forms of an originary language. In this case, it is the lack of communication and an accidental form of translation that leads to the rediscovery of a written past and the property rights generated by it.

The novel's play with fantastical linguistic origins is reflected in financial ones. Its most important locality, in plot terms, is the grave in which the two caches of 'treasure' are found. According to legend, this is the resting place of Malcolm Misbegot, or Misticot, an illegitimate Wardour ancestor who gives his name to Misticot's Tower. At the centre of the financial plot is a name that is differential and whose genealogy is illegitimate – a bastardised origin very far from the continuities and correspondences between ancient Caledonia and modern British Scotland that Chalmers had taken such pains to set up. This grave is an engraving in more ways than one. It holds an inscription, but one that is far from the reliable toponymy of the antiquarians. As part of his plan to maintain the conman Dousterswivel's interest in the grave, Edie shows him the words '*Search Number I.*' carved into the lid of the treasure chest and urges him on with, '*Search Number I.* – that is as mickle as to say, search and ye'll find number twa' (p. 200). Edie knows what Derrida was later to point out: that a thing can only be understood as original by means of the succeeding narrative of which it is the supposed origin. The number one is only uniquely singular by virtue of comparison with two, three, four and so on, and thus not unique or original at all. And, of course, the same inscription can be part of more than one narrative. We discover that the '*Search Number I.*' box is a chest from the gun-brig *Search* in which Lovel has left money for Sir Arthur. The novel associates money not so much with value per se as with representation. The lack of authentic treasure in the grave generates multiple narratives and inventions, and Scott is very interested in the relationship between money and fiction, both within the field of antiquarianism and in relation to modern, national contexts.

Critics have rightly pointed to the importance of objects in *The Antiquary*'s critique of antiquarian history and its economic situation. Shawn Malley observes that '[t]he capitalistic recovery of material history – the ownership and monetary valuation of the past based on rarity and absence – locates objects marked as "historical" within the professional and genealogical consciousness of those who own and, in Scott's case, write them'.[34] Yoon Sun Lee makes a powerful case for the novel's exposure of the financial contracts at the heart of antiquarianism:

> the practice of antiquarianism made manifest the latent resemblance between historical value and market value: both were contingent on the relation between scarcity and a generalised demand. Far from constituting an undivided and priceless ideal legacy, relics of the national past were bought and sold – exchanged for money or less tangible profits.[35]

Lee's argument shows how antiquarianism's commercial base exceeds national boundaries, allying itself with the international practices of trade and profit. My account of the novel continues this discussion by exploring how Scott's foregrounding of etymology as the business of antiquarians also shows how *both* the symbolic value of antiquarian finds, *and* their economic function, may be part of larger systems of representation.

The Antiquary interweaves Oldbuck's obsession with etymology with Wardour's need to shore up his troubled finances and casts both as a kind of treasure-hunting – the quest for lost, slightly mysterious goods, whose discovery generates friction or even antagonism. In fact, the novel draws together ideas about money and language from the start, observing that Oldbuck and his fellow antiquarians are fond of writing 'essays upon medals in the proportion of twelve pages to each letter of the legend' (p. 15). The mention of 'essays on medals' calls up in particular John Pinkerton, author of the best-known essay in the field of numismatics which gives us a clear example of the way antiquarianism sought to produce a nationalist form of money, seemingly untainted by the uneasy internationalism of commerce.

Pinkerton had suffered from an obvious drawback in the toponymy argument with Chalmers: he was almost always wrong. But he had other strings to his historical bow. In 1784, he had published a book that made even more extravagant claims for the universality of a form of inscription than those represented by Chalmers' place-names. Pinkerton's *Essay on Medals* (Oldbuck's favoured guide) makes the claim that of all antiquarian records, the most reliable and universally accurate are coins. Throughout the eighteenth century, coins had been associated with civic values and public forms of knowledge. David Jennings's *Introduction to the Knowledge of Medals* of 1764, though chiefly an account of the rarity value of coins, had introduced the connection between numismatics and the naming of places: 'Geography hath been greatly beholden to this Science, for ascertaining the Names of Ancient Places, the Founders of

Cities and Colonies; and sometimes their situation, by the neighbour-hood of some noted river, mountain, &c. expressed by some device on a Medal.'[36] Pinkerton was to make the geographical scope of coins one of the main themes of his *Essay*. Not only are they useful for ancient top-onymy, but they also allow the specificity of place-names to be under-stood far beyond the original act of naming. Documents, he argues, are fragile and 'subject to innumerable accidents, mutilation, and utter loss' or do not circulate internationally. Public buildings have merit but are not found 'in remote countries'. So, Pinkerton concludes, 'medals alone remain as the principal proofs of historic truth, their evidence reaching at once to the most remote ages, and the most remote countries'.[37] By this neat argument, the circulation of money, the very thing that made commerce problematic as a national phenomenon, can be indicative of national qualities through the agency of geography. Medals transcend any conflict between the local and the global by virtue of their distribution; they remain material things representative of particular cultures but suffer none of the limitations of other antiquarian objects, tied to their local discovery, as their function is to circulate through space.

Behind the claims for public knowledge of Pinkerton's *Essay* lies Joseph Addison's *Dialogues Upon the Usefulness of Ancient Medals* (published posthumously in 1721 but written in the late 1690s and early years of the eighteenth century). Addison's dialogues confront the relationship between coins as antiques and those in modern circulation, or, as he puts it, the 'difference between Money and Medals'.[38] This difference is seen in the *Dialogues* as a modern invention, pointing to a split between the coin as a quotidian object, now tainted by commercial and private interest, and the medal, issued only on rare occasions to commemorate public events. A century later, Pinkerton was also to argue for the end of this distinction and, with it, the patina of antiquarian uselessness that the collecting of medals had acquired. Pinkerton brings coins out of the antiquarian cabinet and into the public sphere. Not only do medals give evidence about the events and objects of the past, but they also contribute to what Pinkerton sees as that most modern of disciplines – what we now call sociology: 'Medals almost present an history of manners, an article but very lately cultivated, yet perhaps the most useful and interesting of all the provinces of history' (p. 33). In opposition to the idea that anti-quarianism was unable to address ideas of historical continuity and progress, Pinkerton subsumes the state of national coinage into the need for better social regulation, and public reform: 'any effectual improve-ment of our coinage must be left till GOD help us; together with the more important improvements of the police of London, of our waste lands, and of parliamentary representation' (p. 224). Antiquarians, so far from being irrelevant as social historians, are now, by virtue of having improved their understanding of civic society by the study of medals, the very people to influence public policy.

For Pinkerton, coins are the master signifiers of culture: 'besides its service to history, the science of medals is certainly of considerable use to geography; to natural history; to the illustration of ancient writers; to architecture; and to the knowledge of a connoisseur, or that of ancient monuments, busts, statues, ceremonies, and the like' (p. 19). This cultural capital is deeply imbricated with national status, and, Pinkerton says, 'the decline of money is justly esteemed a sure symptom of the decline of the state' (p. 220). The free global circulation of coins to which Pinkerton first introduces us turns out to be really the space of empire. Coins represent a nation's imperial status, and Pinkerton uses a Roman example:

It affords patriotic satisfaction in particular to a Briton, to see his native island always represented, upon the earliest imperial coins, sitting on a globe, with the symbol of military power, the *labarum*, in her hand, and the ocean rolling under her feet. An emblem almost prophetic of the vast power which her dominion over the sea will always give her, providing she asserts her element of empire with due vigor and perseverance. (p. 26)

We can pause on these quotations to untangle what is at stake for Pinkerton's construction of medals as a form of national status. Pinkerton claims (or feigns) ignorance of the way an economy works, alleging that he cannot understand 'why gold encreases in its value and pre-eminence over other metals' (p. 54). When he says that the decline of money is a symptom of the decline of the state, he means a decline in the quality of coins, not inflation. Yet, the whole of the essay is written in the language of eighteenth-century finance, with its dependence on credit and an awareness of the promissory function of economic exchanges increasingly detached from the material status of bullion. The inscription on Roman coins acts as guarantor for Britain's national status but must be paid back with the 'vigor and perseverance' of future acts of imperial force.

Marc Shell's history of the epistemology of money as a form of belief shows how this history is driven by changes in 'the relationship between face value (intellectual currency) and substantial value (material currency)'.[39] The function of ideology in this uneasy relation between currency as material thing and currency as inscription leads, Shell argues, to 'the transformation from the absolute adequation between intellectual inscription and real substance to the complete disassociation of them'.[40] In a climate of growing concern about the insecurity of an economic system based on the movement of money away from the tangible forms of land and cash, Pinkerton boldly asserts the symbolic power of money but disguises it as a form of socially useful aesthetics. To accomplish this, Pinkerton must sidestep the problem inherent in representation: its dependence on acts of interpretation. Inscriptions on medals, he argues, should be self-evident. In a move that recalls Chalmers' invention of a Britain based on Scottish models, Pinkerton thinks that coins must be immediately legible and draws a parallel between this idea and the mission of the King James Bible:

> The legends ought always to be in the language of the country where the coin is struck; for the money is made for it, and not for foreign nations; and every inhabitant ought to be enabled to read the legends of the coin, which is made for him, and every day passes thro his hands. It is surprising that, when the scripture was given in English, the coin was not likewise translated [. . .]. (pp. 222–3)

The ideal of coinage is not only national but also a specifically Scottish ideal of writing – the Calvinist principle that a population should be able rationally to grasp divine authority without the need for mediation or mysticism. Of course, it soon becomes apparent that this does not work very well for Pinkerton's own argument, which has previously furnished the reader with an example of a Roman symbol and Latin text acting as a symbol and translation of British imperial greatness. The model of the King James Bible works in two ways: it is written in a 'native' language, but it is also a translation. Pinkerton's theory of the historical importance of coins depends upon their translatability in the movement from originary country to antiquarian collection. In order to reveal the general truths about history and society to which medals bear witness, their inscriptions cannot emerge autonomously but must be recontextualised and translated.

Together, Pinkerton and Chalmers offer a sophisticated and dense form of national antiquarianism that seeks to present historical truths of language and inscription while avoiding any problem concerning the act of interpretation. Both Chalmers' faith in the autochthony of place-names and Pinkerton's insistence on the clarity of originary historical context refuse to consider their subjects as texts which might be subject to a difficult process of reading. Both antiquarians need their inscriptions to be treated as writing, because this is what will allow them to link past and present and to make them educative in the institutions of modern civic society, but neither is willing to think very long about the nature of writing itself. Walter Scott, however, makes this the subject of *The Antiquary* to which we can now return to see how ideas about coins are woven into those about place, language and history.

When Oldbuck grasps the relation between the seemingly fragmentary signs of the ship, the box and the money, he uses a typically antiquarian simile: 'I see it all [. . .] as plain as the legend on a medal in high preservation' (p. 344). The irony is, of course, that it has taken him most of the novel to piece together the meaning of the various discoveries in Misticot's grave and that the method he has used finally to read the situation is much more like his narrative of the 'A. D. L. L' at the Kaim of Kinprunes than a plain legend. The novel, in fact, goes some way to insist that coins rarely have plain legends. The financial plot turns on the misfortunes of Sir Arthur Wardour. Already in debt, he cannot draw on the traditional locus of aristocratic financial power – land – because his estate is heavily entailed. He quickly becomes the victim of the grotesque swindler Herman Dousterswivel, who lures him to invest in phoney projects by planting coins for him to find in the ruined abbey and then claiming to have been led to them by divination. While sympathetic characters work to foil Dousterswivel's plans, Sir Arthur is increasingly harried by his creditors. Scott situates *The Antiquary* very precisely in the history of economics. For all his antiquarian elaborations, Oldbuck has a clear sense of the finer points of 'the present state of the money-markets' (p. 182) and gives Wardour, who is looking for a loan, details of the price of land and the levels of the stock market. Here, the novel turns its attention to the contemporary debate about money and what guarantees its values. Throughout the eighteenth century and into the nineteenth, paper money had been deemed a secondary signifying system, of value only when backed up by the 'real' presence of bullion. But Scott rejects the idea that any one form of money is more real than any other. Wardour offers to pay back the loan in the form of bullion, by which he means 'the precious metals,—gold and silver' but which Oldbuck interprets in terms of its use-value: 'Bullion? I suppose you mean lead – [. . .] But what could I do with a thousand points worth, and upwards, of lead?' (p. 182). So far from providing a real substance to guarantee the imaginary value of a more representative sign system, bullion is 'real' only in so far as it functions with a particular context – in this case, as Oldbuck goes on to explain, the practical one of roofing, which is of no immediate use to him in any case.

Richard Gray has identified in the theory of the German economist Adam Müller the expression of a form of Romantic dynamism that moves away from Smithian economics, with its insistence on substance, facts and quantities. Müller, by contrast, sees money as a relation system in continual circulation between commodities and consumers, here described by Gray: 'in Müllerian economics there are no positive terms, no objects that have inherent value; rather all economic value is the product of a differential system, of reciprocal relationships among objects and consumers'.[41] In such an economy, the apparent lack of historical connectivity in antiquarian objects becomes less of a problem. If we activate the monetary function dormant in Pinkerton's championing of coins as artefacts that move between localities and are not bounded by national locations, we can see how closely his aesthetic model mirrors the economic one. In Gray's analysis of the semiotics of post-Enlightenment economy, 'if money only has value when circulating, when mediating between distinct objects and different individuals, then it can never be the basis of private property.'[42] In *The Antiquary*, the older model, which identifies the source of wealth in land, is an outmoded one. Wardour's estate is heavily entailed, and he can neither sell it nor raise funds on it. A linear form of wealth that depends on original sources, it is now in competition with modern commerce in which wealth must circulate. The act of returning to the source of money is figured in the novel not only as the dead wealth of the grave but also as a series of substitutions whose 'value' can only be determined as a form of transaction (Dousterswivel's swindle or Lovel's secret gift).

Pinkerton's insistence on the aesthetic and representative qualities of medals, rather than their weight or metallic purity, emphasises their condition as signs. And this close relationship between coins and inscriptions is also integral to Scott's historiography in *The Antiquary*. In one sense, the novel gives a voice to contemporaneous fears of a national credit-based economy, that, as Patrick Brantlinger puts it, appears as 'a false, insubstantial sort of prosperity that is really only debt disguised as wealth'.[43] But, in another reading, *The Antiquary* recognises that all history, and all historical fiction, is itself a form of credit based not on a substantial, recoverable or quantifiable past but on acts of belief and the circulation of narratives.[44] When the two antiquarians come to examine the coins planted by Dousterswivel, Wardour invites Oldbuck to take 'such coins or medals as will suit your own collection' (p. 185). Oldbuck insists that he should pay the current market value of the coins and offers to consult them in Pinkerton's *Essay on Medals*. Sir Arthur demurs:

I do not mean you should consider them as any thing but a gift of friendship, and least of all would I stand by the valuation of your friend Pinkerton, who has impugned the ancient and trust-worthy authorities upon which, as upon venerable and moss-grown pillars, the credit of Scottish history[45] reposed. (p. 185)

Scott invites a pun on the conspicuously overdrawn Wardour's use of 'credit' to mean reputation. History works as credit, an anti-teleology in which the future becomes a gamble. The 'facts' of the past do not reappear unchanged in the present but accrue the interest of incremental readings.

The 'credit of Scottish history' brings us back to a passage from Chalmers' *Caledonia* in which he triumphantly asserts the power of topography to preserve Celtic language and to ensure that both act as 'the indubitable vouchers' of Scottish history:

Yet, at the end of seven centuries of different changes, the Saxon colonists, and their descendants, have not been able [. . .] to annihilate the Celtic people, to silence the Gaelic tongue, within proper Scotland, nor to obliterate the Celtic topography, which all remain the constant reproach of the Gothic system, as well as the indubitable vouchers of the genuine history of North-Britain. (vol. I, p. 613)

'Voucher' here refers to a note attesting to the value of something, although in the light of Scott's novel, we may recall an earlier slang meaning of someone who puts counterfeit money into circulation. As much as he presses place-names to confirm the documentary reality of the historical record, Chalmers also lets through their status as signs which are subject to misreading and appropriation. History is subject to the same laws as a modern economy offering neither a recoverable past nor a predictable future but, rather, a system predicated on the uncertainty of speculation. History as credit, then, is also the form of the text and a matter of credit, as its value, or 'worth', is a matter of speculation on the part of their reader who must decide how far to credit it and how much interest will be gained. And this, Scott knew very well, is also how novels work, both fictionally and economically, in the early nineteenth century. *The Antiquary*, like the other Waverley Novels, was sold to its publisher as credit. Scott received pre-publication payment in the form of bills which could be sold on to the banks, the granters of the bills (here Scott's publishers) being liable for the amounts due.[46] Scott was to write to John Ballantyne wondering if the reputation of *The Antiquary* would suffer from having appeared so quickly after its predecessors: 'I am afraid the people will take me up for coining.'[47] The suggestion that novel-writing is not only a profitable activity but also potentially a counterfeit one brings together the novel's own preoccupation with language and money and the relevance of both to its own form. In order to end a plot that he has suggested is endlessly inventive and circulatory, Scott has to produce a monetary transaction that seems to evade representation altogether. Only Lovel's ingots work as money because they are not inscribed: 'There was neither inscription nor stamp upon them' (p. 193). The novel brings about its financial resolution by reasserting the pre-modern value of pure, material goods, but the textual ending is much less confident about the possibility of absolute financial values, offering Oldbuck's notes for publication by 'any one who chuses to make them public, without risk or expence to THE ANTIQUARY' (p. 356) – a highly implausible economic proposition.

Fantastical and palimpsestic, antiquarianism can nevertheless become modern in its novelistic form. During the course of *The Antiquary*, Oldbuck keeps pressing Hector McIntyre, Sir Arthur's nephew, to write a long poem, to be entitled *The Caledoniad*, which will narrate the fictitious defeat of Agricola by the Scots. Just as the geographical site of this battle remains a mystery in *The Antiquary*, the poem, whose goal is to invent a seamless, continuous history, never gets written. Yet all the while, the novel, with its heterogeneous generic conventions and multiple subject matter, is progressing. Scott takes antiquarianism's notoriously fragmentary and static condition and recasts these terms in novelistic form as heterogeneity and synchronicity. If Scott's two central inscriptions of place-names and medals fail to generate the national histories promised by Chalmers and Pinkerton, they nevertheless show how language practices work in the present and how it is that linguistic present that constitutes modern historiography.

CHAPTER 5

Ultima Thule: *The limits of the north*

The geometries of Great Britain, calculated by the uneasy relations of time and space, and by the pressure of the local on the national, reveal a nation whose cultural discourses both produce and destabilise the division of the kingdom into North Britain and South Britain. As I have argued, Scotland in the late eighteenth and early nineteenth centuries sought the parity that such a symmetry offered, yet simultaneously revealed the spatial fissures and temporal discontinuities inherent in the attempt to describe Britain as a northern nation. In the final two chapters, I want to explore what happens when the sense of geographical totalities becomes relaxed, when nations, states or continents are not viewed as necessary or discrete wholes. In the current chapter, I look at two texts that address their own situation at a nominal margin and do not assume that a nation radiates from its national capital, and in the subsequent chapter I explore James Hogg's radical dissolution of the premises of Enlightenment spatiality altogether. Although the Hogg stories are the latest to be published of any in this study, we should not assume a clear transition from the Romantic tensions between local and global, scientific and empirical space to what I shall describe as the post-Enlightenment space of Hogg's imaginative world. Rather, I hope to identify the imbrication of these models in the early nineteenth century, either when the rational structure of Enlightenment spatiality cracks at the seams – as we shall see in the case of Hogg – or when, as in the present chapter, localities are not deemed to be fixed or static in the first place.

The current chapter investigates two texts, produced within a year of each other, about the extreme north of Great Britain: Walter Scott's journal of his 1814 visit with the lighthouse inspectorate to the northern isles of Orkney and Shetland and Margaret Chalmers' *Poems* of 1813. Neither of these are texts that anticipated a large readership or offered themselves as important cultural documents. Scott did not intend to make his journal public, and Chalmers, who needed money more than acclaim, had her volume printed for subscribers by a small firm in Newcastle upon Tyne. Yet, they both have a good deal to say about the possibility of fixing a limit position within British geography.

Both Scott and Chalmers write about the northern isles, the archipelagos at the far north of Scotland. Scott was a visitor, while Chalmers lived in Lerwick, the capital of Shetland. The islands have an interesting position within and in relation to the rest of Britain. In one sense, they are continuous with the absorption of Britain into northern Europe. Although the northernmost part of Britain, they are also at the southern reaches of Scandinavia and bear traces of the language and legal customs of Norway which governed them until 1468 (Orkney) and 1469 (Shetland). The islands form a visible link with other northern nations, and their importance in the whaling trade, contributing men and supplies, makes them pivotal for Britain's participation in a specifically northern economy. The western islands of the United Kingdom, by contrast, are associated with finality, depopulation and immigration – a lost culture or a last stage before a voyage of no return to the New World. On the other hand – and perhaps because of the ways in which this sense of western finality could be translated into myth and romance – the northern isles were not as commonly represented in literary culture as their western counterparts. Unlike the Celtic Hebrides or Ireland, Orkney and Shetland were not widely absorbed into what Katie Trumpener calls 'Bardic Nationalism'.[1] Norse mythology, as I indicated in Chapter 1, was of growing importance as a foundational British myth, but there was no equivalent to the success of Ossian and the subsequent romanticising of the Highlands. Most significantly, the northern islands were not a destination for cultural or aesthetic tourists, partly because of their isolated situation in dangerous waters. There was no regular packet service between Leith (Edinburgh's nearest port) and Lerwick until 1758, and at the time Scott visited the islands in 1814, the two regular packets sailed about six times a year.[2] Until 1812, there had been a monthly postal service, but in that year the company to which the contract had been given put up the costs, and the Post Office abandoned this franchise, sending the mail on a more ad-hoc basis until the resumption of the Post Office packet in 1839. The English traveller and geologist Samuel Hibbert remarks that the journey to Shetland could be done in about two days and nights with a favourable wind, but that it was more usual for vessels to have to put into harbour on the east coast of Scotland, driven there by contrary winds.[3] The alternative, a crossing from the north coast of Scotland to Orkney, confronted the traveller with the treacherous waters of the Pentland Firth.

Although one of the packet boats was equipped to take passengers, Hibbert comments on the 'humble cabin accommodations'; the northern isles were not on the tourist route, and most contemporary accounts of them tend to detail their natural history, and, in the eyes of most commentators, their failure in agricultural improvement. The packets' main function was to carry the post and to facilitate trade between Shetland and Scotland, but Hibbert suggests that commerce was not extensive: 'fishing materials, grain, woollen and linen goods, and spirits are sent from Scotland, whilst this country receives in return dried fish, hosiery, oil, and some little kelp'.[4]

The texts I discuss in this chapter offer both contrasting and complementary views of the far north. In some ways, Scott and Chalmers are each other's opposites. Scott, the famous poet, is taking time out of his literary career while he awaits news of the success of his latest venture, *Waverley*. Chalmers was – and largely remained – an unknown author publishing for the first time. Scott situates himself as a detached observer, moving freely in a space with which he has no personal connection, acknowledging no political inflection and assuming no form of agency. Chalmers is writing about her native location and working to establish Shetland as a significant part of Great Britain. Setting these two authors – in an immediate sense so close in space and time – alongside each other allows us to think about their status in terms of gender and their places in literary culture and about the way these different narrative voices express themselves in spatial discourses. Despite these differences, both are aware of the peculiar situation of the northern isles as the point where the nation ends, and both address the questions of geographical limit that consequently arise.[5]

The northern limit of the nation had a history of uncertainty. 'Thule', that mysterious shifting point that marked the far north, was sometimes used as a term for Shetland. But the 'correct' positioning of Thule, as Samuel Hibbert muses, is impossible:

Thule was long a term of general application, to denote a place either in Britain, Ireland, the north of Scotland, or in regions even still further north, which was supposed to be involved in darkness, whilst its seas were washed by a boisterous ocean; its situation, therefore, always varied with the uncertain geographical information which Roman writers possessed of the British or Caledonian Seas.[6]

Hibbert's remarks nicely point up the problematic location of 'the north' as residing in 'Britain, Ireland, the north of Scotland, or in regions still further north'. Not only is Britain deemed to exclude Scotland, which has its own separate category, but it is not at all clear whether the Shetlands are deemed to be north of Scotland itself, or constitutive *of* the north of Scotland. John Pinkerton cites Pliny's *Natural History* to describe the Hyperboreans, a race of people living 'beyond the beginning of the north', a suitably vague location which avoids the question of where 'the north' begins.[7] Orkney and Shetland were not part of George Chalmers' 'proper Scotland', and Arthur Edmondston, although a native of Shetland, seems unsure about its place in the relations of north and south, nation and empire. Shetland was formerly socially and economically backward, he argues in his 1809 *View of the Ancient and Present State of the Zetland Islands*, until 'the act of the twentieth of George II brought them on a level with their fellow citizens in the southern part of the empire'.[8] Are the Shetlanders now equal with the English, or, despite shaking off their backward ways, only thus far on a par with England's imperial subjects? It was into these waters – not yet firmly fixed on the political or cultural maps of Great Britain – that Scott sailed in 1814.

TO THE LIGHTHOUSES: SCOTT'S NORTHERN VACATION

Scott's journey sprang from a singular opportunity. His friend Robert Stevenson, lighthouse engineer and grandfather of Robert Louis Stevenson, was about to embark on an inspection of the lighthouses round the coast of Scotland, and he invited Scott to accompany him and the other Commissioners of the Northern Lights on the yacht *Pharos*. Aboard the *Pharos*, Scott kept a diary, which he claimed was intended for the eyes of a 'few friends', one of whom, the Duke of Buccleuch, was the addressee of a verse epistle Scott composed during his stay in Lerwick.[9] The diary was not published in Scott's lifetime, but after his death it was included in his son-in-law John Gibson Lockhart's biography, *Memoir of the Life of Sir Walter Scott, Bart.* Scott's northern tour is then midway between a public and private document, designed only for 'a few friends', albeit highly influential ones, and, as we shall see, it is an intermediary text in other ways, moving between the disavowal of previously held knowledge and the imposition of ideas upon the land- and seascapes through which Scott moves. Scott's lighthouse tour sites itself in other liminal positions, particularly regarding space and locality, and we can read his diary as an exploration of the relationship between islands and not-islands (the latter clearly a difficult concept) as well as a voyage north. The meanings of both these trajectories – the voyage north and the voyage through the archipelago – resonate off the stage on which Scott performs his journey as we explore some of these meanings and how they construct the time and the place of the lighthouse journey.

The party set off at the end of July 1814, an interesting time for both Scott and Europe in terms of nations and islands. Islands were highly advantageous for British domination in Europe and expansion in the Empire. In May of that year, Napoleon Bonaparte had been exiled to the island of Elba, and the following year Britain was to consolidate its strategic domination of the globe by the acquisition of further islands at the Congress of Vienna. Britain gained or retained, among others, Ceylon, Malta, Mauritius, Trinidad and the North Sea island of Heligoland, all of which could be used as trading or naval bases. Scott's own literary career was at a turning point. Hitherto celebrated as a poet, he had just anonymously released his first novel to the public. In the journey of its impressionable English protagonist to Scotland, *Waverley* had provided one narrative about the act of going north. The novel had narrated the painful history of the reforging of Britain in the aftermath of the Jacobite Rebellion of 1745–6, and the British reading public was about to give its response to this version of England and Scotland finally accepting an identity as a single, island nation.

A tour to Scotland's own northern islands under these circumstances might be expected to propose questions about Britain's state as a nation. But Scott does not address these directly: the diary does not offer itself as a survey or a scrutiny and, in fact, is difficult to pin down generically. It has no very obvious discursive category. How should we term Scott's journey? A trip? A tour? Or, as its most recent publisher has it, a 'cruise around Scotland'?[10] Scott himself called his account *Vacation 1814: Voyage in the Lighthouse Yacht to Nova Zembla, and the Lord Knows Where*, and these terms set the scene for the spatial structure of the narrative. The voyage is designated a 'vacation' – a holiday space outside the government of normative social codes and conditions. It is also to be a site of newness, of uncharted territory – a voyage to an island named for its newness (Novaya Zemlya off the coast of Russia). And even beyond this, Scott will venture 'the Lord knows where' into the uncharted space of new perspectives. Scott writes in diary form as he goes along, much of it in the present tense, as if in imitation of this teleology-free progression. Events appear as if spontaneously generated from the objects and scenes that present themselves to the eye of the traveller. Scott's diary is not, as earlier Tours of Scotland had been, a *conscious* attempt to narrate the nation, nor is it a way of circumscribing Scotland topographically, although, as we shall see, Scott's narration turns out to be unable to avoid matters of national identity. The title echoes the lines from Pope's *An Essay on Man*, which I quoted earlier in this study to illustrate the long-standing association of the north with a relative structure that has no fixed endpoint:

> Ask where's the North? at York, 'tis on the Tweed;
> In Scotland, at the Orcades; and there,
> At Greenland, Zembla, or the Lord knows where
> No creature owns it in the first degree
> But thinks his neighbour farther off than he.[11]

Pope's north is an ever-receding point which cannot be grasped and which defies attempts to delimit it, a space without ownership that retreats further the more anyone might try to possess it. But any position based on a principle of relativity must be relative to something else. To imagine Greenland in Pope's lines as further north than Orkney, one must first have a sense of where Orkney is, and so on. And, of course, this voyage to the north also imagines the south in that most problematic of positions: a point of origin. It is this tension between a political centredness and the play of possibilities that characterises the lighthouse journal. The 'vacation' of the title was also a legal vacation for Walter Scott, Writer to the Signet, and, at the same time as he is investing in the utopian possibility of fresh perspectives needed to think through the conception of newness, he is also under the sway of the recognition that freedom is an effect of the law and that the exploratory space which the lighthouse tour clears is produced by the discourses already embedded in it.

Scott's party also visited the Hebrides and, briefly, Antrim in Ireland, returning to Glasgow on 8 September. His journal of the western islands changes in tone to include a much greater sense of the already written, including histories of the escape of Charles Edward Stuart and earlier battles fought by the Lords of the Isles. Where the islands of the north will be strange and unfamiliar, here there are 'Unnumbered islets and holms, each of which has its name and its history' (p. 226), and a visit to the ruins on Iona prompts Scott to quote Webster: 'You never tread upon them but you set / Your feet upon some ancient history' (p. 243).[12] But his northern journey is narrated much more as a voyage into uncharted territory. As the party sets off towards its northern destination, Scott begins to blur received cultural opinions about the relationship of north and south. Microdivisions start to appear in received cultural oppositions. As he moves towards the unknown north in the direction of 'the Lord knows where', so he narrates his own sense of becoming increasingly strange from the point of view of the south. As they travel up the east coast of Scotland and visit Slaines Castle, the party meets an old man whose discourse Scott inhabits in a kind of free indirect speech, moving in and out of the old man's words as if to evade the act of narrating them. The old man tells him that Slaines is now inhabited by a Mr Bowles, who comes 'so far from the southward that naebody kends whare he comes frae. "Was he frae the Indies?" – Na; he did not think he came that road. He was far frae the southland. Naebody ever heard of the name of the place' (p. 140). Whatever the 'south' may previously have stood for (Lowland Scotland, England, southern Europe, Britain's colonial possessions in the southern hemisphere) becomes wiped out or transformed into a space that cannot be known because it cannot be named. But this seemingly effortless dissolution of spatial identity cannot be sustained, as Scott brings with him the political questions he had apparently left behind. His narrative considers the possibility that the north is not only a destination but also an origin, not only a free space to which Scots can travel but also the very point of their genesis, if they are to be characterised as 'North Britons', that term that speaks both of Wilkesian eighteenth-century Scotophobia and of the enthusiastic participation of Scottish institutions in the wider context that defines Island Britain – the British Empire. In the epistle to Buccleuch, Scott explicitly opposes this northern origin to the more usual as the 'cradle of civilisation': the classical south of European culture:

> For ne'er for Grecia's vales, nor Latian Land,
> Was fiercer strife than for this barren strand—
> A race severe, the isle and ocean lords,—
> Loved for its own delight the strife of swords [. . .]. (p. 28)

The northern islands, Norwegian territory until the fifteenth century, offer an alternative point of origin to the Rousseauist south, and the north also offers Scotland a contiguous origin, untroubled by the obligation to pass through any other country as would be necessary on a journey south. And this northern origin also offers a simpler prospect than the more problematic Celtic West, already inscribed by competing and often acrimonious claims in the fields of history and mythology. On Orkney, Scott visits the ancient stone circle of Stenness and takes the opportunity to remark on its metonymic status as social origin. The once primitive or barbaric north now becomes the originary model of British democracy itself:

Stonehenge excels these monuments, but I fancy they are otherwise unparalleled in Britain. The idea that such circles were exclusively Druidical, is now justly exploded. The northern nations all used such erections to make their places of meeting, whether for religious purposes or civil policy; and there is repeated mention of them in the Sagas. *See* the Eyrbiggia Saga [. . .]. (p. 199)

But once again, north and south dissolve any stable order of priority. This rare attention to the reader of the diary reminds us that a British readership would be obliged to '*See*' this Icelandic saga in Scott's own English abstraction of it which had just been issued by Ballantynes, the printing firm in which Scott was a partner, in a collection of *Illustrations of Northern Antiquities*.[13] The southern literary origin supervenes upon the northern one. What was supposed to be the site of new discoveries turns out to be already inscribed by the literary culture of cosmopolitan Edinburgh.

An interesting anecdote further deconstructs this northern origin, featuring an appearance of those famously interstitial antecedents, the Picts – the illusive, impossible key to language and society.[14] Scott regrets that weather conditions prevented him from visiting North Ronaldsay, the furthest north of the Orkneys. He had particularly wanted to visit the island as he believed it most clearly showed the Norse origins of the Orcadians in which he was interested. In place of the hoped-for visit, Scott narrates an earlier trip made by Robert Stevenson (an anecdote of which Scott was evidently so fond that he included it in the notes for the *magnum* edition of *The Pirate*):

A missionary preacher came ashore there a year or two since, but being a very little black-bearded unshaved man, the seniors of the isle suspected him of being an ancient Pecht or Pict, and *no canny*, of course. The schoolmaster came down to entreat our worthy Mr Stevenson, then about to leave the island, to come up and verify whether the preacher was an ancient Pecht, yea or no. (p. 195)

Stevenson, unable to get out of this tricky situation, goes to visit the supposed Pecht who turns out to be a man named Campbell, an iron-monger he had known in Edinburgh. Campbell is let off the charge of Pechtism, but Stevenson takes the schoolmaster back to the mainland of Scotland to be 'examined for his office' (p. 196). The schoolmaster, how-ever, is happy with this arrangement on the grounds that 'he was extremely desirous to see a tree; and, on seeing one desired to know what *girss* it was that grew at the top o't – the leaves appearing to him to be grass' (p. 196).[15]

Here the absent Norse or northern origin is replaced by the comedy of displaced origins in which the aboriginal northern other turns out to be represented by the commercial south, and the supposed Pict an Edinburgh ironmonger. Furthermore, in another twist of supplementary logic, Scotland, now the south, is transformed from Samuel Johnson's northern treeless desert into the very place to witness trees. As part of the comedy, the schoolmaster mutates into the anthropological other whose own curiosity *becomes* a curiosity or oddity. He becomes the 'native' of that colonial discourse, whose own subjectivity can never take precedence over that of the coloniser. But, in another sense, the schoolmaster's desire to establish the nature of being 'an ancient Pecht yea or nay' positions him alongside other Scottish nationals – the antiquarians who debated the origin of the Picts, what happened to them, and what was their relationship to the Celts (a debate to be satirised by Scott himself in his next but one novel: *The Antiquary*). North Ronaldsay, as isolated islands are wont to do, offers us a microcosm not of anthropological truths but of anthropological discourse. An island which seems to offer insights into original states in fact reveals the impossibility of origins themselves. Not least, the episode of the Pecht reminds us of Shakespeare's *The Tempest* and of the idea that to be native is not the same as being indigenous or autochthonic.

Scott's vacation space not only complicates the idea of a voyage north but also reflects on Britain's island status. We might suspect Scott of using this narrative to reinforce the constitutive position of Scotland within the island of Britain. In post-Union Britain, there was no chance of asserting John of Gaunt's sceptred isle as purely English – if England wanted to portray itself as an island fortress triumphant in Europe and resisting invasion, Scotland would have to be part of the deal. Such models were readily available to Scott. James Thomson, writing at a time when Scotland's importance to the Union was a case that needed strenuously to be argued, appeals in *The Seasons* for some force which might

> wing
> The prosperous sail, from every growing port,
> Unchalleng'd round the sea-incircled globe;
> And thus in soul united as in name,
> Bid BRITAIN reign the mistress of the deep.[16]

Thomson's trope is an interesting one. Britain's gathering together of itself in an island identity grafts her imperial status onto the modelling of a United Britain as the whole globe, itself a sea-encircled island. Throughout the second half of the eighteenth century, there had been already a strong literary tradition of incorporating Scots into Imperial Britain, often as warlike Highlanders who could swell Britain's military might. Scott himself, anti-Jacobin and Tory, had already made such a move in an 1804 poem, 'The Bard's Incantation', in which a Celtic warrior poet is seen patrolling the British shoreline and repelling the French 'Spectre with his Bloody Hand'.[17] The lighthouse journey, while it recognises the fact that the northern islands had long supplied the British Navy with accomplished sailors, does not seek to represent British Scotland in this way. Instead, Scott seems to draw on an image of Scotland as another kind of island nation – a nation whose frame, so far from being discrete and defensive, is porous. His account makes the island strange – not the better to comprehend it in a formal act of defamiliar-isation, but to stress its otherness and detached position. Scotland, so far from completing England, thwarts its definition. Unlike England, Scotland's coastline is surrounded by islands that create problems of definition. Archipelagos break up continuity. The topography presents gaps and dots instead of straight lines. Islands introduce a logic of sup-plementarity into the attempt to define which is the mainland and which the islands. Scott's own narrative technique evokes the archipelago in this way. Instead of using the lighthouse tour to inscribe the circumnavigation of Scotland in a continuous narrative, his descriptions are a series of observations often unrelated to each other. His piecemeal itinerary depends on the contingent circumstances of tides or of weather. The islands' own rugged coastlines blur the clear lines between land and sea, a pheno-menon which seems to Scott to have affected the commercial choices of their worryingly amphibious inhabitants. He regrets the lack of clear distinctions between farming and fishing and hopes that 'This separation of trades will in time take place, and then the prosperous days of Zetland will begin' (p. 154).

The model of the self-contained island is also a frightening or isolating one. The Fair Islanders, Scott notes, have little truck with either the Shetlanders or the Orcadians; they intermarry among themselves and are hostile to strangers. The tacksman of Fair Isle is described, in that most familiar of island tropes, as living 'like Robinson Crusoe, in absolute solitude as to society' (p. 172). The wife of one of the lighthouse-keepers has a baby to whom she had to give birth unassisted, which Scott notes down as 'a dreadful inconvenience of an island life' (p. 178). Islands are not only frighteningly isolated but also, conversely, confusing and mul-tiple. So far from being unique and central, islands tend to reproduce themselves, as Gillian Beer has noted, in a kind of fractal geometry.[18] Scott observes how the ancient Zetlanders miniaturised their own island state by building towers on artificial islets in lakes and that to Orcadians the term 'mainland' applies not to Scotland but to the largest of the islands. Shortly before setting out on the trip, Scott wrote to his friend J. B. Morritt that he would be visiting 'all that is curious on continent and isle': the relationship between Scotland and its islands replicates the position of Britain as an island off the continent of Europe. Scotland, no longer a supplement to England, becomes the continent, the containing power.[19] The imperial status of the northern isles is subject to the tensions of their status both as north and as archipelago. Samuel Hibbert confidently casts the Shetlands as the topmost boundary of Britain as island fortress: 'The cluster of Islands and Rocks which, under the name of SHETLAND, form the northern barriers of the British Kingdom.'[20] But, of course, 'a cluster of Islands and Rocks' is not contiguous as a barrier. Much may slip through it, not least the vessels of nations with whom Britain was at war. Scott comments that Britain's northern barrier has already been breached: American privateers stalk the waters surrounding the archipelago looking for prizes.

It is striking how this image of the porous archipelago recurs in Scott's diary, which is much more interested in islands than it is in lighthouses, the official purpose of the trip. Scott barely discusses the trip's official purpose: to inspect existing lighthouses and to review plans for new ones. He makes little use of the lighthouse as a metaphor or even as a landmark. Robert Stevenson, introduced as 'a most gentlemanlike and modest man, and well known by his scientific skill' (p. 136) remains a shadowy figure who is always disappearing off from the main party to attend to some unspecified lighthouse business.

The lighthouse 'vacation' turns out to be less of a holiday from Scott's literary environment than he had claimed, as the narrative plays inconsistently between the pure space of northern discovery and the sense that the north has already been colonised by the literary cultures of the south. Furthermore, like many a colonising force, Scott was unable to disguise the fact that his own presence had left its mark on the northern islands, in his case in a most dramatic fashion. On the trip, he met Alexander Peterkin, Sheriff-Substitute of Shetland, who furnished him with a great deal of the information about the history of Orkney and Shetland that he was later to use in *The Pirate*. Peterkin went on to publish his own account:

Hoy-head, or the Keam of Hoy, being the most westerly hill and point of the island, and of great height, is also supposed, when viewed from the manse of Stromness, to present a profile likeness of one who may justly be distinguished as the living poet *of Scotland*,—Sir Walter Scott. I mention this as a proof of the extent to which his name and image have penetrated in the recesses of his native country, and of the impression which has been stamped by his genius on the minds of Scotsmen in every region and in every sphere. The mantle of Burns has descended on him. Like his more humble, but eminently illustrious precursor, he is deeply imbued with the 'prophet's fire', which has illustrated the manners and character of his countrymen. His inspired hand has touched the rocks of our native land: a stream has gushed forth; the heart of Scotland is gladdened and refreshed; and all its highest, and deepest, and most patriotic sympathies, have been powerfully awakened by the magical powers of his imagination.[21]

In Peterkin's extravagantly flattering scene, Scott is not merely engraved on the landscape, he *is* that landscape. Not only has his 'inspired hand' called the landscape forth, the geography has reciprocated by reduplicating him in itself. And it is this mere presence in the landscape that finally links the islands to the 'continent' that Scott himself was to become. Scott's apparently own free-floating narrative to 'the Lord knows where' leaves him carved into the Orkney hillside, both subject and object, both tourist and attraction – the Mount Rushmore of Scottish literature.

MARGARET CHALMERS AND THE OPTICS OF THE NORTH

If, for Alexander Peterkin, Scott had absorbed Orkney into a vast literary nation linking the 'mantle of Burns' in the south-west with the far north, the northern isles themselves did not have a very developed reputation for literary productions. Arthur Edmondston conceded that there had been some 'native Zetland poets' of the Norse era whose 'poems have been preserved, and celebrated by succeeding historians' but adds that 'there is no contemporary production in any other department of literature.'[22] Yet, just a few years after Edmondston's account, a Shetland author produced a volume of poetry that had a great deal to say about the contemporary situation of the islands.

Margaret Chalmers' *Poems* were published by subscription in New-castle in 1813.[23] The publication process was evidently not a happy one, and the subscribers had to wait some time to receive their copies. From the biographical details contained within the poems and notes, we know that Chalmers' father, dead by the time of publication, had been Collector of Customs at Lerwick and that her brother William, a master in the Royal Navy, was killed at Trafalgar. Chalmers was fifty-five when her *Poems* were eventually published. Despite the economic difficulties the family had suffered, Chalmers' tone is generally optimistic, depicting an idealised, benevolent and cooperative society on the islands, capable of overcoming physical hardship. Her island community is, in this sense, a miniature version of Britain as a whole, whose island status, according to environmental determinism, makes it a harmonious state. William Falconer writes that 'The inhabitants of islands [. . .] have a higher relish for liberty than those of the continent' because islands are small and 'one part of the people cannot be so easily employed to oppress the other'.[24] At first glance, Chalmers' poetry can seem conventional (particularly in its topical patriotism) and her language straightforward. But this lack of surface difficulty disguises the complex structures of her poems and their often delicate ambiguities and shifts of meaning. Chalmers is eager to situate Shetland as part of the nation – not a distant or peripheral part, but as British as anywhere else. She effects this largely through the depiction and manipulation of spatial relationships, which she configures in a way very different from the reified space of charts or the pure extension of mathematics. Unlike the geography of the *Statistical Account*, Chalmers' space is not something that precedes experience and thus cannot be easily divided into discrete parts. Instead, Chalmers assumes a spatial sense which is always produced or mediated by the consciousness that experiences it or by the social transactions that form it. In the following discussion of her poetry, I want to think about these forms of spatiality as ones that address her situation as a 'provincial' woman writer.

Chalmers is much more interested in geography than she is in historiography. The volume contains a few references to the past influence of Scandinavian countries upon Shetland but very little history other than recent events. Her most 'historical' poem, 'On an Ancient Obelisk', tackles the question of history directly, and, although typically polite about forms of inquiry other than her own, Chalmers betrays a certain scepticism about the usefulness of historical investigation. The poem starts with a reference to Pope's lines from the third of the *Moral Essays* describing the inscription on the London Monument that erroneously blamed Catholics for the Great Fire of 1666:

> Thou monument equivocal, say, why
> Dost thou in *silence* rear thy top on high?
> In grandeur rude, and 'pointing to the skies',
> Thou 'lift'st the head', but who can say 'it lies'. (p. 126)

The act of hearing the story of the past is so complex as to be impenetrable. The obelisk bears no inscription, but even if it did, Chalmers observes, it might be lying. Then again, even though there might be the

possibility of lying, there would remain the impossibility of strictly determining historical truth, which must finally depend on interpretation: 'who
can say "it lies." ' In any case, the task of the antiquarian is at best pointless
and at worst slightly sinister. The poem alludes to a Mr Mollison of Glasgow
who has invented a way of reading defaced inscriptions. But the monument
cannot be 'induced' by Mollison to impart its purpose and thus evades his
'strictest scrutiny' (p. 126). The rest of the poem is taken up with versions of
history in the form of a series of historical questions which the obelisk is
evidently unable or unwilling to answer. Having dismissed antiquarianism,
Chalmers (here using typically spatial metaphors) is further doubtful of the
usefulness of conjectural history: 'From Probability's wide track we change, /
And Possibility's vague empire range' (p. 128). The poem ends inconclusively, with the suggestion that perhaps the obelisk 'faintly hints' (p. 128) at
the scene of a religious sacrifice.

If Chalmers was not greatly convinced by the utility of history, she is
extremely interested in space and position, despite these being the very
things that would seem most to marginalise her as a female author from
the 'periphery'. But having cleared her ground of the determining influence
of history, Chalmers is able to use space to situate Shetland in a global
sphere of synchronic, economic modernity. Her recognition that readers
may associate her with a specific, peripheral locality turns into a detailed
study of the nature of place in a national context. Many recent studies of
Scottish Romanticism, including my own first chapter, have pointed to
Scotland's role in the British project of defining itself as a modern nation
while simultaneously identifying those pre-modern 'peripheries' that
could define the modern centre. But Chalmers' Shetland is conspicuously
not one of those 'fractured, disjointed, and disruptive temporalities', as
Saree Makdisi describes them, that render uneven the smooth synchronicity of modernity. In fact, of all the writers in this study, it is Chalmers –
in a surprising way – who seems most to aim at Benedict Anderson's
identification of the modern nation with Benjamin's 'homogeneous empty
time' in which distant subjects can be seen to share a common identity.[25]
Following Anderson's *Imagined Communities*, we are used to the idea of
this communality as a product of widening transport links that stand-
ardise time and reading matter. But Chalmers offers us an opportunity to
think about the space of the nation in a different way: the imaginative
construction of national homologies from a point usually conceived to be
peripheral or idiosyncratic.

In a straightforward sense, Chalmers does correspond to the idea of
the local writer, offering an 'insider' picture of social life on early

nineteenth-century Shetland and one that differs markedly from the perspective of most of the published tours by visitors to the islands. Arthur Edmondston's 1809 account identifies the isolated northern islands as an early kind of Galapagos of human society ready to instruct the scientific mind:

The history of a country circumscribed in extent, and detached in its situation, by exhibiting its varied internal relations in an isolated form, is, perhaps, the best calculated of any, for the attainment of correct notions of human society. Under such circumstances, the whole range of the political system appears, as it were, spread out before us, and its various branches can be studied, either in detail or in conjunction.[26]

One of the more widely read narratives, John Laing's *Voyage to Spitzbergen*, which went through four editions, tends to treat the Shetlanders as anthropological specimens whose remoteness throws into relief the curious nature of their customs. A Malthusian, Laing regards Shetland as a useful test case for the relation of population to environment: 'It is curious to observe how the principles of Mr Malthus accommodate themselves to, and receive illustration from, the smallest societies.'[27] Here is his unflattering account of middle-class Shetland women:

The women above the common rank, lead a very sedentary life, and seldom appear out of doors, unless at church, which, probably on account of its great distance from them, they do not often visit. Besides, tea has found its way into these dreary regions, a constant use of which is the well known enemy of those who lead sedentary lives, and do not take exercise sufficient to promote the necessary secretions. Hence come on relaxation of the solids, indigestion, flatulency, glandular obstructions, hysterics, &c.[28]

Laing's women are the inevitable, factual, somatic products of their zonal environment. A subscriber to climate theory's belief in meteorological categories, Laing believes that *all* Shetlanders are unhealthy because of their cold, damp climate, and that the women are particularly susceptible. A low population, a consequence of the bad climate, further leads to a sedentary lifestyle, which is only exacerbated by female over-indulgence in tea.[29] Compare this with Chalmers' description of teatime (published just one year after Laing's):

And now arrives the hour which brings the board
With China's fragrant leaf and porcelain stor'd,
Where British cups with China's porcelain vie,
(What cannot British industry supply?) (pp. 91–2)

Where Laing sees tea as a superfluity, harmful to the physical specimens in their remote regions, Chalmers restores it to the status of social
phenomenon, no longer bound to the body for its significance or to the
zonal locality of that body. Released from its local exemplarity, tea
becomes the signifier that links the Lerwick drawing room to the mobility
of global trade. The ill effects of tea were seen by a number of commentators to threaten the strength of the population in general. William
Falconer fears that 'it has had the effect of enfeebling and enervating the
bodies of our people, and of introducing several disorders that arise from
laxity and debility.'[30] But Chalmers seizes upon tea as an example of the
vigour of the modern commercial nation. By means of the synecdoche of
the tea table, the everyday activities of the Shetlanders are seen to take
place in a series of overlapping spatial identities. The same place, the tea
table, exists in multiple, simultaneous spaces: Britain, the world of empire
and global trade, and Shetland, here represented by some locally produced jam, 'the native produce of our ground' (p. 92). Chalmers' space is
a shifting model that does not work very well within the structure of
statistical inquiries. For eighteenth-century travellers such as Pennant
or geographers such as Sinclair, the delimitation and identification of
localities were basic groundwork. Units of space were legal and social and
could easily be represented by a small number of spokesmen, usually the
parish minister. Through this form of positivist description, the locality
could be described and its relation to the economy, population and
natural history of Scotland as a whole could be reckoned. But Chalmers'
sense of place differs from this in two important respects. First, she does
not imagine a prior whole – whether of the nation or the globe – which
can be subdivided into contiguous units and reassembled through
description. Rather, Chalmers conceives of space as performative and
experiential, defined by the transactions that take place in the present and
not restricted to prior borders or subdivisions. Second, unlike the male
reporters of the survey, Chalmers is self-consciously writing as a woman
poet and produces versions of female experience that inflect her sense of
spatiality.

In Chalmers' poetry, the local is no longer synecdochal for the nation
but produced by economic transactions that fracture prior boundaries.
Chalmers moves apparently peripheral Shetland into a position where it
can be easily connected with a wide sphere of global trade. Documented
in the long poem 'Johnsmas', the local economy of Lerwick is dependent
partly on the arrival of the Dutch fishing fleet in time to reach the annual
sale of hosiery at the midsummer fair of Johnsmas. These locally made

goods are the principal manufacture in the islands, and Chalmers underlines the fact (emphasising with insistent footnotes) that an important
element of Lerwick's commercial stability is the work of 'of female labour
and of commerce' (p. 52, n). In fact, the contributor to the *Statistical
Account*, Lerwick minister James Sands, points out that 'the only manufacture, carried on in the parish, is the knitting of woollen stockings, and
in this almost all the women are more or less engaged.'[31] This is in marked
contradistinction to the Edinburgh-based Patrick Neill's 1806 account
of Lerwick in which he states that a straw-plaiting business, run by 'a
London Company' is the only viable female industry in the town: 'Before
its introduction, there was no kind of manufacture in Lerwick, in which
young women could advantageously exert their industry,—the knitting of
stockings being only a waste of time.'[32] For Neill, the Shetland women
have no autonomy in the generation of wealth, their independent labours
are worthless, and they can only contribute to the economy when organised
by the London company.[33]

Chalmers' decisive assertion of Shetland women as participants not only
in the economy of the island but also in a form of international trade,
circumvents the model of national centre and periphery and imagines an
economic sphere not tied to spatial hierarchies. This non-hierarchical
model of space occurs throughout Chalmers' verse:

> May useful traffic still extend her smiles
> Around our bleak, detach'd, sea-circled Isles.
> Some genius whisper to the patriot's mind,
> The profitable market where to find,
> For Thulian produce; point where to explore
> Ready acceptance for our woollen store,
> Of texture such as 'woven, drest, and clean',
> By female industry, 'may clad a Queen'. (p. 144)[34]

As so often in Chalmers' writing, the social significance is suggested by
geographical relations. Economic continuities (between the female producers and the Queen) are seen to be a product of geographical *discon*-
tinuities. The 'detach'd' condition of the Shetland islands loosens them
from topographic homogeneity and allows them to become part of economic
movement and circulation. In another example of the fractal geometry
of Britain's island geography, it is not clear if the isles are detached from
each other or from the rest of Britain, whether 'our' Isles are the
Shetlands or appear as all the islands of Great Britain to 'the patriot's
mind'. Notably Chalmers does not specify London as the ideal market,

despite that being the place where the Queen is most likely to be found, as if she is depicting a nation without obvious centres and peripheries and within which markets are points of renewal and, to use her term, exploration. Chalmers sublimates causal relationships between production, distribution and consumption into a virtual space that represents circulation and commerce as a formal principle rather than a set of practices. When Adam Smith wrote 'As by means of water-carriage a more extensive market is opened to every sort of industry than what land-carriage alone can afford it, so it is upon the sea-coast [. . .] that industry of every kind naturally begins to subdivide and improve itself',[35] he may not have had Shetland in mind. But Chalmers takes Smith's version of modern commercial space to a condition of radical spatial contemporaneity, removing the history of the linkage of centres of consumption with regional sites of production and replacing both with continuous circulation where points are not fixed but can replace each other.

In an influential essay, Doreen Massey writes about the interrelations of the local and the global in a way that might describe Chalmers' geography as a form of modernity:

Space is created out of the vast intricacies, the incredible complexities of the interlocking and the non-interlocking, and the network of relations at every scale from the global to the local. What makes a particular view of these social relations specifically spatial is their simultaneity. It is a simultaneity also, which has extension and configuration.[36]

The spatial configuration of modernity takes the form of a radical contemporaneity in which social spaces can emerge and reconfigure themselves at any point on a network of global reach. Place is the point at which these interactions can be performed. To reinforce how remarkable Chalmers' poetry is in this regard, we can briefly set her alongside another Shetland author, Dorothea Primrose Campbell, whose *Poems* appeared in London in 1811 with a reprint, adding more poems, in 1816. Campbell is a different kind of poet altogether, and it would clearly not be proper to characterise all Shetland writing from a sample of two. But Campbell participates in a broader category of writing – the tropes of the national tale and of the traditional poetry associated with regional ballads. The early poems in the collection draw on folklore and superstition, and the volume opens with the lines 'It was on Burray's seabeat Isle, / Where Fairies dwelt in days of yore',[37] and, in the manner of Edgeworth's or Scott's explanations of folk beliefs to the more enlightened reader,

Campbell footnotes the title, 'The Spirits of the Hill' with some information about 'certain fantastical beings' known as Bokies. Chalmers, by
contrast, starts with some alternative lines for the tune of 'God Save the
King'. Where Chalmers confidently asserts the contemporary importance
of Shetland, Campbell follows the pattern of detailing local and traditional peculiarities as they begin to be subsumed into national homogeneity. Many of Campbell's poems are about the inevitability of leaving
(unlike Chalmers, Campbell did leave Shetland, moving to London), or
the passing away of childhood experiences. The landscape is often seen as
a romance space, tinted with loss and death. Her Shetland-set poems are
mixed with Highland ones, the more usual source of imagery for national
tales, and 'To the Northern Islander' both addresses and identifies the
author with that overarching embodiment of silenced cultures, the bard:

> Minstrel! the harp which thou hast deign'd to praise,
>   Ere yet its humble notes are hush'd for ever,
> Would gladly thank thee for thy gen'rous lays
>   Then sleep in silence, and awaken never.[38]

Not surprisingly, Campbell went on to publish a full-scale national tale,
Harley Radington (1821), in which the title character, born in London, visits
his mother's former home in Shetland.

  Chalmers' interest in the spatiality of modern commerce is interwoven
with her sense of herself as a woman author. She renders Shetland a
female sphere in which women are both producers and consumers and in
which class differences are blurred by being placed on a smooth continuum that links the manufacture of staples to the consumption of
luxuries and their common eighteenth-century exemplars, wool and tea.
In fact, Chalmers often sees the entire economic function of a society as
female even where its participants are male. The poem that ends the
collection, some lines 'To the United Trades' Society of Lerwick', blurs
gender roles. The society is at once a 'fraternal fund' (p. 140) and a
maternal body that gestates philanthropy, Chalmers' italics emphasising
the female nature of trade:

> Twelve winters now have roll'd on whirling storm,
> Since Lerwick *her* Society did form.
> The embryo benefit now ripening stands [. . .]. (p. 140)

Chalmers' attentiveness to her own status as an author encompasses
not only the importance of gender but also the relationship between the
kind of abstract space of circulation I discussed above and the more

empirical space generated by her surroundings. As she notes in the collection's preface, 'She has drawn the principal part of the imagery and scenery from the objects around her' (p. v). Chalmers is interested in space both in its geographical sense as the inscription, direction and delimitation of locations and also in a more phenomenological sense that asks questions about the way the mind synthesises experience to form a sense of place. Sometimes these come together in the same poem as her verse registers a hesitation between a world that is given to the mind fully inscribed with social and political meanings and a sense that the experience of place is shaped by consciousness. In an elegant answer to the question of whether subjects are formed by their locations or place is constituted socially, J. E. Malpas describes a form of subjectivity very like that which occurs in Chalmers' poetry:

Place is [. . .] that within and with respect to which subjectivity is itself established – place is not founded *on* subjectivity, but is rather that *on which* subjectivity is founded. Thus one does not first have a subject that apprehends certain features of the world in terms of the idea of place; instead, the structure of subjectivity is given in, and through, the structure of place.[39]

The social, Malpas argues, may be brought about by the forms in which any society orders time and space, but time and space are not essentially products of the social because there cannot be an a priori social that precedes spatiality.

We can see how this works in one of Chalmers' best poems. 'Description of Sound, near Lerwick' finds her standing on a steep hill and surveying the surrounding view. The poem starts off as a fairly standard example of natural theology working through the aesthetic experience as the beauty of the scene 'conspires / to lift the soul from nature to its God' (p. 102). It is not long, however, before this perspective is complicated as Chalmers speculates on the lack of trees in Shetland:

> Let us impartiality evince,
> By owning, that the wide surrounding view
> No envious (envy'd) forests intercept,
> Waving, in boastful pride, to mar our plan;
> Yet, who that looks around, but must confess
> A crown of British oak would well become
> Bressa's majestic Ward Hill. (pp. 102–3)

The reader is lulled into a false sense of simplicity by the promise of an objective world guaranteed by 'impartiality'. But the phrase 'envious (envy'd) forests' makes the genesis of this space unclear as it hesitates between two forms of agency. Do the imagined trees come from a pre-existing world of political agency that can be envious of the Shetland landscape, or are they called up by the desire of the viewer? The ambiguity of the word 'plan', which could refer either to the mapping of a given space or, in phenomenological terms, an intention of the mind towards the landscape, is similarly fluid, moving between a charting of a pre-cultural world in the present and a future imagining of the 'British' scene brought into being in the next lines. And even if this uncertainty could be resolved, it is again disturbed by the word 'become'. The primary meaning of 'to suit' coexists with the sense 'to turn into', again making the order of priority between the given and imaginary landscapes unclear. The instability of the language here further complicates the notion of Britishness, asking whether it is an assumed characteristic or an innate quality. Is national identity something that can be added to a discrete local landscape by association, or is it possible for the landscape to be constructed out of patriotic ideas – for the British oaks, to turn into the Shetland hill and absorb it into a homogenised nation?

These questions do not seem to require answers, as Chalmers assumes a shifting sense of place. Her sense is that metaphor is how we see the world anyway and not necessarily illustrative of some underlying material reality.[40] The recurrent theme of the lack of trees on Shetland, so far from confirming Johnson's evidence of Scottish deficiency, become for Chalmers a function of imaginative vitality:

> The harbour view'd, from where obstructing heights
> Conceal the vessels' hulks, yet show the masts,
> Mimics a wintry forest stript of leaves,
> A *floating* forest Thulè only boasts. (p. 54–5)

Even the dominant metaphor/metonym of British nationalism patriotism (with its echoes of Pope's 'Windsor-Forest') connecting patriotic feeling to material military might, Garrick's famous patriotic song 'Heart of Oak Are Our Ships' can be adapted to treeless Shetland:

> Tho', on our hills around,
> No shady woods are found,
> With the *Oak* graceful crown'd,
> We boast the *Hearts*. (p. 3)

The trees on Shetland are doubly produced by the practices of representation: they are represented metonymically by the ships manned by

Shetland sailors (including the late William Chalmers) and imaginatively in the mind of the poet. And this projection is itself doubled as Chalmers imagines the trees reflected in the sea:

> Pines and elms
> Would with superior beauty grace these shores,
> Would grace them twice, for liquid groves would wave,
> In soften'd foliage, in the crystal flood. (p. 103)

This is very common in Chalmers' verse, which assumes that mirrors and reflections are part of the quotidian life of the Shetlands. She describes the drawing room of the Linklater family who have placed a mirror there to reflect views from the garden inside the house:

> Dispos'd by the judicious hand of taste,
> A mirror view to such advantage plac'd,
> As to reflect the garden in full bloom,
> Seen as an antichamber to the room,
> Which 'twixt the real and shadowy garden seems,
> Whilst thro' the whole bright dart the sunny beams.
> It must be own'd that in our Northern clime
> Summer is rather chary of his time,
> His tardy visit transient and sweet,
> Slow in advance, but in retreating fleet;
> What can we more to counteract his haste
> Than doubly view his beauties while they last. (p. 91)

The mirror is a social artefact placed there by 'the judicious hand of taste', but it is also part of Chalmers' perceptual world in which the subject constantly repositions itself in a space of reflections, relative distances and effects of light. This particular mirror stage is very different from Jacques Lacan's famous formulation, because it never lures the subject into identifying with its own image. The garden mirror amplifies and moves the space around the gazing subject, allowing the visual to be produced by spatial configuration and not the other way round. Unlike the narcissistic gaze, which produces a gestalt in the imaginary world corresponding absolutely to the subject, the Linklaters' mirror reflects light, the impersonal ground for vision rather than the formed image.

We might also think of this as a female space. In modern feminist theory, Luce Irigaray describes the phallocentric position of the flat mirror that 'privileges the relation of man to his fellow man' with its 'effects of linear projection, of circular turning back onto the self-(as the) same'.[41] Chalmers' mirror, instead, creates a liminal space that acts as an 'antechamber', not giving back and confirming the image of the spectator but complicating the idea of flat or empty space against which the identity of the view could be asserted. Objects, in Chalmers' landscape, are rarely fixed or given. They are often posed between metonymic and metaphoric states, like the masts that transform into trees or are produced by effects of light and reflection. Consequently, space is not a field upon which objects can be displayed. Rather, it is something that is generated by individual consciousness or social interactions. Chalmers' world takes place "twixt the real and shadowy', a space where objects are 'doubly view'd' and the distinctions between depth and surface, inside and outside are not enforced.

This is how Chalmers forms her ideas of patriotism through spatial relations. Notions of centre and periphery, up and down, inside and out are everywhere in her work, produced and inflected by angles of sight and positions of viewing. She is intensely interested in positionality but works this out through multiple perspectives that complicate or avert the divisions and power relations often implicit in the establishing of positions. Keenly aware of the prior social demarcations of her own position as a woman author and a Shetlander, Chalmers complicates the spatial identity of the periphery so that it can no longer be seen only in relation to a perceived social or national centre. Recent work on women's writing of the eighteenth century has shown the emergence in the later decades of the century of a form of female, middle-class patriotism which argued, as Harriet Guest puts it, 'that patriotism was a necessary part of women's education, and [. . .] that middle-class women's exclusion from paid labor allowed them to cultivate a statesmanlike knowledge of the world that was not longer available to professional or landed men'.[42] Ann Grant, whom I discussed in Chapter 1, clearly sees herself in this tradition, but Chalmers occupies a different place in patriotic verse. She has no qualms about claiming to speak for Shetland on a world stage, but her poetry replaces the politics of events with the sociology of space. Many of her poems are strongly patriotic, and the three that open the collection are on the subject of the 1809 Jubilee of George III. 'Congratulatory Lines on the Jubilee' calls for patriotic feeling throughout the nation:

> Be Julius' towers exulting heard around,
> And join'd throughout Britannia's circling bound,
> Till royal Charlotte's cannon echo back the sound. (p. 4)

'Julius' towers' are the Tower of London, reputedly founded by the Romans and here rescued from their less flattering appearance in Gray's

'The Bard' as 'towers of Julius, London's lasting shame', and Fort Char-
lotte in Lerwick is, as a footnote tells us, 'the most northern garrison of
the Empire' (p. 4, n.). But Chalmers' vision of a national harmony that
unites the north–south extent of Britain is not so much linear as circular.
'Circle' or 'circling' are among Chalmers favourite words, occurring
eighteen times in the volume's thirty-four poems. As is so often the case in
her verse, single words are not as simple as they at first appear, and subtle
ambiguities lurk in the term here. 'Circling', on the one hand, means
'encircling', emphasising the bounded or enclosed spatiality of the nation.
But the term also implies 'circulation' or a boundary that is not fixed but
forms a moving point not tied to a particular position on a circumference.

The Linklaters' mirror, drawing the outside indoors, creates a space
between public and private, but Chalmers assumes the normality of
reflection on wholly public occasions as well. 'Verses on the Jubilee
Night, at Lerwick', the third poem in the collection, is also the third and
final celebration of the King's Jubilee, moving the generalised perspectives
of the first two to the specific location of Lerwick. The poem describes a
complex spatial arrangement that depends on proximities, trajectories,
refraction and reflections rather than discrete objects or localities. In a
prefatory note, Chalmers explains that the closeness of Lerwick to the sea
means that displays of lights in the town are reflected in the water of the
harbour, unless the moon is full. On the occasion of the Jubilee, there was
a full moon, but its luminosity 'made ample amends' (p. 8) for the loss of
the reflected lights. The poem plays with the fluidity between states of up
and down, land and water, night and day, nature and culture. The gaze of
the various participants or positions in the drama is multiple rather than
being directed on single objects. The moon occupies three positions: the
sky, the water that reflects it, and the land for whose lights it substitutes.
Chalmers' poems take place in a world which is not visually available in a
continuous way across its extent. The globe of climate theory and the
nation of the statistical account have an embodied existence prior to
scrutiny, and it is unnecessary always to specify the physical means by
which they appear to the observer because they do so by uniform laws. In
a section on the climate-induced ailments of the Shetlanders, Arthur
Edmondston writes, 'It is vain to contend against the influence of natural
powers, which are uniform and steady in their operation.'[43] But Chalmers'
poetry gives a visual form to the recognition that it is not only places
that differ, but the act of seeing them is also subject to discontinuity. She
expresses this as a quality of light: to live in Shetland is to recognise visual
experience as normally indirect, mediated or doubled.

The conclusion of 'Verses on the Jubilee Night' finally associates patriotism with a dependable British masculinity: although successful on this particular evening, Cynthia, the moon, is too flighty to be depended upon for public occasions, and only Neptune can be absolutely relied on as 'our friend in need'. But in the poems which do not seek the official status of occasional verse, Chalmers further explores the specific spatiality of the female body. The 'Description of Sound' muses on the relation between the landscape and gendered bodies:

> Shall I the North or Southern Isthmus choose?
> Both stretch their white and curving arms of beach
> To lead me to it by the eastern course.
> The opposing Isthmuses, the western knolls,
> And the Peninsula a circle form
> Around a Loch, whose pure transparency,
> Opposing boundaries of white and green,
> And site sequester'd, pleasing union form.
> Slender these barriers on the north and south,
> Which here divide the near approaching bounds
> Of Neptune, and the gentle Arethuse;
> Who seems as she enjoy'd protection from
> The power marine, save when fierce conflicts rise
> 'Twixt him and Æolus; haply in the strife
> The beach's limits all-unequal prove [. . .]. (p. 111)

Describing her walk home, Chalmers touches on a trope usually coded as female, the 'white and curving arms' of the beach, but here taken out of the symbolic field. The body is not only a vehicle for traversing the different spaces on Chalmers' walk, it also becomes a way of thinking about experiencing space itself. Or, to put it another way, there is no absolute distinction between embodied space and the conceptualising mind. The landscape is female not because it is inscribed in that way but because it is the experience of the female observer and not reliant on a clear distinction between subject and object which might divide the gaze. The mind is contiguous with the landscape, a space that is neither culture nor nature as it precedes these categories. Unburdened with the freight of socialised sexuality, the female body becomes associated with what looks at first like freedom of choice between opposing spatial relations ('Shall I the North or Southern Isthmus choose?'), but in fact introduces oppositions only to dispel them. The 'opposing boundaries' become 'slender barriers' that form a 'pleasing union' at a point at which bounded, material space gives way to space as conceptual and imagined, and where – in

Chalmers' most frequent spatial trope – oppositions become circular. It is only when the body becomes once again historicised and socially inscribed – in this case mythologised and personified into the figures of Neptune and Aeolus competing over the nymph Arethusa – that the landscape becomes once again part of a clearly gendered symbolic order, here touched with the threat of sexual violence. The beach's 'white and curving arms' are no longer the projection of female experience but the sign of women's cultural representation, and the 'beach's limits' become important only when they are transgressed and when power becomes the determinant of space.[44] Again, Chalmers contemplates both a space that is politically inscribed and given to the subject, on the one hand, and a lived space, a property of the affective relations of a moving, experiencing, body that would later be theorised by phenomenology: 'I am not in space and time, nor do I conceive space and time; I belong to them, my body combines with them and includes them.'[45] There is no permanent distinction in Chalmers' work between a material world and a perceiving mind. The poem as a whole traces a walk through a rapidly changing landscape in which place is expressed as a journey: it is the movement of the body through the landscape that produces the changing views and perspectives, rather than the landscape being a spectatorial collection of impressions from an external viewpoint. There is no obvious priority in the act of seeing; the speaker views a landscape which has its own ability to attract: 'Here the charm'd eye a pleasing magnet finds' (p. 110). It is also, Chalmers suggests, a lived landscape, made social not in prior inscription of social symbolism, as in the gendered isthmuses, but by the activities of the people who live there. The speaker has a sense of the landscape as 'incomplete' without the acts that constitute the lives of its inhabitants:

> Still seems the landscape incomplete and tame,
> That lacks result which hill and dale bestow;
> Though Flora and Pomona, emulous
> Each other to outvie, should deck the scene;
> Here sports that gay diversity at will,
> The corn fields sweep not here in wide extent,
> But portion'd into *rigs* varying in shape and size;
> While fallow ground, meadow and pasturage,
> Irregularly interspers'd between,
> In chequer work, please fancy and the eye. (p. 104)

The external personifications of Flora and Pomona who 'deck' the scene from outside it, are seen as less significant in giving the nature of the landscape than the activities of the humans who are there to experience it and interact with it – what geographers following Heidegger refer to as 'dwelling'.[46]

It is not my intention to claim Chalmers for contemporary pheno-menological geography but to show how her thoughts on the relation between mind and space characterise her own peculiar sense of writing as a woman author in early nineteenth-century Shetland. All these come together in one of her finest poems, which forms an extended meditation on her themes of space, position, nation and gender. 'The Rose of the Rock' is a rather mysterious poem, not least because Chalmers tells us in an endnote that part of it was composed by a 'friend' whom she does not name. In my discussion of the poem, I do not propose to distinguish between the two writers, but their co-authorship is nevertheless itself an interesting detail in a poem about relationships between women which are not fully articulated or, perhaps, not capable of being articulated.

Setting the poem's enigmatic tone, the epigram is Gray's well-known 'Full many a flower is born to blush unseen / And waste its sweetness on the desert air', from the 'Elegy Written in a Country Churchyard', but in the context of Chalmers' poem, this becomes less of an aphorism and more of a metaphysical puzzle that asks about the continuous existence of objects in the material world and their independence of the gaze. The poem begins by quoting an unnamed speaker, perhaps also the narrator, who suggests a journey to the hills outside Lerwick. The narrator then describes the perspective: 'And, in one wide and heart-dilating view, / Gives Thulè's utmost boundaries to the eye' (p. 21). The movement of sudden expansion taking place both in the viewer's heart and the tre-mendous view confuses the perspective. In a move typical of Chalmers' verse, there is no clear distinction between very big and very small, not even a reconfiguring of power as in the Kantian sublime and the Romantic poetry that descends from it. As we saw in the 'Description of Sound', Chalmers' experience of scenery is an act quite unlike the sublime of William Wordsworth or Shelley with its attendant battles between the mind and the landscape, acts of power and usurpation. In 'The Rose of the Rock', the spectator does not re-establish her equilibrium upon rec-ognising her mind's capacity to experience the infinite because this was not a power relation that happened in the first place. Unsurprisingly, the idea of an 'utmost boundary' is not as fixed as it first seemed. Although the limits of the view are given to the eye, the imagination continues to expand the view 'Eastward, beyond where keenest sight can pierce' and north-west towards Iceland. Despite the prominent landmarks that are listed in the poem ('Vaalifield's high ridge and Saxaford' [p. 21]), this is not only a landscape in which objects are non-discrete bodies in a spatial field. Chalmers' favourite term, 'circling', takes on double meanings that confuse subject and object: 'The circling still the penetrating gaze, Lo! Fitful lifts on high his aged head' (p. 22). It is not clear whether the gaze is circling Fitful Head (a promontory) or vice versa. Space is itself a causality that produces or shapes objects which exist in it as specular images. It can even take on its own agency: 'yonder space, that points to Faro's Isles' (p. 22).

On the other hand, Chalmers' geographical reach is never far from the locality of Shetland itself. Here the elevated position and the confusion of big and small seems to situate Shetland at the top of the world with a view of the extent of northern Europe, again disrupting conventional geographies of centre and periphery. Situating herself on one elevation and using its height to identify others, Chalmers decisively employs a visual structure that claims the apparently outlying Shetlands as central, familiar and of real geographic importance. Barbara Maria Stafford points to a fundamental difference in two sorts of mapping in this period: coastal drafting, which was 'to provide as clear an indication of the shape of unmapped land [. . .] as the distance from the ship would permit', and panoramic views, which 'were connected with triangulation surveys that sighted on important landmarks from the interior'.[47] These distinct forms also mark the difference between Scott and Chalmers.[48] Scott's northern isles are mapped in the first way: his tracing of the coastline is an exterior view that chronicles an unknown sequence of fragmentary views whose coherence – if it has any – must be conferred by his own narrative. Chalmers, by contrast, assumes an interior position whose importance is *already* given. She triangulates a landscape connected by points of acknowledged national significance.

In the next scene, we see a flock of birds disturbed by the speaker and 'whirling a thousand ways'. The birds are 'fluttering parents', anxious about their young, but then the word 'parent' becomes transferred from the birds to the landscape:

> The billows' rage, aiding the power of time
> To which full oft yields even the solid rock,
> Had, from the parent island, wide disjoin'd
> A craggy cliff, whose deep resounding base
> Was insulated by the circling wave. (p. 23)

This image, casting human relationships in nature, may remind us of another poem by a 'regional' female author, Dorothy Wordsworth's

'Floating Island at Hawkshead', where the apparently solid ground has let loose a part of itself which is both separate from the originating land and still connected in unseen ways as its 'lost fragments shall remain, / To fertilize some other ground'.[49] But where Wordsworth's poem seems to indicate the hidden interconnectedness of women with communities, Chalmers' speculates on a more intractable problem about the recognition of female subjectivity and sexuality. First, Chalmers removes the possibility of distinguishing gendered experience through aesthetics:

> Half way adown the bleak and rugged steep,
> Secur'd from most intrepid schoolboy's reach,
> Nature, amid a scene whose wild sublime
> Might chill the blood and even to horror rouse,
> Had dropt a lovely solitary flower,
> As remembrancer of another style
> Of beauty, by full contrast heighten'd seen. (p. 23)

What seems to be a clear distinction between the 'wild sublime' of the cliff and the beautiful flower is deconstructed and along with it the association of these modes of affect with masculine and feminine principles. At first, we think that the 'lovely' rose is small compared with the towering cliff, but the poem states that the contrast actually has the effect of making the beauty of the rose seem 'heighten'd'. Thus, the rose is beautiful because, in Kantian terms, beauty is a property of the form of the object. But it also mimics the experience of the sublime in which what is apparently small (the observer) is immensely heightened by its ability to conceptualise the experience that first appeared to diminish it. Kant puts it:

But because there is in our imagination a striving to advance to the infinite, while in our reason there lies a claim to absolute totality, as to a real idea, the very inadequacy of our faculty for estimating the magnitude of the things of the sensible world awakens the feeling of a supersensible faculty in us; and the use that the power of judgment naturally makes in behalf of the latter (feeling), though not the object of the senses, is absolutely great, while in comparison to it every other use is small.[50]

The rose, typically in Chalmers' writing, is placed uncertainly between subject (the experiencing consciousness of the sublime) and object (the form of the beautiful). It does not occupy a space that is mathematically commensurable outside the mind, being both big and small at the same time, but neither does Chalmers restore the possibility for comparison, or the 'absolutely great' in Kant's terms (our capacity to think the infinite), to assert the power of the mind's judgement over what we can measure through the senses.

It is these forms of indeterminacy which Chalmers tends to cast as a redistribution of female space. The rose is clearly associated with women. As an object, it is for their attention only, being 'Secur'd from most intrepid schoolboy's reach'. The narrator decides not to tell her friends about the rose as it would be too dangerous if any of them, particularly a young girl who is in the party, were to seek for it. But she is not sure this is the right decision and stands 'mute, / Lingering, absorp't, irresolute' (p. 24) while the secret escapes anyway. In contrast with Chalmers' patriotic poetry, in which women take an active public role, this poem about female desire is itself tentative in its conclusions. The speaker traces a mythological narrative that might contextualise and socialise the young girl's dangerous desire:

> Not Eden's fair, amid the fragrant bowers,
> More ardently desir'd forbidden fruit,
> Than now, with disappointments arrow stung,
> Her young descendant doth forbidden flower. (p. 24)

But, as with the isthmus scene in the 'Description of Sound', which also explores the uneasy correlations between empirical female experience and narratives of female behaviours, the poem does not make a clear distinction between the female gaze and the female object. It is not clear if the rose is a referent for female sexuality or female desire or both. Neither is it entirely clear from the syntax that 'flower' in the quotation above is exclusively a noun – as a verb, it carries the suggestion that the young girl's curiosity about the world is a form of flowering that that world restricts. The child is a 'blooming traveller' (p. 24), the rose is a 'blooming stranger' (p. 23); subject and object are not clearly separated. If the poem is about sexuality, it resists the spatial distribution of the gaze into these categories.

Although I am reluctant to push this puzzling poem into specific readings, we can nevertheless conclude that it is a way for Chalmers to explore the possibility of an exclusively female spatiality. 'The Rose of the Rock' ends with a return to the geography of Shetland, which now becomes an immense landscape contained within the imagination of the women in the poem in a final dialogue between the narrator and the young girl:

> 'Reflect, we either twice must cross the sea,
> 'And o'er two islands must retrace our steps,

'Or we must brave the surge 'round Bressa's Ord,
'And stem the impetuous force of Baarda stream,
'Ere we can reach the spot from whence 'tis seen.'
'I care not, I would travel Zetland o'er,
'To see the Rose that grows amid the Rock.' (p. 25)

Instead of the anthropological perspective of Laing or Edmondston, which pictured the women as creatures of, and contained by, terrain, the landscape here extends from the women's consciousness. And Shetland itself, instead of being a set of small, distant islands, becomes a broad expanse of lands and seas, site of travel and exploration.

For Scott, a margin is a place one visits from the centre and discovers that, however much one romanticises that margin as a place of newness and discovery, it will turn out to be inscribed by the centre from which one has left.[51] Chalmers, on the other hand, from her starting point of conventional patriotism, deconstructs the opposition between margin and centre, inside and outside. Her optical north plays with spatial hierarchies, allowing supposedly distant northern isles to become panoptical positions and central surveying points, but ones that do not exert power over the islands' population. Despite her claim to be only a 'Thulian quill', Chalmers' sense of spatiality is perhaps the most complex and radical of any in this study.

CHAPTER 6

Norths: James Hogg and post-Enlightenment space

James Hogg was 'The Ettrick Shepherd', but not in the same way that Robert Burns, a generation earlier, was 'The Ayrshire Ploughman'. Burns certainly did not think of himself in the conventional terms of the eighteenth-century 'peasant' poet and, as I have argued, makes very individual play with the conventions of the poetry of rural place. But his verse was nevertheless expected by his readership to follow the traditions of a neoclassical pastoralism and georgic exposition of humble rural life, and Burns could write in this vein when he chose. 'The Cotter's Saturday Night' was his most popular poem among contemporary readers and throughout the nineteenth century.[1] But if 'The Ayrshire Ploughman' was the sign of Burns's periodic interpellation by a prior discourse of labouring-class poetry, Hogg was self-consciously and provocatively the Ettrick Shepherd. By the time his literary career was taking off in the 1820s, the fashion for 'peasant poets' was diminishing. Hogg was more interested in using the term 'the Ettrick Shepherd' as a brand name to further his career and in keeping his readers guessing as to how far his shepherd-persona was identical with a naïve resident of the Ettrick Valley.[2] While Burns's popular celebrity now rests partly on his apparently universalisable humanity, Hogg's reputation declined in the twentieth century to that of a local writer, of interest largely through his associations with the poems and traditional stories of the Scottish Borders. Hogg's most significant work comes in the 1820s when the Romantic local was increasingly drawn into a discourse of domestic tourism and ethnographic objectification, and it is in response to a readership that looked for material that was, in the terms of one of his own subtitles, *Collected among the Cottagers in the South of Scotland*, that he produces his own particular complications of the possibility of the local. In this chapter, then, I argue that Hogg is not so much a local writer as a writer about locality and about the impossibility of fixing it.

161

The local contains its own paradox: ostensibly a particular place, it is nevertheless open to generality. We recognise in the local a certain universal affect, associated with familiarity and homeliness, but when we go on holiday, 'the locals' are the people other to ourselves. We might say that the 'local' is what we expect through past experience, whereas a 'locality', on the other hand, would be something not readable through these terms of expectation and identification but, rather, a position that cannot be constituted relationally, a place that can be experienced once, in one time and space.

The difference between the local and a locality has something in common with Peter Hallward's distinction between the specific, the position of the individual subject in relation to the species, and the singular, a way of articulating how the singular subject maps the world rather than being mapped by demographic coordinates:

the words singular and specific designate two abstract poles of distinction, i.e. two fundamentally divergent conceptions of individuation and differentiation. Roughly speaking, a singular mode of individuation proceeds internally, through a process that creates its own medium of existence or expansion, whereas a specific mode operates, through the active negotiation of relations and the deliberate taking of sides, choices and risks, in a domain and under constraints that are external to these taking. *The specific is relational, the singular is non relational.*[3]

Hallward proposes the specific and the singular as two distinct individuating logics and argues that the truly post-colonial would constitute a singularity in which individual identities can transcend the world-ordering properties of the specific and become absolutely self-sufficient.[4] Although it would be possible to read Hogg through post-colonial thinking, I want rather to think of him as a post-Enlightenment author, reacting to the appropriation or invention of popular culture by a middle-class, urban readership.

'Singular' is one of Hogg's favourite words, but he also exploits its ambiguities, rather than concentrating it in a distinct sphere. Singular things are, on the one hand, curiosities, examples of the antiquarian project of cataloguing diverse examples of the national past. Hogg had worked for Walter Scott in the ballad-collecting operation that produced the *Minstrelsy of the Scottish Border* and was well aware of Scott's taxonomic impulse to systematise his *'historical and romantic ballads, collected in the Southern counties of Scotland, with a few of modern date, founded upon local tradition.'*[5] In this sense, the singular is local and specific, producing examples of the types of the rural labouring class. But the singular in Hogg is also singular in another sense. Singularity is whatever is not explicable through relations of difference. Hogg is explicit about this in the opening of the short tale 'Adam Bell', where he argues that a unique event may be true, that is, experienced by an individual, but that it cannot be explained through 'facts that have been discovered relating to it' and is therefore 'singular', fully present only to those who experienced the tale as a 'primary cause', the event itself at the moment of its unique occurrence:

This tale, which may be depended upon as in every part true, is singular, for the circumstance of its being insolvable either from the facts that have been discovered relating to it, or by reason: for though events sometimes occur among mankind, which at the same time seem inexplicable, yet there being always some individuals acquainted with the primary causes of those events, they seldom fail of being brought to light before all the actors in them, or their confidants, are removed from this state of existence.[6]

Rather than reducing the supernatural to a historical category, Hogg obstructs the transcendent position of the antiquarian who would identify the supernatural as superstition. Hogg leaves open the possibility of the supernatural as the medium of its own existence, not tied to specific coordinates of time and space but behaving according to the criteria for its own operation. The reality-transforming power of magical spells works through the moment of their utterance – not through the explanatory medium of history but according to the immediate logic of their enunciation. If magic is not determined by anything outside itself, then it is singular and cannot be predicted by the relational schemas of antiquarianism or ethnography.

In Hogg's stories, the supernatural is often what undercuts apprehension of the local. Hogg insists that the local is not familiar by virtue of its being reproducible within a ideological systematisation of locality, in which each apparently local point would be recognisable through external narratives (the local as homely, as natural, or as non-cosmopolitan). His writing stands in contrast to the national tale in which the ethnographic exploration of the local is what allows the reader to understand the national.[7] In Hogg's case, the local is not really knowable in any repeatable, recognisable way but is something that occurs once in one space and time. Local traditions, in Hogg, can challenge spatial locatedness altogether, airily waving aside the Kantian idea that 'I cannot conceive anything as located outside me unless I represent it as in a space different from the space in which I myself am.'[8] Hogg offers an alternative to space as extension and introduces us to supernatural worlds in which one might be occupying one space yet be in two different places at the same time. We might take, for example, the protagonist of 'The Mysterious Bride', who manages simultaneously to be in Scotland and Ireland, for reasons that cannot be explained through physics or empiricism. Hogg is particularly fond of using this technique to discomfort the expectations of his metropolitan readers who might associate the rural with the familiarity of tradition by shocking them with corpses that come back to life to re-narrate their own deaths ('Some Terrible Letters from Scotland') or children who apparently cause each other's deaths by dreaming about them ('Cousin Mattie').

A number of Hogg's short stories are about localities not as places recognisable from outside themselves but as instances that recreate their own situatedness in particular circumstances. Typically, Hogg plays to and then discomforts his readers' expectations of the familiarity of the traditional, local story. 'John Gray o' Middleholm', first published in the collection *Winter Evening Tales* in 1820, sounds as if it should be a story that unites the local and the typical into the specific, but Hogg immediately juxtaposes two irreconcilable positions: 'He was altogether a singular figure, and a far more singular man. Who has not heard of John Gray, weaver and feuar in Middleholm?'[9] If John Gray is really singular, then he cannot be the generally known individual specimen of weavers and feuars that the narrator offers us. This apparently local story troubles the idea of locality itself, and Hogg moves gleefully between a set of apparently recognisable local Scottish Border places and the local hero's own difficulty in recognising them. In a dream, John Gray, an avid treasure-hunter, is given precise instructions by a monk as to the whereabouts of a hoard of treasure buried in Kelso Abbey, but when he goes there, 'he found that nothing was the same as it had been shown to him in the dream' (p. 239) and that the landmarks he has been given are all slightly out of place. While awake, John meets the dream figure, now a cobbler, who tells him that he has in turn dreamed of treasure in John's own orchard. Returning home, John finds some old coins buried beneath one of his apple trees, although (in a motif typical in Hogg where information disappears up a blind alley) he keeps this quiet from his wife and neighbours.

The story positions the reader at a point of hesitation between ways of identifying individual places. Kelso, a Borders town, is a local spot, readable through the antiquarian discourses of local history and fiction. It was the site of the first publication of Scott's hugely successful *Minstrelsy of the Scottish Border*, and the comic search for treasure in the Abbey recalls Scott's own jokes about antiquarian treasure-hunting at the ruins of the Abbey of St Ruth in *The Antiquary*, which we saw in Chapter 4. Even more specifically, Hogg reminds us of Borders treasure-hunting escapades at nearby Melrose Abbey in Scott's *The Monastery*, published the month before *Winter Evening Tales* in March 1820. This Abbey is both local – recognisably a portrait of the 'real' Melrose – and singular, referred to in Scott's novel as Kennaquair ('don't know where'), a place conjured up by the fictions of the novel and a locality not to be recognised through outside knowledge. In Hogg's story, the treasure turns out to have been in John Gray's own orchard all along although, unlike Kelso Abbey, not recognisable through any historical relations. It lies in 'an old pan filled with coins, of a date and reign John knew nothing about' (p. 254). Not visible from outside, John's own home becomes a singular locality, magically reconstituted. The treasure is there not because orchards, like abbeys, commonly contain treasure, but because John decides to dig for it there. The act of looking magically creates its own object. Yet, Hogg never quite lets the reader decide between the singularity of his fictions and the specificity expected by his audience: the exchange-of-dreams story is itself a traditional model, made comprehensible through prior readings and tellings.[10]

It is this dissolution of structures of locating that characterises Hogg's norths; the same unknowability of place through relational identity collapses ideas as much about a global spatiality as about local Borders spots. The next two northern stories under discussion here act retrospectively on the Enlightenment system-building that has been the subject of this book, so before turning to them, it might be helpful to sum up the relations of history and geography that Hogg proceeds to unravel.

'A MOST ABOMINABLE COUNTRY': NORTHERN EUROPE

In Chapter 1, I discussed how Enlightenment geography depends on the enfolding of geography into history. We can trace this from Montesquieu's dictum in *The Spirit of the Laws* that laws are derived from the nature of things – these 'things' including religion, means of subsistence, terrain, population number and climate. History and geography are codependent as forms of sociology: historical narratives 'account for' national difference over the globe, while geographical variation is what allows history to take place as laws develop according to natural diversity. A globe that could be mapped in terms of zones and climates could also be read historically; laws were not wholly politically contingent principles but existed as 'spirit', a general inclination emanating from physical, not moral, causes. For Montesquieu, history and geography are foundational, but they do not require to be represented in detail. As Richard Sher points out, peoples represent for Montesquieu 'a single "type" of society regardless of whether they are considered as they were at a given time in the past or as they are in the present.'[11] But advances in the technologies of cartography exerted pressures of representation on the epistemological conditions of Enlightenment geography. With demand for new forms of representational 'accuracy', it became no longer possible to assume an imaginary static position from which to view a 'great map of mankind', as Edmund Burke sees it, where there 'is no state or Gradation of barbarism, and no more of refinement which we have not at the same instant under our View.'[12] As John Pinkerton claims, a *Modern Geography* such as his own is determined by precise conditions of the temporality of spatial difference and the provisional nature of historical inscription. His work is 'modern' partly because of its recognition of the topographic nature of geography: his book will not just describe the physical globe but will also recognise that what is being described is itself a process of writing as the world is determined by the shifting claims of politics: 'Whole kingdoms have been annihilated; grand provinces transferred: and such a general alteration has taken place in states and boundaries, that a geographical work published five years ago may be pronounced to be already antiquated.'[13]

What comes between the broad stadial contours of Burke and the topographical volatility of Pinkerton is partly a reaction to the cartographic function of warfare. For Scottish Enlightenment historians, Europe had been a balanced system of commercially sophisticated nations in which temporary disparities of power are sorted out by wars concluded by treaties that more or less restore the initial distribution of territory and authority:

But when nations are in a similar state, and keep pace with each other in their advances towards refinement, they are not exposed to the calamity of sudden conquest. [. . .] Other states interpose, and balance any temporary advantage which either party may have acquired. After the fiercest and most lengthened contest, all the rival nations are exhausted, none are conquered. At length a peace is concluded, which re-instates each in possession of almost the same power and the same territories.[14]

Behind this is an argument about warfare conducted by Hume and Robertson, and more equivocally by Adam Ferguson, that advanced commerce will protect a nation from internal conflict while strengthening its capacity for external warfare, should this prove necessary. War is not something that disturbs zonal divisions but rather is produced by the very categories they set. Only despotic regimes indulge in wasteful, unruly war, argued Adam Smith; commercial peoples could conduct sophisticated campaigns to protect the very concept of national sovereignty. Adam Ferguson, more ambivalent on the subject of warfare and civilisation, nevertheless states: 'Without the rivalship of nations, and the practice of war, civil society itself could scarcely have found an object, or a form.'[15] For Robertson, the peace treaties that conclude wars are not primarily topographic themselves but are a function of the equilibrium of nation-states, an equilibrium in turn brought about by the predictable, causal relations of history and geography. For Pinkerton, on the other hand, treaties are a form of writing that destabilises global geographical narratives: 'These treatises not only influence the descriptions of European countries, but of many in Asia, Africa, and America.'[16]

These shifts in post-Enlightenment geography offer a context for Hogg's foray into the spatial politics of northern Europe. The long story 'The Adventures of Captain John Lochy' casts a cynical eye upon versions of Imperial Britain and its epistemological legibility in historical geography. The story takes place in the early eighteenth century. John Lochy, the narrator, is discovered by the banks of the river Lochy in the Scottish Highlands with a note claiming that he is 'nobly born' and is brought up under the sponsorship of the Earl of Breadalbane. After some youthful adventures involving kidnapping, he joins the British Army and fights in Marlborough's campaigns during the War of the Spanish Succession in the Netherlands and Germany. A Highlander named Finlayson accompanies him during these exploits. Fitted up for theft, Lochy deserts and joins the Swedish Army of Charles XII as it advances on Moscow. He teams up with an Asian prince and a Jewish woman but becomes disillusioned with the war and returns to Edinburgh. Here he falls in with the Jacobite side in the 1715 rebellion but becomes disenchanted with its leadership and switches sides again to that of the Duke of Argyll. Losing interest in his mercenary career altogether, he proposes to head off out of his own story to join his erstwhile eastern companions. As a postscript, an editor observes that he may in fact have remained in or returned to Scotland to dispute a land title. Some letters to Scottish newspapers are then printed claiming his birth was the result of an elopement in the aristocratic Wharton family.

The commercial foundation of warfare, in this tale, is entirely a matter of theft or fraud, at the opposite extreme from Adam Smith's ideal of commercial self-interest engendering social discipline. Lochy changes

sides at every turn, and the story describes a state of affairs more like
Adam Ferguson's nightmare vision of a mercenary army wholly aban-
doning any idea of civic virtue or even identity, the dark double of
Robertson's Europe held in check by political treaties:

In Europe, where mercenary and disciplined armies are everywhere formed, and
ready to traverse the earth, where, like a flood pent up by slender banks, they are
only restrained by political forms, or a temporary balance of power; if the sluices
should break, what inundations may we not expect to behold? [. . .] Every state,
by the defeat of its troops, may be turned into a province; every army opposed
in the field to-day may be hired to-morrow; and every victory gained, may give
the accession of a new military force to the victor.[17]

In 'John Lochy', European military logic is not a matter of commercially successful states fine-tuning the balance of power, and warfare itself
is unable to support a self-sustaining economy. The soldiers routinely loot
everything in their path:

We often plundered and burnt from twenty to thirty rich towns in a day; and it
was said that upwards of three hundred such were utterly consumed. The riches
that some men got were immense; but they were mostly in goods of high value,
and a good part was again lost before they could be turned into money.[18]

War here is an economy out of control; consumption has turned to
excess (another of Adam Ferguson's worst fears), and commodities have
fallen out of their financial structure. Like a kind of hyperinflation, the
looted goods prove worthless before they can be cashed in. The division of
labour is no help here as everyone throughout the army hierarchy is engaged
in a system of kleptocracy: John Lochy steals some horses only to have his
own beast forcibly removed from him by the Duke of Marlborough.

Lying behind this economic meltdown is a radical tearing apart of the
bonds that had held time and space together in Enlightenment writing.
The story maps out a historiography that is not linear or developmental
but one that returns to and retraces earlier narratives, superimposing and
rearranging them to dissolve causalities and to introduce discontinuities
in Enlightenment narratives of geography as well as history. As Gillian
Hughes points out in her edition of *Altrive Tales*, John Lochy is not only
an account of Charles XII's march on Moscow but also an analogy for
Napoleon's later adventure in that direction and back, a connection made
by a number of early nineteenth-century commentators on Napoleon's
mad enterprise. But in Hogg's case, the two campaigns are not so easily
seen as mutually illuminating. Hogg is writing against a tradition that

celebrated Napoleon's disastrous campaign as a kind of natural restoration of European geographical harmony. As I discussed in Chapter 1, Anne Grant's lengthy verse account of the retreat from Moscow and the Battle of Leipzig goes right back to Montesquieu in suggesting that it was the French Army's southern characteristics, their timorousness, physical weakness and susceptibility to tyranny, that made them unable to resist the challenges of the northern climate. She makes an explicit comparison between the armies of Napoleon and Charles XII, observing that it is only an accident of a failure in the supply chains that does for the 'iron Swedes to polar climes inured', while the French seem to perish from the climate itself.

Hogg's story resists Grant's causal geography of difference, and historical narratives are collapsed into each other by the removal of causality. Napoleonic territorial war, early eighteenth-century wars over dynastic succession and Jacobite antagonisms over religion and nation are confused with each other. Hogg's northern European armies are not clearly differentiated: Lochy has pretty much the same experience in all of them, and they all end up mixed 'promiscuously' together on the battlefield and afterwards: 'the Protestant Cathedral [of Smolensk] was given up to them as an hospital, where they lay, Russians and Swedes promiscuously, entirely at the mercy of the poor inhabitants' (p. 111). The landscape does not offer differential landmarks or contours but is 'a most abominable country, without either hill or dale, but covered with interminable woods and morasses' (p. 107). So far from the bird's-eye view-survey of Burke's great map, or Grant's epic overview, Lochy's Europe is seen from the ground up – literally so, as he finds himself describing events while stuck in a ditch following an engagement with the Tartars. The narrative is shaped like an early picaresque tale and was received as such by its reviewer in *Fraser's Magazine* who read it as 'a very happy imitation of De Foe.'[19] But 'John Lochy' also looks forward to Stendahl's Waterloo in *The Charterhouse of Parma*, published just seven years later, in its dissolution of the idea of history as collective event. In his commentary on Fabrice's inability to 'find' the battle, even while taking part in it, Nicola Chiaromonte writes:

What underlies this reduction of every occurrence to the immediate and the immediately felt is not the rejection [. . .] but the simple deflation of the idea that events have any rational (i.e., causal) relation to each other. Rationality is present only when events are reduced to a web of concepts in an abstract construction designed to give them a single meaning. But to do this, one must completely disregard the specificity of the event whose 'true' meaning one claims to be seeking.[20]

Chiaromonte reverses Peter Hallward's terms – 'single' is here a conceptual consensus, while 'specific' takes on the meaning of singular – but the passage usefully draws attention to Hogg's and Stendahl's post-Enlightenment dissolution of causal or collective history.

Looking back to Anne Grant's Europe, divided between north and south, Hogg retells this story by tipping the world of zonal difference round by ninety degrees. Instead of a clearly legible north, he opens up his story to the much less easily described difference between the west and the east. Because of their shared latitudes, east–west distinctions did not fit very well into Montesquieu's primary somatic distinctions between bodily responses to heat and cold, and, generally, the difference had to be constituted as that between a varied landscape that presented a formative set of natural challenges and an unvariegated one that did not encourage social change. Ferguson remarks that 'The unbounded plain is traversed at large by hordes, who are in perpetual motion, or who are displaced and harassed by their mutual hostilities.'[21] But in the world of 'John Lochy', it is the European nations that this sentence describes, and, not surprisingly, Hogg peoples his story with a set of characters that defy national and even racial clarity: Prince Iset, the sophisticated 'Baschkeir' (in Pinkerton's *Modern Geography* the Bashkirs occupy a space right on the traditional divide between European and Asian Russia), a Chinese Jew resident in Smolensk and a Jewish woman confusingly named Araby. Asia makes porous the boundary between east and west and opens up the borders of Europe.[22] Earlier Enlightenment geography had insisted on the physical continental unity of Europe as a teleological support for its global dominance. William Guthrie cites climate and surface variety as an example of this geographical guarantee, circumstances which, he concludes, 'have had a considerable tendency in giving it the superiority over the rest of the world.'[23] As J. G. A. Pocock points out, the expansion of the Russian Empire had produced a literature of stadial history that located the earliest forms of human settlement in Siberia and northern Eurasia.[24] But 'John Lochy' refuses this unifying discourse to insist on a north that cannot be absorbed into narratives of progress.

This is, then, a map of mankind that has no point of orientation, least of all that traditional compass point pictured on maps, the north. Hogg chooses a supposedly marginal starting point, Highland Scotland, but, rather than moving it to the centre as we follow Lochy's travels, he shows the fragility of *any* kind of global reckoning from a prior position. Throughout his travels, Lochy is accompanied by Finlayson, a character who appears in numerous guises, foreshadowing the more famously polymorphic Gil-Martin in Hogg's later *Private Memoirs and Confessions of a Justified Sinner*. Despite his shape-shifting proclivities, Fin has one characteristic that apparently defines him as a Scot: he is 'a strange character, and such a one as the Highlands of Scotland only can produce, – a being void of any moral principle, save inviolable faith and attachment to a superior' (p. 98). As it turns out in the story, however, this is not attachment to just any superior but an absolute and inviolable attachment to Lochy himself. In a parody of the idea of national character, which would normally be expected to reveal itself more clearly by remaining consistent against a changing geographical background, Scottishness turns out to be a rootless, peripatetic identity that can adapt to any geographical context: Fin passes as Sir Ranald Finlayson, General Finlay, Baron von Kui, Baron Steinburg and General Count Fleming. What should be geographically typical and specific – Fin's Scottishness – turns out to be another kind of singular locality. Instead of being loyal as a principle of individuality (that is a *specific* loyalty to what someone stands for), Fin's loyalty is *constitutive* of his relation with Lochy so, thus, cannot really be explained by any Humean concept of national character. Fin is local not because he exemplifies Highland characteristics but because he continually generates his own point of identification with Lochy as a singular individual: his loyalty is not to Lochy as a fellow-Scot or (despite Lochy's claims) as a superior officer, but to Lochy himself, an identity without defining relations.

Returning to Scotland, the narrative refuses to clarify the basis of any geographical of difference. Edinburgh becomes a place of such heterogeneity that the reader is sent on a dizzying trail that merges distinct places into each other:

> The search was then renewed for Iset with more ardor than ever, and by some means it was discovered that he had been removed from Smolensko by General Count Fleming. An express was sent to Dresden, and there it was found that the count had not been in the czar's dominions that year. But at Smolensko they found the Jew, who gave the marks of the prince, and then with ease they traced him to Leith. (p. 122)

Multilingual Edinburgh is suddenly full of people speaking Gaelic, Russian, Scots and Northumbrian, not in order to mark these languages as different from a standard of English but to break down clear linguistic demarcations altogether as points of origin. Human diversity, which had been the initial driving point of Scottish Enlightenment anthropology, is no longer the causal point of teleological history but a strange kind of modernity, cut free from stadial progress or regional demarcation. Hogg resists the identification of locality with the individuality of the species and produces something more singular, something that generates its own medium and, thus, is not conceptual in the available narratives of time and space.

'NO POLE NOR PILLAR': THE ARCTIC NORTH

My last story takes us even further north, to a point that both produces and challenges the possibility of singularity and is, thus, a location of considerable interest to James Hogg. This story, the latest of all the fiction that I have been considering in this book, carries a strong sense of the irretrievable mapping of Enlightenment geography and pitches the very possibility of a global imagination into the realm of the absurd. In the upsurge of Arctic exploration after 1815, it was no longer possible to assume with Pope of the Arctic that 'No creature owns it in the first degree.'[25] Throughout the nineteenth century, each unsuccessful attempt to reach the extreme north, the pole, could boast of having established a new 'furthest north' accompanied by a new set of bearings. To adjust Pope's phrase slightly: it had become very important for one creature to own the first degree. The pole inaugurates a collision between two different kinds of singularity – a distinction which Hogg seizes upon and gleefully allows one term to disrupt the other. First, there is the idea of the singularity of the pole as a form of sovereignty, the first degree as a position which gains its singular power and authority from its place in a hierarchy. But this is set against the Hoggian singularity of the non-representable, the space that cannot be defined by its relation to other spaces. Hogg's Arctic narrative *The Surpassing Adventures of Allan Gordon* returns us to Pope's question, 'Where's the North?', but recasts it for the 1820s into the question 'What's the North?', questioning the very possibility of locating a directional point.

Michel Foucault famously argues that the attempt of any culture to establish its own modernity has always privileged history over geography:

The great obsession of the nineteenth century was, as we know, history: with its themes of development and of suspension, of crisis and cycle, themes of the ever-accumulating past with its great preponderance of dead men and the menacing glaciation of the world. The nineteenth century found its essential mythological resources in the second principle of thermodynamics. The present epoch will perhaps be above all the epoch of space. We are in the epoch of simultaneity: we are in the epoch of juxtaposition, the epoch of the near and far, of the side-by-side, of the dispersed.[26]

Foucault observes elsewhere that in history-privileging cultures, space is rendered 'the dead, the fixed, the undialectical, the immobile',[27] and we can see how this might be read in Arctic explorers' sensations that they were confronting a space that was peculiarly liable to resist discourse. Efforts were made to counter this state of affairs, and reports of Arctic exploration try valiantly to situate themselves within history. Such accounts are typically given the sense of chronological sequence by being entitled 'narratives' and by specifying the sequence of years of their duration. But the trouble with this approach was that there did not seem to be much time *at* the Arctic: no visible effects of chronology, no lost civilisations, no history and no myth.[28] The 'menacing glaciation of the world' that Foucault detects as a comfortable nineteenth-century tele-ology was already there, seemingly outside temporal process altogether. Instead of time, the north consisted of a great deal of unvariegated space, reducible only by its expression in geographical bearings. This, then, was a space that challenged nineteenth-century time-bound certainties, and the problematic localities of the extreme north were not easily adapted to existing discourses.

There is a striking allusion to contemporary Arctic adventuring in Hogg's poem 'The P and the Q, or the Adventures of Jock M'pherson'. A curious precursor of Virginia Woolf's Mr Ramsay, who charts his intellectual achievement along an imaginary alphabet, Jock's academic development is arrested in a more literal sense when he fails to learn any letters beyond O. After this educational impasse, Jock is sent to sea and has several exciting adventures including the circumnavigation of the whole globe. The reader is given a mad visualisation of a world wheeled around by giants 'like a kirn on a standish', and rotating on polar axles lubricated with bear's grease. The narrator cautions:

> Let Barrow, and Parry, and Franklin, commence
> From this as example, and learn to speak sense.[29]

Barrow, Parry and Franklin, polar heroes popular in the first half of the century, are invited, in a grand inversion of sense and nonsense, to learn a new way of speaking; that is, a new subject position that radically con-fronts received notions of global space and a topic that afforded Hogg plenty of material. In his responses to the proliferation of reports on Arctic exploration that appeared in *Blackwood's Edinburgh Magazine*, we can see how Hogg, the notable disturber of the historical, throws himself with equal vigour into the disruption of global space.

The pole is, on the one hand, the north as absolute position, the 'true north' from which all other localities take their spatial identity. Yet, on the other hand, because it is an imaginary and impossible position occupying only theoretical space, the pole dissolves identities based on separation and distance. Hogg's polar narrative provides an implicit commentary on Arctic reportage that identifies the problem of knowing where one is, both in the sense of global spatial organisation and in the primary sense of the epistemology of the subject in space. Through Hogg, we can read how geographical space conjured up by the nineteenth-century Arctic can be translated into the spaces of the body.

The plot of *Allan Gordon* is a strange one. Allan, the son of an Aberdeenshire farm servant, is apprenticed to a tailor (thus following the same career path as Jock M'Pherson) but runs away to sea after a violent altercation with his master and ends up on a northbound whaling vessel. The drunken captain claims to have reached the North Pole, where the ship becomes surrounded and then crushed by pack ice. Allan is the sole survivor and goes on to survive an attack by polar bears, killing one and adopting its cub whom he names 'Nancy'. Allan and Nancy live happily together on the ice before setting out for Greenland where they fall in with a Norwegian colony now 'gone native', and Allan has some amorous adventures. After another ferocious bear attack on the colony, Allan is rescued by Nancy and finds a ship to take him back to Scotland, leaving Nancy behind.

Like 'The P and the Q', *Allan Gordon* offers a gleefully Gothic picture of the north, satirising the efforts of more sober reporters to account for their presence in the Arctic. In the early nineteenth century, Britons were in the Arctic for one of two reasons, both of them commercial.[30] They were either there, like William Scoresby, a source for Hogg's tale, as whalers, or they had been financed by the British Government to look for the North-West Passage: a way round the north of Canada into the Pacific which, it was hoped, could be established as a trade route. Yet, the nature of being there, as a state which could be represented, was much less certain. Early nineteenth-century polar narratives tend to site their own narratives in a very indeterminate field that challenged the grounds of perception itself. At stake in the description of this perplexing and threatening Arctic space is a discourse of power that manifests itself in different ways. This is sometimes expressed as an assertion of European imperial power, an obvious theme of Arctic travel to which I will turn later, and often in the discourse of the sublime, the confrontation between a threatening material world and the creative imagination. *Allan*

Gordon addresses both these issues, laying bare the power relations on which both are predicated. More political than Allan's narration some-times admits, the story sees power at the heart of the reconstruction of the individual in the crisis of alien Arctic space. Freed from his slave-like existence with his master the tailor, Allan uses the discourse of the sublime to imagine political empowerment on his solitary iceberg: 'I [. . .] could not but deem it eminently sublime for me to be living in a chrystaline palace on this elemental mountain.'[31] But the north as the first degree, the top of a spatial hierarchy, is precisely what it challenged in the encounter between Arctic space and European topography.

Contemporary accounts describe Arctic travel as the colonisation of the unknown by a newly scientific exploration. William Scoresby was com-plimented patronisingly in *Blackwood's:*

True philosophy indeed regards with a loving eye the faithful labours of her least inspiring followers; but he who would pursue her spirit beyond those sublime barriers which the timidity of less gifted minds have assigned to her domain, assuredly deserves to be rewarded with her most radiant of smiles.[32]

(As both a professional whaler and a student of natural history at Edinburgh University, there is the suggestion that Scoresby is to be taken as both the faithful labourer and the philosophical traveller beyond the sublime barriers.) Needless to say, the equation of knowledge and power is an extremely precarious one in the Arctic. Everything that can be *said* about the pole is qualified by the impossibility of *imagining* it. The physical properties of ice fields are such that they cannot be delimited by human perception, and no objects can emerge from them. The spatial configuration of the pole – or rather the difficulties of configuring it – challenge the very basis of subject formation. One returned explorer from the John Ross expedition of 1818 describes: 'a vast extended plane, of alabaster whiteness, and to which the eye can assign no limits.'[33] William Scoresby positions the Arctic beyond any European means of measure-ment. A learned system of relative distances here breaks down: 'Any strangers to the Arctic countries, however well acquainted with other regions, and however capable of judging of the distance of land generally, must be completely at a loss in their estimations when they approach within sight of Spitzbergen.'[34]

The pole is, thus, a region both of the imagination and of the failure of an imagination confronted by an impossible topography. J. Hillis Miller, here following Jacques Derrida, points out how mapping rests upon a concomitant stability in the relationship between the figurative (maps) and the spatial (places):

Topography, the graphing of a place, presupposes arithmetic and geometry, and by implication the rest of the seven liberal arts, too. [. . .] Topography is a logocentric practice through and through. It depends, for example, on the law of non-contradiction. A place is either there in a given place or not there, and no thing, a building for example, can be in more than one place at once.[35]

The nineteenth-century Arctic is not like this. Sometimes it is difficult to say whether things are there or not there, as in the case of the mountains John Ross either imagined or claimed to have seen blocking Lancaster Sound. (Ross's notorious decision to turn back cost him the command of any other Arctic expedition for ten years.) Even when visual objects are more materially present, it is hard to say *where* they are present in a landscape in which the ice is constantly breaking up and shifting position. Ice makes mapping difficult, interfering with practices based on the rational manipulation of space and time: the coastline cannot be traced in a linear or chronological way; it is not easy to distinguish an inlet from a strait open in both directions. The Arctic interferes with the figurative stability of topography. Contemporary maps of the known Arctic are strange, ghostly affairs with stray lines unconnected at either end, aporias of the visual.

The spatial discourse available to talk about these geographical questions was equally uncertain. In the writing about the Arctic of this period, it is possible to detect a tension between two opposing geographical trajectories: to go *into* something or to go *beyond* something. Thus, on the one hand, there was much talk of 'penetrating the icy fastnesses of the north.' It was sometimes thought that the proximity of the sun must melt the ice at the pole, and many people believed in an open polar sea into which it might be possible to sail. This was later taken to a rather startling extreme by the American John Cleves Symmes who believed that there might be an entrance point at the pole into a hollow earth.[36] On the other hand, the pole was thought of as lying beyond known territory, just at it lay beyond the imagination, an idea picked up in the title of *The Surpassing Adventures of Allan Gordon*. One writer, commenting on opposition to polar exploration, remarks: 'some go as far as to say, that the attempt was nothing less than impious, to pass the frozen boundary which God has been pleased to set to man's researches',[37] and I have already noted William Scoresby's philosophical flight 'beyond those sublime barriers'.

This pole, lying beyond known space, is more difficult to describe than the interior version because it had no ready model in colonial adventure, and it introduces spatial tensions into the description of the Arctic. A *Blackwood's* reviewer is forced to turn to the vocabulary of African travel (widely known through Mungo Park's *Travels in the Interior of Africa* of 1799) to offer a contrast with the idea of the pole: 'And most earnestly do we wish that Mr Barrow [. . .] may yet be as successful in the interior of Africa, as he has thus at length been on the exterior of North America.'[38] (John Barrow, Second Secretary at the Admiralty, was a notable fixer of Arctic expeditions.) These concepts cannot be part of any transcendent logic but, like North and South Britain, succumb to that of supplementarity. The 'exterior' of North America is also the 'interior' of the icy fastnesses. 'North' itself is a provisional position when 'North America' becomes south relative to the North Pole. To be at the pole further disrupts the logic of polarity; at the extreme north there is no north or south. And in the physical mapping of the coast, the boundary that would mark 'North America' from what lies beyond is broken and incomplete.

Arctic explorers did not, of course, think they were merely milling about in unmappable space. On the contrary, and particularly as the century wore on, the idea of the North Pole as a discrete and absolute locality took shape out of the earlier tendency to use the term as synonymous with 'Arctic regions'. As it became suspected that even if the North-West Passage were established, it would lie too far north to be a practical commercial route, attention began to transfer to the pole as position. This pole is ideal, abstract and aspirational. It is a unique point in space, and its temporal position similarly attracts ideas of singularity: the pole can only be 'discovered' once. Another way of looking at this would be to say that the pole is phallic, the primary object of desire and location of authority. Much has been written of the gender implications of the penetration of the white, male explorer into the interior of 'darkest Africa', and in the Arctic, the gender question invites ideas about the construction of masculine sexual identity and the role of narcissism. Arctic exploration often takes refuge in an optimistically phallic narcissism that can find its way into the scientific vocabulary of the time. One *Blackwood's* article comments with evident excitement that Ross and Buchan 'have measured the length of the pendulum in regions where the pendulum had never vibrated before.'[39] Fictional polar narratives interact with this triumphant attempt to overcome the problems of Arctic epistemology: in *Frankenstein*, a text which bears an interesting relationship to *Allan Gordon*, Captain Walton is in search of 'the wondrous power that attracts the needle.'[40] He soon meets up with the well-mannered and beautiful Victor in whom all the sailors immediately take an interest. Similarly, the fragility of the assumption of phallic masculinity, and what lies beyond it, is one of the main concerns of *Allan Gordon* that transforms the somatic spaces of the female north into surreal forms.

In *Allan Gordon*, the captain's assumption of the pole lays claim to a geographical vanishing point, the convergence of all directions and a position that appears to transcend the limitations of space: 'Am I not resting on the pole of the world and can run from hence into any of its divisions I chuse' (p. 4). Hogg here literalises the metaphorical positional singularity of Burke's great map of mankind, but the captain's assumed spatial authority also expresses itself in a gendered way. Captain Hughes is a drunken, post-Enlightenment version of *Frankenstein*'s Captain Walton. Walton's polar conquest will result in an 'inestimable benefit which I shall confer on all mankind to the last generation',[41] and Captain Hughes seeks a similar 'discovery which will hand down my name to all generations' (p. 4). For these men, the North Pole is not only unique but also an origin: primary, potent and naming. Yet, the problem with occupying the vanishing point upon which all trajectories converge is that things tend to vanish into it, not least the creature in *Frankenstein* who floats off towards the icy horizon 'lost in darkness and distance'.[42] Any seizing of power based on singularity as sovereignty is a risky project in the works of James Hogg. Captain Hughes's imaginary identification with the phallus is proved the illusion that it was always bound to be. His assumption of the absolute oneness and singularity of the pole is, literally, ruptured by his gruesome fate and reduced to a *corps morcelé*. He is multiply fragmented, being first 'crushed to pieces' (p. 5) by the ice and his corpse later observed by Allan as it is eaten by bears who are 'rugging and riving at the body of my late captain which I knew to be his from the shreds and patches of his clothes' (p. 9).

Allan's own anti-heroic status, contrasted with the overconfident Captain Hughes, parodies the strategies available in Arctic narratives for this kind of empowerment in the face of the unimaginable Arctic regions. In straightforward terms, Allan's topographical sense is dim at best; adrift on the iceberg which is his 'resistless vessel' (p. 23), he has only a vague suspicion that he is going round in circles. Lacking any confrontational intentions, and uninterested in technical data, Allan is the antithesis of the masculine polar hero. His early job as a tailor marks him out with the popular belief that this was not a manly occupation, and he himself comments: 'whether or not it was from having been bread a tailor I cannot tell but I certainly had something rather cowardly and timorous in my nature' (p. 12). Later in the story, the captain's desire to 'hand my name down to all generations' is inverted into comic excess by Allan's discovery that all the unmarried Greenland women claim him as father of their children, his supposed mistress having played multiple bed-tricks on him, and that he is now 'a butt of ridicule to the whole tribe' (p. 46). But Allan Gordon's exploration of sexual identity in Arctic space is more complex than this straightforward parody. The erosion of the grounds for subjectivity makes prophetic the mate's words: 'if we lose our ship we lose ourselves' (p. 4). Hogg is interested in what happens when distinctions fail and differences are not observed, and one such difference is that of language itself and the play between the literal and the figurative. Allan is saved from ruin by the old joke that there is no actual pole at the North Pole: 'there was no pole nor pillar of any kind to be seen; neither was there any axletree or groove which there behoved to have been had we been at the pole of the world' (p. 3). This is an interesting statement in two respects: first, to return briefly to Foucault's history of spatial epistemes, we can recognise in Allan's conception (which he shares with Jock M'Pherson of 'The P and the Q') of a pre-modern cosmology, in which things have their designated places. Foucault calls this 'the space of emplacement', which was to be disrupted by Galileo's opening up a space of extension in which 'a thing's place was no longer anything but a point in its movement.'[43] This may remind us that *Allan Gordon* is not just a joke about masculinity but also one about modernity, or at least about a Frankenstein-like overconfidence in the capabilities of an enlightened scientificism.

The second point about Allan's global conceptions is that they resist any metaphorical implications; the literal-minded Allan calls a pole a pole, and if you can't see one, it's not there. In fact, Allan is, throughout his narration, very resistant to metaphor: he misses the possible pun on tailor's needles and compass needles, and when he accidentally stumbles on a trope, he goes out of his way to admit its uselessness. On observing that a footprint is 'as apparent as the sun at noonday', he feels obliged to point out prosaically that this is an 'inapt simily' on the grounds that 'there was no sun and no noonday there' (p. 28). The joke here is not just on Allan but also on a more general problem experienced by polar explorers: the question of how the seemingly limitless pole could support a signification which depends on borders and differences, and of the plurality and metaphoricity of representation.

The epistemological crisis engendered by the Arctic was sometimes deferred by polar explorers in an attempt to transfer problems of perception and meaning to other races. *Allan Gordon* addresses indirectly the way in which the inhabitants of the Arctic regions were appropriated to underscore the Europeans' spatial dilemmas. To live in such regions, it was assumed, would be to suffer in an extreme form the epistemological confusion experienced by the writers of Arctic narratives. In this region of sameness, the colonial aspiration to characterise indigenous peoples as other is infused by a sense that the extreme north produces extreme versions of the same. In one memorable encounter, the failure of symbolism experienced by the Ross expedition is transferred onto the native people. On meeting some 'Esquimaux', Ross runs up a flag 'on which was painted a hand holding a green branch of a tree.' This friendly gesture is, not surprisingly, ignored. The officer on Ross's ship who is describing the incident comments without any apparent irony that these were 'a colour [. . .] and an object not very common in this part of the world.'[44] Yet, it does not seem to be so much the *specific* cultural signification of the olive branch that the Inuit are deemed to have failed to understand as the process of signification itself. Amid the 'vast, extended plane, of alabaster whiteness [. . .] to which the eye can assign no limit' objects cannot be clearly distinguished. Parry complained of 'the want of objects to afford relief to the eye.'[45] The Europeans believe the Arctic peoples to have infantile perceptions, unable to recognise objects or even their own reflection:

they seemed like men who distrusted the sense of sight, and could not satisfy themselves of the reality of objects, until they had grasped them; to view themselves in a looking-glass, but more especially in a concave mirror, made them almost frantic with joy and wonder, and drew such bursts of laughter, and exclamations of surprise, as were never heard before.[46]

Against these tenuous subjectivities, *Allan Gordon* plunges its readers into a comically grotesque vision of the failure of power, of the self, of sexuality and of language. The story takes place in a world of violence in which distinctions are often violently disturbed. Allan comments that for long periods of the year there is no day or no night, and both he and Nancy fall into spells of a kind of suspended animation. The familiar binaries of sleeping/waking, alive/dead, male/female, human/animal, eater/eaten seem no longer in force. The polar bears, which lurk round every corner of this story, are habitually mistaken for 'naked human creatures' (p. 9), and Allan's relationship with Nancy is both parental, replacing her lost mother, and coyly eroticised: 'Yes she lay in my bosom and though certainly a most uncourtly mate she being the only one I had I loved her most sincerely I might almost say intensely' (p. 16). In one nightmare moment, Allan kills Nancy's mother, leaving her stuck half in and half out of the ship's window and then hears strange munching noises (later revealed to be Nancy) from without: 'I was more frightened than ever and began to think that nature was all reversed in that horrible clime for how a creature could be dead and frozen in its hinder parts and munching and eating with its foreparts was to me quite inconceivable' (p. 13).

At the extreme north, even the most primary or archaic space, that of the body, takes on Gothic qualities far removed the rational divisions of Enlightenment geography. The Arctic becomes a gigantic maternal body: Nancy searches her dead mother's skin for her teats; Allan uses an iceberg as his water supply: 'I sucked and sucked till I could hold no more' (p. 6). Later, Allan plunders the Captain's liquor store by sucking it up through the ship's bellows. The maternal body of the extreme north has its own history that frays the edges of Enlightenment spatiality. Fretting (as usual) about the circumstances and dangers of human reproduction, Tristram Shandy returns to Pope's impossible Nova Zembla, but this time characterising it as a space of monstrous anti-gestation where human reason is suppressed:

Indeed there is one thing to be considered, that in *Nova Zembla, North Lapland*, and in all those cold and dreary tracks of the globe, which lie more directly under the artick and antartick circles,—where the whole province of a man's concernments lies for near nine months together, within the narrow compass of his cave—where the spirits are compressed almost to nothing—and where the passions of a man, with every thing which belongs to them, are as frigid as the zone itself;—there the least quantity of *judgment* imaginable does the business—and of *wit*—there is a total and an absolute saving,—for as not one spark is wanted,—so not one spark is given.[47]

Tristram's thoughts here are part of a longer speculation on climatic determination, mining the absurdity that already lurked within that theory. Hogg's story looks back on the history of Enlightenment theories of global demarcations altogether, replacing a masculinised concept of discrete spaces with his strange, dyadic Arctic relationships.

The bodily space of the Arctic resists even simple oppositions such as inside and outside, focusing particularly on eating. Significantly, Allan's reading in the Bible, to which he frequently draws attention, is quite selective. He is fond of the 'historical parts' but 'as for the tedious ceremonial law I accounted that perfect nonsense' (p. 33–4). The 'tedious law' refers presumably the Judaic laws, including dietary restrictions, of Leviticus, which, as Mary Douglas has pointed out, function as 'an act of recognition', allowing distinctions to be made between physical classifications in the animal world and to keep separate clean (whatever can be categorised) and unclean (whatever crosses categories).[48] But these laws do not hold sway in the Arctic where Allan continually fears attack by cannibals who 'might flay and eat Nancy and I even without the ceremony of letting out the life blood' (p. 27). In the social world of Leviticus, the spilling of blood is so transgressive of bodily integrity that it must be carefully managed by either scientific or religious ceremony. *Allan Gordon* evokes the terror of the body stripped of its social containment. Such unregulated incursions on the body's frame trouble the subject's dependence on the body as a primary means of recognising self: the delimitation of the individual from the space that surrounds it.

The narrative is haunted by the threat of cannibalism: a reciprocal relation between drawing in and assimilating the other (the final dissolution of the borders of corporeal space) and the rejection of such an incorporation as taboo. Maggie Kilgour describes it thus: 'the idea of return is both idealized as a return to communion with an originary source and a primal identification, and demonized as regression through the loss of human and individual identity.'[49] Allan is tempted to search for and eat the bodies of his shipmates but later considers himself spared by a super-ego-like 'Almighty' when he is unable to find any. Hogg picks up on incidents of cannibalism from contemporary accounts, and among William Scoresby's details about polar bears is the following remark: 'Bears, though they have been known to eat one another, are remarkably affectionate to their young.'[50] The maternal and the cannibal, two archaic forms of incomplete bodily subjectivity, are found together at the Arctic. The anthropomorphic bears in *Allan Gordon* carry traces of both these activities. They gobble up the ship's crew, but Allan is moved by the sight of Nancy's dead mother, realising 'I had taken a mother from her starving offspring' (p. 13).

In the Arctic narratives of the nineteenth century, cannibalism lurks round every corner but is never present, as it were, in the flesh. Cannibalism is the fugitive other, always a potential in language but never substantiated. In one of its narrative forms, cannibalism introduces a split between narration and its objects: it either happens but cannot be spoken of or is spoken of but cannot be found to happen. Arctic anthropologists became familiar with the idea that cannibalism is always alleged to be practised by 'other' tribes: John Ross encountered groups who claimed that the far north was inhabited by a race of giant cannibals. Cannibalism is unspeakable in that it cannot be incorporated directly into testimony. On John Franklin's Arctic foray in the early 1820s, the returning expedition split into two, one party being led by the Scottish surgeon, John Richardson. Richardson himself narrates this part of the story in Franklin's *Narrative of a Journey to the Shores of the Polar Sea*. The men, suffering from severe exhaustion and starvation, have meat brought to them by their native Canadian guide, Michel. Michel says that the meat is from a wolf killed by the horn of a deer. Richardson comments: 'We implicitly believed this story then, but, afterwards became convinced from circumstances, the detail of which may be spared, that it must have been a portion of the body of Belanger or Perrault.'[51] Later on, Richardson suspects that Michel has become violently deranged and shoots him through the head as a precaution. As evidence of Michel's dangerous insanity, Richardson notes that he has been claiming that white people ate some of his family. In sparing us the unspeakable 'detail' which would prove his own cannibalism, Richardson refuses to realise his action in narration. And, in refusing to believe that Michel's relatives have been eaten, he consigns cannibalism to an imaginary world that exists in narration but not in fact.

The Arctic, the most extreme of Hogg's northern positions, renders the articulation of space – global, local or bodily – no longer possible through Enlightenment geometries. Poles, axes, directions and zones exist in Hogg's work only as bizarre propositions which cannot be absorbed into human experience or which can only be understood by transformation into absurd comedy, like Jock M'Pherson's churn spinning precariously on its stand. The Arctic may seem a long way from the Borders. Yet, two years after the publication of John Richardson's narrative, Allan Cunningham paid tribute to his fellow Dumfriesian in the introduction to his collection of ballads and other songs, *The Songs of Scotland, Ancient and Modern*. Modernity, Cunningham laments, has narrowed the scope of poetic invention, replacing inspiration with mathematical exactitude and the imaginary space of balladic storytelling with the spatial strictures of science:

Our steps are regulated by the compass, and our motions by the quadrant; and the Muse has no nearer resting-place where she may indulge her inventions than on some few acres of untrodden snow, near the North Pole, around which she may yet see the marks of the feet of my townsman, Richardson.[52]

'Yet' is here ambiguous. Does it mean that Richardson's footprints are still visible, contrary to the assertion that the snow is untrodden? Or does it mean that the muse will one day see Richardson's marks on the pristine snow? Time and place are again uncertain in this most ambiguous of localities. As Cunningham brings together the literary spaces of Hogg's Borders with those of his North Pole, he also reflects back on the literary geography of North Britain that has been the subject of this book. The investment in spatial modernity that produced the *Statistical Account*, or a stadial history that could be scientifically predicted through geography, does not exclude forms of Romantic or amorphous space. Indeed, as Hogg and Richardson demonstrate, it is the very impulse to know the world geographically that produces imaginary spaces that cannot be accounted for. Cunningham's Richardson and Hogg's Aberdonian sea captain are both Scots who move the impossible geometry of Scotland to the extreme north, but the fictions of geography that they discover there are those that were already at work in the long history of North Britain.

CONCLUSION: POST-ENLIGHTENMENT SPACE

To end a study of Scotland and geography with James Hogg is to see not only how spatiality changes across the period but also how those changes still have their roots in the mid-eighteenth century. We have come a long way from Samuel Johnson's advice that 'no man should travel unprovided with instruments for taking heights and distances'[53] to Hogg's poleless north with its impossible mathematics. Where Johnson is apt to see Scotland's spatiality as a troubling, ungrounded territory, in need of demarcation, Hogg gleefully promotes the idea of Scotland as nowhere – on the understanding that nowhere else is anywhere either. Yet, the reason that I have described Hogg as a 'post-Enlightenment' rather than a 'Romantic' writer is that he remains fascinated by the possibility of measurement and its limits. For Hogg, the incommensurable, which finds its way into most of his writing, is always an effect of the impulse to take distances and heights. Ideas of boundlessness are always the product of the failure of measurement. His games with the singularity of space engage directly with a continuous history of navigation and a myth of progress based on mathematical precision. I would like, then, to end with some general thoughts about the place of Scottish writers in what we think of as Romanticism.

Hogg's Arctic is produced by the failure of limits, yet this is not exactly the Kantian or Wordsworthian sublime but something altogether more ironic. For Allan Gordon, the sublime is the social elevation of a 'chrystaline palace', just as, in Scott's novels, there is the suspicion that the sublime is always something produced, rather than an unsummoned encounter with the infinite. When Edward Waverley experiences the seemingly archetypical moment of the sublime encounter with nature – emphasising the human figure against a vast ravine and waterfall – it is already a set-up, staged by Flora MacIvor with a view to impressing him into joining the Jacobite cause. It is this ironic detachment from spatiality that makes Hogg one of the clearest examples of the way national geography is shaped. His interest in the inexpressible nature of singularity (or what Peter Hallward calls its non-relational status) exposes the necessary interdependence, yet unavoidable lack of fit, between the local and the general, between place and space and between point and structure. These insoluble geometries interfere with clear distinctions between periods and movements in Scotland. A recent collection of essays explores how Scotland found itself on the 'Borders of Romanticism', a space that provides material for, but never fully participates in, what we think of as a mainstream Romantic 'movement'. This is a Scotland, the editors point out, in which '"Classical" and "Romantic" cultural forms occupy the same historical moment and institutional base, rather than defining successive stages or periods.'[54] The field of spatiality and the means of identifying place form one way in which these fluid stadial boundaries and overlapping intellectual forces can be read.

One well-worn story about Romanticism is that it marks a retreat into local, rural, recuperative places from the stresses of the industrialising nation. But this concept does not fit the whole of Great Britain very well, and a Romantic period viewed from Scotland tends rather to emphasise the impossibility of individual, localised places, from Burns's inscriptions to Hogg's extra-physical localities. For Burns and Hogg, ideas of the new, the local and the affective do not constitute a retreat but have an active relationship with those other forms of modernity: systems of national and global mapping. Ideas about place as something experiential or individual – ideas we might associate with Romanticism – are produced through the Enlightenment systems that they interrogate. What, I hope, has emerged in these pages, is the recognition that terms such as 'Romanticism' and 'Enlightenment' are very closely involved with each other in the period and that the former can rarely replace the latter. As we saw in Chapter 3, Scotland's geography, at least from the mid-eighteenth century, always divides itself between a mapped, political space and its Romance alternative and then proceeds to blur these spaces at their edges. The 1760s and 1770s mark both the popularity of James Macpherson's unmappable space and the call for national surveys to advance the insights of Adam

Smith and the new political economy. Scotland calls both these into
being through a tradition of stadial history that simultaneously tracks the
growth of the nation as a modern, commercial system and requires acts of
the imagination to construct the 'primitive' prehistory of the modern
nation. Scotland's geography is, thus, always imaginary even where that
act of imagination is presented as one of logical rationality. It is this
continual engagement, on the part of Scottish writers, with the Enlightenment project of putting the nation, and the globe, in place, that opens
up the contradictions in Enlightenment itself.

Scotland's social geography, then, puts pressure not only on Romantic
places but also on Enlightenment theories of spatiality, posing the
question of what happens when stadial history encounters lived experience. Mary Poovey argues that the 'modern fact' found one of its most
confident articulations in the economic theory of the Scottish Enlightenment, which, resting on the secure substrate of stadial history, seemed
able to unite the observed detail and general knowledge through a conviction that 'a systematic order underwrote the particulars individuals
could see.'[55] Yet, the literature of the period – as well as a great deal of
travel writing – undermines this confidence geographically. The local will
never fully act as a synecdoche for the general. Place will never emit a fully
present history. Geography will not comfortably exemplify history.

If Scotland unsettles the relations of geography and history, it also
introduces discontinuities into the national contours of Britain. Projects
of an economically united kingdom, or a globe unified across its surface
by navigation or climatic gradations, are not only contradicted by the
writers under discussion here but are already unstable, unable to bear the
demands of national identity placed upon them. In order to explore these
discontinuities, the relationship of England and Scotland in the period is
sometimes seen as a form of 'internal colonisation'.[56] But the geography
of supplementarity complicates this model somewhat, raising questions
about orders of priority into the struggle to define 'Britishness'. At a most
basic sense, we can see how the mapping of the nation as a whole disrupts
the sense of imperial, island Britain. While the south coast was drawing
up its defences against the French, the north coast of the nation was a
much less defined limit, visually tailing into archipelagos and linguistic-
ally and commercially blurring into European states still further north.
Scotland completes island Britain but resists insular Britain. The north
itself – as we have seen – becomes an impossible location, just as Britain
starts to identify itself as a northern nation. The antiquarian project to
map a discrete Ancient Britain is, as we saw in Chapter 4, divided by the

demands of the modern nation. The final chapters of this book uncover an island that leaks at the top and draws attention to the geographical continuities and fluidity of trade. The boat that takes Allan Gordon to the North Pole is a whaler, travelling through a network of northern seas, harbours and nation-states. In the work of Margaret Chalmers, the regionality of Scotland is subsumed by the openness of global trade and panoramic views, seemingly untied to material locations.

In a more complex sense, Scotland draws attention to the way place is a form of national representation in the period, not only in the sense of what is represented but also how geography itself is used to make the nation visible. The re-drafting of Scotland after 1746, and its subsequent rapid production of forms of cultural and economic capital, make geography less descriptive than performative. In an often-quoted passage from *Waverley*, Scott writes: 'There is no European nation which, within the course of half a century, has undergone so complete a change as this kingdom of Scotland.'[57] The rapid historical changes that Scott describes can be read in the geography of the nation. In a sustained burst of enthusiasm for geography itself, Scotland breaks down the possibility of discrete spaces. This pulls in two directions as it leads to the growing appropriation of a single landscape (misty, mountainous, Highland) to stand for 'Scotland' in general. The lack of specificity here turns Scotland into a homogeneous commodity to be repackaged and sold, leading towards the stasis of Victorian representation of the country. Yet, at the same time, Scottish geography is changing very rapidly. The impetus to map Scotland, by new roads and statistical surveys, was not only to link existing places or to describe what was already there but also to change the country by improving it; geographical knowledge is itself an active agent of social change. As we saw with the various tourists and border-crossers of Chapter 3, Scotland is infused with an anxiety of expectation for the Romantic traveller. 'Scotland' is caught between its pre-inscription as a source of Romance history or the picturesque and the fact that it is continually in a state of becoming, the product of changes in land use, population and the creation of modern urban spaces such as Edinburgh's highly visible New Town. It is this anxiety of expectation (so fertile to James Hogg among others) that gives Scottish Romanticism an edgy, self-reflexive quality, a consciousness of history both as something to be produced and as an ancient national past. The tension between these is the driving force of North Britain.

The example of Scotland offers a process – whether dialectic or deconstruction – that examines the paradoxical nature of the singular, the problem of boundedness and the relation of discrete places to predictable structures. In fact, it could be argued that the ever-present tensions between the local and the national, between the singular place and conceptualised space, that we notice everywhere in Scottish writing of the period produce some of the most intense discussions of location in British writing as a whole, inviting us to read Hogg and Chalmers alongside Wordsworth and Coleridge as key Romantic authors. But these texts should also be read as themselves constitutive of British Romanticism and of a Romantic irony that resists the possibility of the single expression of situation. Scotland's reclamation of its identity as 'North Britain' not only makes Britishness a contested and divided identity but also asks questions about where precisely 'Britain' is, and how its citizens might articulate their sense of living between history and geography.

Notes

INTRODUCTION

1 Samuel Johnson, *A Journey to the Western Islands of Scotland*, ed. Mary Lascelles (London and New Haven, Conn.: Yale University Press, 1971), p. 13.

2 Richard Gough, *Anecdotes of British Topography* (London: W. Richardson and S. Clark, 1768), p. 617.

3 William Smellie, *Account of the Institution and Progress of the Society of the Antiquaries of Scotland* (Edinburgh: William Creech, 1782), p. 23.

4 Letter to William Robertson, 9 June 1777, *The Correspondence of Edmund Burke*, 10 vols. (Cambridge: Cambridge University Press, 1958–78), vol. III, ed. George H. Guttridge, pp. 350–1.

5 Although highly influential, Montesquieu was also a subject of debate among Scottish Enlightenment philosophers. For a summary, see Christopher J. Berry, *Social Theory of the Scottish Enlightenment* (Edinburgh: Edinburgh University Press, 1997), pp. 7–8 and 74–90. See also Richard B. Sher, 'From Troglodytes to Americans: Montesquieu and the Scottish Enlightenment on Liberty, Virtue, and Commerce', in David Wootton (ed.), *Republicanism, Liberty, and Commercial Society 1649–1776* (Stanford, Calif.: Stanford University Press, 1994), pp. 368–402.

6 Franco Moretti, *Atlas of the European Novel 1800–1900* (London: Verso, 1998), p. 5.

7 See, for example, Maureen McLane, 'Ballads and Bards: British Romantic Orality', *Modern Philology* 98 (2001): 423–43; and Susan Oliver, *Scott, Byron and the Poetics of Cultural Encounter* (Basingstoke: Palgrave, 2005).

8 William Wordsworth, *A Guide Through the District of the Lakes: The Prose Works of William Wordsworth*, ed. W. J. B. Owen and Jane Worthington Smyser, 3 vols. (Oxford: Clarendon Press, 1974), vol. II, p. 174.

9 John Kerrigan, 'Wordsworth and the Sonnet: Building, Dwelling, Thinking', *Essays in Criticism* 35 (1985): 45–75; p. 50.

10 Jonathan Bate, *The Song of the Earth* (Basingstoke: Picador, 2000), p. 206.

11 John Lucas, 'Places and Dwellings: Wordsworth, Clare and the Anti-Picturesque', in Denis Cosgrove and Stephen Daniels (eds.), *The Iconography of Landscape* (Cambridge: Cambridge University Press, 1989), pp. 83–97; p. 87.

12 John Barrell, *The Idea of Landscape and the Sense of Place 1730–1840: An Approach to the Poetry of John Clare* (Cambridge: Cambridge University Press, 1972), p. 120.

13 *Coleridge's Poetry and Prose*, eds. Nicholas Halmi, Paul Magnuson and Raimonda Modiano (New York and London: W. W. Norton, 2004), p. 120.

14 Michael Wiley, *Romantic Geography: Wordsworth and Anglo-European Spaces* (Basingstoke: Palgrave, 1998). Wiley demonstrates an impressive range of political resonances in Wordsworth's landscapes but nevertheless indicates that the poems foreground his 'conviction that the central characteristics of places do not emerge from the people who have economic rights over them, but from the people who live most upon them, working their soil, suffering hardships, enjoying family life or even traveling on foot over them' (p. 84).

15 Walter Scott, *Waverley*, ed. Claire Lamont (Oxford: Oxford University Press, 1981), p. 329.

16 Thomas Newte, *Prospects and Observations on a Tour in England and Scotland: Natural, Œconomical, and Literary* (London: G. G. J. and J. Robinson, 1791), p. 322. A shorter version of the work originally appeared as *A Tour in England and Scotland, in 1785, By an English Gentleman* (London: G. G. J. and J. Robinson, 1788). 'Thomas Newte' was, however, neither English nor apparently much of a gentleman. The name was one of the many pseudonyms of William Thomson from Perthshire, who, after unsuccessful careers as a librarian and a minister (when he received complaints from his parishioners about his social excesses), settled in London to become a professional writer.

17 William Wordsworth, *The Borderers*, ed. Robert Osborn (Ithaca, NY and London: Cornell University Press, 1982), p. 814.

18 Scott, *Waverley*, p. 296.

19 Jane Millgate reads Edward's three returns to Tully-Veolan as emblematic of his education through romance into history. *Walter Scott: The Making of the Novelist* (Edinburgh: Edinburgh Press, 1984), pp. 43–6.

20 I am indebted here to Robert P. Irvine's argument that the narrative structure of *Guy Mannering* reveals that 'conservative organicist political ideology is reaffirmed by a narrative form that is itself conservative in its recuperation of an original social unity and organicist in presenting a member of the lowest social caste as the agent whereby this restoration can take place.' *Enlightenment and Romance: Gender and Agency in Smollett and Scott* (Bern: Peter Lang, 2000), p. 113. Miranda Burgess further suggests that the novel's 'magical symbiosis of laird and land' is a fragile one that simultaneously exposes the exhaustion of the natural rights of the aristocracy. *British Fiction and the Production of Social Order, 1740–1830* (Cambridge: Cambridge University Press, 2000), p. 191.

21 Cairns Craig, *Out of History: Narrative Paradigms in Scottish and English Culture* (Edinburgh: Polygon, 1996), p. 11.

22 From an advertisement circulated in Europe, cited in the introduction to Donald J. Witherington and Ian R. Grant (eds.), *The Statistical Account of Scotland 1791–1799 edited by Sir John Sinclair*, 20 vols. (East Ardsley: E. P. Publishing, 1983), vol. I, p. xv.

23 Newte, *Prospects and Observations*, p. 430.

24 Thomas Pennant, *A Tour in Scotland 1769* (Chester: John Monk, 1771), p. 287.

25 Robert Jameson, *Mineralogy of the Scottish Isles*, 2 vols. (Edinburgh: W. Creech and London: B. White, 1800), vol. I, p. vii.

26 Jameson, *Mineralogy of the Scottish Isles*, vol. I, p. 29.

27 Jameson, *Mineralogy of the Scottish Isles*, vol. I, p. vi.

28 This book will not discuss the question of Ireland in any detail because to include Ireland in a study of the supplementary relationship of England and Scotland would not be appropriate for the complex nature and chronology of the politics of Union. The relation of Ireland to Romantic national cultures has been recently and impressively discussed by Ina Ferris in *The Romantic National Tale and the Question of Ireland* (Cambridge: Cambridge University Press, 2002).

1 NORTH BRITAIN

1 *The Complete Poems of Thomas Gray*, ed. H. W. Starr and J. R. Hendrickson (Oxford: Clarendon Press, 1966), pp. 131 and 133.

2 The geographer Mark Billinge writes: 'For its widest sustenance, the articulation of a North-South divide [of England] might be held to rely, in part, on a largely unconscious thesis which links urbanism, the Industrial Revolution and the economic philosophy which underpinned them both to a northern ethic'. 'Divided by a Common Language: North and South, 1750–1830', in Alan R. H. Baker and Mark Billinge (eds.), *Geographies of England: The North–South Divide, Material and Imagined* (Cambridge: Cambridge University Press, 2004), pp. 88–111; p. 101. Although I disagree with Billinge's contention that 'Intellectual abstractions are not the stuff of which real geography is made' (p. 111), he clearly demonstrates the ways in which an oppositional north–south division in England was not uniformly available as a cultural assumption until the mid-nineteenth century when Elizabeth Gaskell can entitle a novel set in Manchester *North and South*.

3 Robert Burns, *Poems and Songs*, ed. James Kinsley (Oxford: Oxford University Press, 1969), poem 38, ll. 57–60 and 65–70.

4 For Wilkes and *The North Briton*, see Linda Colley, *Britons: Forging the Nation, 1707–1837* (London and New Haven, Conn.: Yale University Press, 1992), pp. 105–32; George Nobbe, *The North Briton: A Study in Political Propaganda* (New York: Columbia University Press, 1939); and Adam Rounce, 'Stuarts Without End: Wilkes, Churchill, and Anti-Scottishness', *Eighteenth-Century Life*, 29 (2005): 20–43. For the wider political context, see Colin Kidd, 'North Britishness and the Nature of Eighteenth-Century British Patriotisms', *The Historical Journal* 39 (1996): 361–82.

5 John Wilkes, *The North Briton*, 3 vols. (London: J. Williams, 1763), vol. I, p. 9.

6 Wilkes, *The North Briton*, vol. I, pp. 19–20. The association of homesickness with the Swiss is discussed in *Acta Germanica, Or the Literary Memoirs of*

Germany and the North, 2 vols. (London: G. Smith, 1742), a collection of translations of texts on various scientific subjects: 'This sickness is more prevalent among the *Swiss* than any other nation' and ascribes the phenomenon both to a hereditary 'disquietude of the mind' and to the fact that the Swiss's 'native air is more pure and rarefied than what they meet within foreign countries' (vol. II, p. 51). Wilkes's claim that the Scots do not possess the attachment to home for which they later become popularly famous, pre-dates the cultivation of a cultural nostalgia stemming from immigration to the New World but may also be related to Scottish historical theory which made a distinction between natural interpersonal affections and love of country, which is weaker because it depends on partial affiliations. See Adam Ferguson, *An Essay on the History of Civil Society*, ed. Duncan Forbes (Edinburgh: Edinburgh University Press, 1966), p. 21. For the relation of Scots and Jews, see Howard D. Weinbrot, *Britannia's Issue: The Rise of British Literature from Dryden to Ossian* (Cambridge: Cambridge University Press, 1993), pp. 481–91.

7 Wilkes, *The North Briton*, vol. II, p. 192.

8 Wilkes, *The North Briton*, vol. II, p. 193.

9 'Albion' is generally used both for England and Britain, whereas Scotland is denoted as 'Alba'. The terms are not, however, exclusive.

10 *The Scots Magazine* 49 (1787): 76–9; p. 78.

11 Hugh Blair, *Lectures on Rhetoric and Belles Lettres*, 2 vols. (London: W. Strahan and T. Cadell, 1783), vol. I, p. 171.

12 James Beattie, *Essays on Poetry and Music, as they affect the Mind; on Laughter, and Ludicrous Composition; on the Utility of Classical Learning* (Edinburgh, W. Creech, 1776), p. 413.

13 John Sinclair, *Observations on the Scottish Dialect* (London: W. Strahan and T. Cadell, 1782), p. 4.

14 Tobias Smollett, *The Expedition of Humphry Clinker*, ed. Lewis M. Knapp, rev. Paul-Gabriel Boucé (1966; rev. edn. Oxford: Oxford University Press, 1984), pp. 199–200.

15 Janet Sorensen, *The Grammar of Empire in Eighteenth-Century British Writing* (Cambridge: Cambridge University Press, 2000), p. 131.

16 John Cleland, *The Way to Things by Words, and to Words by Things* (London: L. Davis and C. Reymers, 1766), p. 54.

17 George William Lemon, *English Etymology or, a Derivative Dictionary of the English Language* (London: G. Robinson, 1783), entries for 'Britain' and 'sinister'.

18 Anne-Louise-Germaine de Staël, *De la littérature considerée dans ses rapports avec les institutions sociales*, ed. Paul van Tieghem, 2 vols. (Geneva: Librarie Droz, 1959), vol. I, p. 182. My translation.

19 James Anderson, *Observations on the Means of Exciting a Spirit of National Industry Chiefly Intended to Promote the Agriculture, Commerce, Manufactures, and Fisheries, of Scotland* (Edinburgh: T. Cadell, 1777), p. 51.

20 Anderson, *Observations*, p. 51.

21 Gray, *Complete Poems*, p. 15.

22 Wilkes, *The North Briton*, vol. II, p. 28.

23 Joanna Baillie, 'Lines on the Death of Walter Scott' (1832), in *The Dramatic and Poetical Works of Joanna Baillie* (London: Longman, Brown, Green, and Longmans, 1851), p. 793.

24 De Staël, *De la littérature*, vol. I, pp. 178 and 180.

25 Edward Jerningham, *The Rise and Progress of the Scandinavian Poetry* (London: James Robson, 1784), pp. 5 and 10. For representations of Norse culture in Britain in the period, see Julian Meldon D'Arcy, *Scottish Skalds and Sagamen: Old Norse Influence on Modern Scottish Literature* (East Linton: Tuckwell Press, 1996), pp. 17–36.

26 Sam Smiles, *The Image of Antiquity: Ancient Britain and the Romantic Imagination* (London and New Haven, Conn.: Yale University Press, 1994), p. 28.

27 Thomas Percy, Preface to Paul-Henri Mallet, *Northern Antiquities; or, a Description of the Manners, Customs, Religion and Laws of the Ancient Danes, and other Northern Nations*, 2 vols. (London: T. Carnan, 1770), vol. I, p. liii.

28 Colin Kidd, *British Identities Before Nationalism: Ethnicity and Nationhood in the Atlantic World, 1600–1800* (Cambridge: Cambridge University Press, 1999), p. 185. See pp. 185–210 for a meticulous account of the gradual separations of Gothic and Celtic as ethnological terms. For the problematic position of modern Germans in the debates about northern ancestry, see Weinbrot, *Britannia's Issue*, pp. 495–504.

29 Nick Groom, *The Making of Percy's Reliques* (Oxford: Clarendon Press, 1999), p. 72.

30 Fiona J. Stafford. *The Sublime Savage: A Study of James Macpherson and the Poems of Ossian* (Edinburgh: Edinburgh University Press, 1988), pp. 137–9. Leith Davis further suggests that Macpherson uses theories of ancient tribal descent to draw England and Scotland together at the origin. *Acts of Union: Scotland and the Literary Negotiation of the British Nation, 1707–1830* (Stanford, Calif.: Stanford University Press, 1998), pp. 85–6.

31 Gray, *Complete Poems*, p. 31.

32 John Pinkerton, *Modern Geography: A Description of the Empires, Kingdoms, States, and Colonies*, 2 vols. (London: T. Cadell and W. Davies, 1802), vol. I, p. iii.

33 Charles W. J. Withers, *Geography, Science and National Identity: Scotland since 1520* (Cambridge: Cambridge University Press, 2001), p. 141. See also Robert J. Mayhew, *Enlightenment Geography: The Political Languages of British Geography, 1650–1850* (Basingstoke: Macmillan, 2000).

34 Pinkerton, *Modern Geography*, p. iv.

35 Robert Mayhew argues that Pinkerton's work is not only modern but also self-consciously British as a geography: '*Modern Geography* was a text which positioned itself as a geography of the world as it had settled after the upheavals of the French Revolution, Pinkerton may well have felt the need to make his geography discernibly British if it was to chime with the public mood of strident nationalism.' 'British Geography's Republic of Letters: Mapping an Imagined Community, 1600–1800', *Journal of the History of Ideas* 65 (2004): 251–76; p. 262. For *Modern Geography* in relation to Pinkerton's politics, see Mayhew, *Enlightenment Geography*, pp. 184–92.

36 John Pinkerton, *Ancient Scotish Poems*, 2 vols. (London: Charles Dilley, 1786), vol. I, pp. x and xi.

37 Pinkerton, *Ancient Scotish Poems*, vol. I, p. xviii.

38 John Pinkerton, *Dissertation on the Origin and Progress of the Scythians or Goths* (London: George Nicol, 1787), p. 200.

39 Pinkerton, *Dissertation*, pp. 202–3.

40 Pat Rogers describes the lure of the scientific north–south axis: 'Real geographical and climatic differences depend upon the latitude, rather than the longitude; seasons relate to the one as they do not to the other. The equator is more than a metaphysical entity, whereas the degree zero of modern cartography had been drawn at an arbitrary point on the globe.' 'North and South', *Eighteenth Century Life* 12 (1988): 101–11; p. 101.

41 James Thomson, *Spring*, ll. 366–7 and 378. *The Seasons* (London: J. Millan, 1730), pp. 27 and 28.

42 Jean-Jacques Rousseau, *Essay on the Origin of Languages*, trans. John H. Moran (Chicago, Ill. and London: Chicago University Press, 1966), p. 39.

43 Alexander Pope, *An Essay on Man*, Epistle II, ll. 208–16. *The Poems of Alexander Pope*, ed. John Butt (London: Methuen, 1968), p. 523.

44 Edward S. Casey, *The Fate of Place: A Philosophical History* (Berkeley, Calif.: University of California Press, 1997), p. 182.

45 John Pinkerton, *An Enquiry into the History of Scotland Preceding the Reign of Malcolm III, or the Year 1056*, 2 vols. (London: John Nichols, 1789), vol. I, p. 10.

46 Peter Davidson describes the subjectivity of the north and the 'tendency of northern frontiers to fade into debatable lands of fog and conjectural map-making' in *The Idea of North* (London: Reaktion Books, 2005), pp. 21–50; p. 25.

47 William Falconer, *Remarks on the Influence of Climate, Situation, Nature of Country, Population, Nature of Food, and Way of Life, on the Disposition and Temper, Manners and Behaviour, Intellects, Laws and Customs, Form of Government, and Religion, of Mankind* (London: C. Dilley, 1781), pp. 169–70. Falconer's Southerners are clearly influenced by long-standing Orientalist (and many of his typical examples are Indians) ideas of Eastern peoples as their somatic oversensitivity makes them irrational, untrustworthy and prone to succumb to the sort of tyranny best supplanted by British rule.

48 Thomas Warton, 'On the Introduction of Learning into England', prefixed to vol. 1 of his *History of English Poetry*, 4 vols. (London: J. Dodsley, 1774), not paginated. For the poetical relations between east and north, see Geoffrey H. Hartman, 'Blake and the Progress of Poesy', in *Beyond Formalism: Literary Essays 1958–1970* (London and New Haven, Conn.: Yale University Press, 1970), pp. 193–205.

49 Robert Colvill was a minister in Fife. For his life and poetic career, see Richard C. Cole, 'James Boswell and Robert Colvill', *Studies in Scottish Literature* 16 (1981): 110–21.

50 Robert Colvill, 'On the Winter-Solstice', in *Occasional Poems* (Edinburgh: Walter Ruddiman, 1771), p. 1. Further page references appear in the text.

51 Suvir Kaul, *Poems of Nation, Anthems of Empire: English Verse in the Long Eighteenth Century* (Charlottesville, Va. and London: University Press of Virginia, 2000), p. 124.

52 Anne Grant, *Eighteen Hundred and Thirteen: A Poem* (Edinburgh: Longman, Hurst, Rees, Orme, and Brown, 1814), p. 5. Further page references appear in the text.

53 See J. R. Watson, *Romanticism and War: A Study of British Romantic Period Writers and the Napoleonic Wars* (Basingstoke: Palgrave, 2003), pp. 144–59.

54 Falconer, *Remarks on the Influence of Climate*, p. 28.

55 Charles Churchill, *The Prophecy of Famine: A Scots Pastoral*, 2nd edn (London: Printed for the Author, 1763), p. 16.

56 Churchill, *The Prophecy of Famine*, p. 14.

57 Wilkes, *The North Briton*, vol. I, p. 15.

58 Robert Colvill, *The Caledonians: A Poem* (Edinburgh: Printed for the Author, 1779), p. 6.

59 Scott, *The Vision of Don Roderick*, Canto 2, stanza 59, in *The Poetical Works of Sir Walter Scott*, ed. J Logie Robertson (London: Oxford University Press, 1906), p. 605.

60 Wilkes, *The North Briton*, vol. I, p. 53.

61 Canto 3, stanza 16, *Poetical Works of Sir Walter Scott*, p. 609.

62 For the career of Thomas Graham, see Rory Muir, *Britain and the Defeat of Napoleon, 1807–15* (London and New Haven, Conn.: Yale University Press, 1996), pp. 306–10. His appearance in Scott's *Vision of Don Roderick* is discussed in Simon Bainbridge, *British Poetry and the Revolutionary and Napoleonic Wars: Visions of Conflict* (Oxford: Oxford University Press, 2003), pp. 165–6.

2 BURNS, PLACE AND LANGUAGE

1 James Currie, 'The Life of Robert Burns', vol. I of *The Works of Robert Burns, with an Account of his Life*, 3rd edn, 4 vols. (London: T. Cadell and W. Davies, 1802), p. 315.

2 Currie, 'Life of Robert Burns', p. 316.

3 Currie, 'Life of Robert Burns', p. 150.

4 Henry Mackenzie, 'Surprising Effects of Original Genius, Exemplified in the Poetical Productions of *Robert Burns*, an Ayrshire Ploughman', *The Lounger*, 3rd edn, 3 vols. (London: A. Strahan and T. Cadell, 1786), vol. III, pp. 278–89; p. 280.

5 James Dunbar, *Essays on the History of Mankind in Rude and Cultivated Ages*, 2nd edn (London: W. Strahan and T. Cadell, 1781), p. 3.

6 'On the one hand, communities can exist without being in the same place – from networks of friends with like interests, to major religions, ethnic or political communities. On the other hand, the instances of places housing single "communities" in the sense of coherent social groups are probably – and, I would argue, have for long been – quite rare. Moreover, even where

they do exist this in no way implies a single sense of place. For people occupy different positions within any community'. Doreen Massey, *Space, Place and Gender* (Cambridge: Polity Press, 1994), p. 153.

7 For the concomitant difficulties of understanding 'region', see Roberto M. Dainotto, *Place in Literature: Regions, Cultures, Communities* (Ithaca, NY and London: Cornell University Press, 2000), pp. 1–33.

8 Anthony Giddens, *The Consequences of Modernity* (Cambridge: Polity Press, 1990), p. 18.

9 References are to poem and line number in Robert Burns, *Poems and Songs*, ed. James Kinsley (Oxford: Oxford University Press, 1969).

10 See, for example, Thomas Crawford's comment that 'Burns's development as a poet was from the local to the national to the universal'. *Burns: A Study of the Poems and Songs* (Edinburgh: Oliver and Boyd, 1960), p. 342.

11 For the globalisation of geographical knowledge in the eighteenth century, see Roy Porter, 'The Terraqueous Globe', in G. S. Rousseau and Roy Porter (eds.), *The Ferment of Knowledge: Studies in the Historiography of Eighteenth-Century Science* (Cambridge: Cambridge University Press, 1980), pp. 285–324. For the construction of totalised systems built on this knowledge, see David Harvey's account of 'the time and space of the Enlightenment project', *The Condition of Postmodernity* (Oxford: Blackwell, 1989), pp. 240–59. For the role of Scottish geographers in a 'universalizing discourse, designed to gather information about the globe', see Charles W. J. Withers, 'Geography, Natural History and the Eighteenth-Century Enlightenment: Putting the World in Place', *History Workshop Journal* 39 (1995): 137–63; p. 142.

12 Geoffrey H. Hartman, 'Inscriptions and Romantic Nature Poetry', in Geoffrey H. Hartman, *The Unremarkable Wordsworth* (London: Methuen, 1987), pp. 31–46; p. 32. See also Jonathan Bate, *Romantic Ecology: Wordsworth and the Environmental Tradition* (London and New York: Routledge, 1991), pp. 85–115.

13 Michel de Certeau, *The Practice of Everyday Life*, trans. Steven Rendall (Berkeley, Calif.: University of California Press, 1984), p. 117.

14 Hartman, 'Inscriptions and Romantic Nature Poetry', p. 40.

15 David Hume, *An Enquiry Concerning Human Understanding*, ed. Tom L. Beauchamp (Oxford: Clarendon Press, 2000), p. 24. Hume does not offer geometrical forms as ideal objects in anything other than the philosophical sense and viewed geometry as a dangerous precedent, which, because of its ability to sustain infinite divisibility, was liable to attract the attention of metaphysicians. For Euclidean geometry in the *Enquiry*, see Marina Frasca-Spada, *Space and the Self in Hume's Treatise* (Cambridge: Cambridge University Press, 1998), pp. 135–40.

16 Hume, *Enquiry*, p. 24.

17 Hume, *Enquiry*, p. 24.

18 These questions of geometry, history and transcendental objects have been revisited in the twentieth century in Jacques Derrida's first published work, his *Introduction to Husserl's 'Origin of Geometry'*, trans. John P. Leavey Jr.

(1978; Lincoln, Nebr.: University of Nebraska Press, 1989). Derrida argues that through inscription, 'Historical incarnation sets free the transcendental, instead of binding it' (*Introduction*, p. 77). See also John Pickles, *Phenomenology, Science and Geography: Spatiality and the Human Sciences* (Cambridge: Cambridge University Press, 1985). For Hume in relation to eighteenth-century geography, see Margarita Bowen, *Empiricism and Geographical Thought: From Francis Bacon to Alexander von Humboldt* (Cambridge: Cambridge University Press, 1981), pp. 134–43.

19 For the context of climate in the human sciences, see David N. Livingstone, 'Geographical Inquiry, Rational Religion, and Moral Philosophy: Enlightenment Discourses on the Human Condition', in David N. Livingstone and Charles W. J. Withers (eds.), *Geography and Enlightenment* (Chicago, Ill.: University of Chicago Press 1999), pp. 93–119; and Clarence J. Glacken, *Traces on the Rhodian Shore: Nature and Culture in Western Thought from Ancient Times to the End of the Eighteenth Century* (Berkeley, Calif.: University of California Press, 1967), esp. pp. 552–605. Interest in climate theory has recently given rise to some important work on eighteenth-century gender and sexuality; see Felicity A. Nussbaum, *Torrid Zones: Maternity, Sexuality, and Empire in Eighteenth-Century English Narratives* (Baltimore, Md.: Johns Hopkins University Press, 1995); and Clare Brant, 'Climates of Gender', in Amanda Gilroy (ed.), *Romantic Geographies: Discourses of Travel, 1775–1844* (Manchester: Manchester University Press, 2000), pp. 129–49.

20 See Arden Reed, *Romantic Weather: The Climate of Coleridge and Baudelaire* (Hanover, NH and London: University Press of New England, 1983).

21 David Hume, 'Of National Characters', in *Essays: Moral, Political and Literary* (Oxford: Oxford University Press, 1963), p. 203.

22 John Millar, *The Origin of the Distinction of Ranks*, 3rd edn (London: J. Murray, 1779), pp. 12–13.

23 Adam Ferguson, *An Essay on the History of Civil Society*, ed. Duncan Forbes (Edinburgh: Edinburgh University Press, 1966), p. 110.

24 William Falconer, *Remarks on the Influence of Climate Situation, Nature of Country, Population, Nature of Food, and Way of Life, on the Disposition and Temper, Manners and Behaviour, Intellects, Laws and Customs, Form of Government, and Religion, of Mankind* (London: C. Dilly, 1781), p. 116. Further references appear in the text.

25 Dunbar, *Essays on the History of Mankind*, pp. 419 and 451.

26 For an overview, see Christopher Berry, ' "Climate" in the Eighteenth Century: James Dunbar and the Scottish Case', *Texas Studies in Literature and Language* 16 (1974): 281–92.

27 Dunbar, *Essays on the History of Mankind*, p. 295.

28 James Beattie, *Dissertations Moral and Critical* (London: W. Strahan and T. Cadell, 1783), p. 523.

29 James Beattie, *The Minstrel*, new edn (London: Charles Dilly, 1784), p. 60.

30 Beattie, *The Minstrel*, p. 4.

31 Tobias Smollett, *The Expedition of Humphry Clinker*, ed. Lewis M. Knapp, rev. Paul-Gabriel Boucé (Oxford: Oxford University Press, 1966), p. 253.

32 Smollett, *Humphry Clinker*, p. 253.

33 Smollett, *Humphry Clinker*, p. 254.

34 'As it departs from the sun [. . .] passion is further composed into a habit of domestic connection, or frozen into a state of insensibility, under which the sexes at freedom scarcely chuse to unite their society.' Ferguson, *Essay on Civil Society*, p. 116.

35 Falconer seems to have thought of Scotland as a northern country, in comparison with temperate England. This, he argues, accounts for the fact that 'the Reformation was conducted with a greater degree of moderation in England, than in Scotland, many parts of Germany, and the North' (*Remarks on the Influence*, p. 147). Whereas Scotland is generally northern in climate studies, England could be northern or temperate depending on the context or political inflection. John Aikin hedges his bets in his topographical description of England: 'With respect to climate, England is situated in the northern part of the temperate zone.' *England Delineated* (London: J. Johnson, 1778), p. 17.

36 Colin Kidd, *British Identities before Nationalism: Ethnicity and Nationhood in the Atlantic World, 1600–1800* (Cambridge: Cambridge University Press, 1999), pp. 205–10. For a very helpful survey of early language theory, see James H. Stam, *Inquiries into the Origin of Language: The Fate of a Question* (New York: Harper and Row, 1976).

37 Dunbar, *Essays on the History of Mankind*, pp. 120 and 118.

38 Jean-Jacques Rousseau, *Essay on the Origin of Languages*, trans. John H. Moran (Chicago, Ill. and London: Chicago University Press, 1966), pp. 30 and 46.

39 George William Lemon, *English Etymology; or, a Derivative Dictionary of the English Language* (London: G. Robinson. 1783), p. xxxiii.

40 James Burnet, Lord Monboddo, *Of the Origin and Progress of Language*, 6 vols. (Edinburgh: A. Kincaid and W. Creech, 1773–92), vol. IV, p. 40.

41 Rousseau, *Essay on the Origin of Languages*, p. 24.

42 William Mitford, *An Essay Upon the Harmony of Language* (London: J. Robson, 1773), p. 59.

43 James Adams, *The Pronunciation of the English Language Vindicated from Imputed Anomaly and Caprice* (Edinburgh: J. Moir, 1799), p. 157.

44 Adams, *Pronunciation Vindicated*, p. 153.

45 Adams, *Pronunciation Vindicated*, p. 158–9.

46 Adams, *Pronunciation Vindicated*, p. 137.

47 Mitford, *Essay Upon the Harmony of Language*, p. 96.

48 Monboddo, *Origin and Progress*, vol. I, p. 325.

49 Rousseau, *Essay on the Origin of Languages*, p. 5.

50 Monboddo, *Origin and Progress*, vol. I, p. 490.

51 Hugh Blair, *Lectures on Rhetoric and Belles Lettres*, 2 vols. (London: W. Strahan and T. Cadell, 1783), vol. II, p. 55.

52 Monboddo, *Origin and Progress*, vol. IV, p. 175.

53 Janet Sorensen, *The Grammar of Empire in Eighteenth-Century British Writing* (Cambridge: Cambridge University Press, 2000), p. 139.

54 Thomas Sheridan, *Lectures on the Art of Reading*, 2 vols. (J. Dodsley: London, 1775), vol. I, p. 112.

55 Rousseau, *Essay on the Origin of Languages*, p. 51.

56 Blair, *Lectures on Rhetoric*, vol. I, p. 108.

57 Anselm Bayly, *An Introduction to Languages, Literary and Philosophical* (London: John Rivington, 1758), p. 181.

58 Edward Jerningham, *The Ancient English Wake: A Poem*, (London: James Robson, 1779), p. 10.

59 William Tytler 'Dissertation on the Scottish Music', printed in his *Poetical Remains of James the First, King of Scotland* (Edinburgh: J. and E. Balfour, 1783), p. 196.

60 Leith Davis, 'At "Sang About": Scottish Song and the Challenge to British Culture', in Leith Davis, Ian Duncan, and Janet Sorensen (eds.), *Scotland and the Borders of Romanticism* (Cambridge: Cambridge University Press, 2004), pp. 188–204; p. 189. See also Roger Fiske, *Scotland in Music: A European Enthusiasm* (Cambridge: Cambridge University Press, 1983).

61 Tytler, 'Dissertation on the Scottish Music', p. 196.

62 David Herd, *Ancient and Modern Scottish Songs*, 2 vols. (London: James Dickson and Charles Elliot, 1776), vol. I, p. v.

63 Herd, *Ancient and Modern Scottish Songs*, p. vii.

64 Joseph Ritson, *Scotish Song*, 2 vols. (London: J. Johnson and J. Egerton: 1794), vol. I, p. lxxix.

65 David Daiches, *Robert Burns*, rev. edn (London: Deutsch, 1966), p. 209.

66 Ritson, *Scotish Song*, pp. lxxix–lxxv.

67 Ritson, *Scotish Song*, p. i.

68 Robert Burns, *Notes on Scottish Song by Robert Burns: Written in an interleaved copy of 'The Scots Musical Museum' with additions by Robert Riddell and others*, ed. James C. Dick (London: Henry Frowde, 1908), p. 6.

69 Jacques Derrida, *Of Grammatology*, trans. Gayatri Chakravorty Spivak (Baltimore, Md. and London: Johns Hopkins University Press, 1976), p. 217.

70 Blair, *Lectures on Rhetoric*, vol. I, pp. 136 and 123.

71 See Monboddo, *Origin and Progress*, vol. I, pp. 313–17.

3 GREAT NORTH ROADS

1 Henry Skrine, *Three Successive Tours in the North of England and Great Part of Scotland* (London: P. Elmsly, 1795), pp. 34–5.

2 Dugald Stewart, 'Account of the Life and Writings of Adam Smith', ed. Ian Simpson Ross, in Adam Smith, *Essays on Philosophical Subjects*, eds. W. P. D. Wightman and J. C. Bryce (Oxford: Clarendon Press, 1980), p. 293.

3 James Chandler, *England in 1819: The Politics of Literary Culture and the Case of Romantic Historicism* (Chicago, Ill. and London: University of Chicago Press, 1998), p. 129.

4 Ian Duncan, 'Primitive Inventions: *Rob Roy*, Nation, and World System', *Eighteenth-Century Fiction* 15 (2002): 81–102; p. 85.

5 Tobias Smollett, *The Expedition of Humphry Clinker*, ed. Lewis M. Knapp, rev. Paul-Gabriel Boucé (1966; Oxford: Oxford University Press, 1984), p. 213.

6 For Scott and tourism, see James Buzard, 'Translation and Tourism: Scott's *Waverley* and the Rendering of Culture', *Yale Journal of Criticism*, 8 (1995): 41–53. For literary accounts of Scottish tourism, see John Glendening, *The High Road: Romantic Tourism, Scotland, and Literature, 1720–1820* (Basingstoke: Macmillan, 1997).

7 John Carr, *Caledonian Sketches, or a Tour Through Scotland in 1807* (London: Mathews and Leigh, 1809), p. 38.

8 John Lettice, *Letters on a Tour through Various Parts of Scotland in the Year 1792* (London: T. Cadell, 1794), p. iv.

9 Lettice, *Letters on a Tour*, p. 23–4.

10 Lettice, *Letters on a Tour*, p. 6.

11 Lettice, *Letters on a Tour*, p. 15.

12 John Millar, *The Origin of the Distinction of Ranks*, 3rd edn (London: J. Murray, 1779), p. 13.

13 Charles W. J. Withers, 'Toward a Historical Geography of Enlightenment in Scotland', in Paul Wood (ed.), *The Scottish Enlightenment: Essays in Reinterpretation* (Rochester, NY: University of Rochester Press, 2000), pp. 63–97; p. 79.

14 Thomas Newte, *Prospects and Observations on a Tour in England and Scotland: Natural, Œconomical, and Literary* (London: G. G. J. and J. Robinson, 1791), p. 426. For the real identity of 'Thomas Newte', see my introduction, n. 16.

15 Sir John Sinclair, *Analysis of the Statistical Account of Scotland* (London: John Murray, 1826), part 1, p. 102.

16 Sinclair, *Analysis*, part 1, p. 97.

17 See William Taylor, *The Military Roads in Scotland* (1976; rev. edn Colonsay: House of Lochar, 1996).

18 Edmund Burt, *Burt's Letters from the North of Scotland*, intro. Robert Jamieson, 2 vols. (Edinburgh: William Paterson, 1876), vol. II, pp. 332–3.

19 Burt, *Letters*, vol. II, p. 336.

20 Burt, *Letters*, vol. II, pp. 336–7.

21 Adam Smith, *An Inquiry into the Nature and Causes of the Wealth of Nations*, eds. R. H. Campbell, A. S. Skinner and W. B. Todd, 2 vols. (Oxford: Clarendon Press, 1976), vol. I, p. 163.

22 Samuel Johnson, *A Journey to the Western Islands of Scotland*, ed. Mary Lascelles (New Haven, Conn. and London: Yale University Press, 1971), p. 9.

23 Johnson, *A Journey to the Western Islands of Scotland*, p. 126.

24 For Macpherson's 'topographical liminality', see Joep Leerson, 'Ossianic Liminality: Between Native Tradition and Preromantic Taste', in Fiona Stafford and Howard Gaskill (eds.), *From Gaelic to Romantic: Ossianic Translations* (Amsterdam: Rodopi, 1998), pp. 1–16; pp. 3–4.

25 James Macpherson, *The Poems of Ossian and Related Works*, ed. Howard Gaskill (Edinburgh: Edinburgh University Press, 1996), p. 18.

26 Macpherson, *The Poems of Ossian*, p. 18.

27 In *Acts of Union: Scotland and the Literary Negotiation of the British Nation 1707–1830* (Stanford, Calif.: Stanford University Press, 1998), Leith Davis argues that Macpherson's Celts 'practiced a kind of democracy which led to representative government' (pp. 84–5). For Macpherson and sensibility, see Daffyd Moore, *Enlightenment and Romance in James Macpherson's 'The Poems of Ossian': Myth, Genre and Cultural Change* (Aldershot: Ashgate, 2003).

28 The geographic imprecision of Ossian also contributed to an exceptional portability that allowed imperial, national and cultural ethnographies to be built on it: outside Britain, Herder read *Fingal* on a sea journey and, famously, Napoleon kept a copy in his pocket during his conquest of Europe. For Macpherson's European reception, see the essays in Howard Gaskill (ed.), *The Reception of Ossian in Europe* (London: Thoemmes, 2004).

29 Richard Warner, *A Tour through the Northern Counties of England, and the Borders of Scotland*, 2 vols. (London: G. and J. Robinson, 1802), vol. II, p. 57.

30 Franco Moretti, *Atlas of the European Novel 1800–1900* (London: Verso, 1998), p. 51.

31 An exception is William Macritchie's 1795 diary which seems not to have been intended for publication but which appeared in an edition by his grandson in 1897. Macritchie does not record the point of crossing the border from north to south, but comments on the bridge at Coldstream on the way back. He includes the engaging detail that 'The Borderers seem to be fond of rhiming', having noticed signs such as 'Bread, beer, / Sold here'. *Diary of a Tour through Great Britain in 1795*, ed. David Macritchie (London: Eliot Stock, 1897), p. 16.

32 James Boswell, *The Life of Samuel Johnson*, 3rd edn, 4 vols. (London: Charles Dilly, 1791), vol. I, p. 231.

33 *The North Briton*, 3 vols. (London: J. Williams, 1763), vol. I, pp. 15–16.

34 Walter Scott, *Rob Roy*, ed. Ian Duncan (Oxford: Oxford University Press, 1998), p. 93. Further citations appear in the text. See also *The Fortunes of Nigel* (1822), where Scott opens with a optimistic vision of 'the south and north divisions of the Island of Great Britain' in which 'the subjects of either side of the Tweed' enjoy friendly relations. *The Fortunes of Nigel*, ed. Frank Jordan (Edinburgh: Edinburgh University Press, 2004), p. 3.

35 *Waverley* is nevertheless very interested in the spatiality of the nation. See Saree Makdisi, *Romantic Imperialism: Universal Empire and the Culture of Modernity* (Cambridge: Cambridge University Press: 1998), pp. 70–99.

36 Walter Scott, *The Heart of Mid-Lothian*, ed. David Hewitt and Alison Lumsden (Edinburgh: Edinburgh University Press, 2004), p. 292. Further references appear in the text.

37 For Scott and Smith see Peter Garside, 'Scott and the Philosophical Historians', *Journal of the History of Ideas* 36 (1975): 497–512; and Kathryn

Sutherland, 'Fictional Economies: Adam Smith, Sir Walter Scott and the Nineteenth-century Novel', *ELH*, 54 (1987): 97–127.

38 Duncan, 'Primitive Inventions', pp. 86–7.

39 Janet Sorensen, 'Internal Colonialism and the British Novel', *Eighteenth-Century Fiction*, 15 (2002): 53–8; p. 56.

40 For the history of road-building in the period, see William Albert, *The Turnpike Road System in England 1663–1840* (Cambridge, Cambridge University Press, 1972); and Eric Pawson, *Transport and Economy: the Turnpike Roads of Eighteenth Century Britain* (London: Academic Press, 1977).

41 See Sidney Webb and Beatrice Webb, *The Story of the King's Highway* (1913; London: Frank Cass, 1963), pp. 121–2.

42 John Louden McAdam, *Remarks on the Present System of Road Making* (Bristol: J. M. Gutch, 1819), p. 17.

43 John Sinclair, *The Statistical Account of Scotland 1791–1799*, ed. Donald J. Witherington and Ian R. Grant, 20 vols. (East Ardsley: EP Publishing, 1983), vol. III, p. 109.

44 Sinclair, *Statistical Account of Scotland*, p. 110.

45 John Sinclair, *Analysis of the Statistical Account*, part 1, p. 233.

46 McAdam, *Remarks*, p. 21. In 1805, another Scottish road-builder, Thomas Telford, was commissioned to build new roads in the Highlands more suitable for modern modes of transport and to stimulate the Highland economy by facilitating the movement of goods. He completed about 1,200 miles of new or improved roads with 1,100 bridges. When Telford's friend Robert Southey visited Scotland in 1819, the roads were a constant locus for observation, at times seeming to supplant even that most usual of focal points, the picturesque: 'These roads when they are cut thro' the rock, or have the high bank turfed on one side, and are walled up and parapetted on the other, are beautiful works of art; and even when they have no picturesque features of this kind, you cannot look forward or backward upon them without a sense of order, and care and fitness, which is a pleasure of no mean degree.' Robert Southey, *Journal of a Tour in Scotland in 1819*, ed. C. H. Herford (London: John Murray, 1929), pp. 211–12. From 1815, travellers could witness at Bonar Bridge a marble inscription inviting them to 'read with gratitude the names of the Parliamentary Commissioners appointed in the year 1803 to direct the making of above 500 miles of roads thro' the Highlands of Scotland' (Southey, *Journal of a Tour*, p. 131). For further information about Scottish road-building, see A. R. B. Haldane, *New Ways Through the Glens: Highland Road, Bridge and Canal Makers of the Early Nineteenth Century* (London: Nelson, 1962).

47 Peter Linebaugh, *The London Hanged: Crime and Civil Society in the Eighteenth Century*, 2nd edn (London: Verso, 2003), pp. 212–13.

48 Duncan, 'Primitive Inventions', p. 99. In a note to the 1829 *magnum opus* edition, Scott underscored the interrelations of modern British and traditional Scottish thievery: 'The introduction of gaugers, supervisors, and

examiners, was one of the great complaints of the Scottish nation, though a natural consequence of the Union' (*Rob Roy*, p. 460).

49 Wade roads crop up in Scott's introduction to the 1829 edition of *Rob Roy*, where Scott prints a letter from Rob to Wade ('at that time engaged in disarming the Highland clans, and making military roads through the country') setting out a contorted expression of allegiance to George I while confessing to 'having played booty during the civil war of 1715' (p. 36).

50 Joanna Baillie, *The Dramatic and Poetical Words of Joanna Baillie* (London: Longman, Brown, Green, and Longmans, 1851), p. 305.

51 Thomas Percy, *Reliques of Ancient English Poetry*, 3 vols. (London: J. Dodsley, 1765), vol. I, p. xxi.

52 John Pinkerton, *Ancient Scotish Poetry*, 2 vols. (London: Charles Dilly, 1786), vol. I, p. xvii.

53 Walter Scott, *The Letters of Sir Walter Scott*, ed. H. J. C. Grierson, 12 vols. (London: Constable, 1932–5), vol. I, p. 174.

54 Allan Cunningham, *The Songs of Scotland, Ancient and Modern*, 4 vols. (London: John Taylor, 1825), vol. I, pp. 129 and 131.

55 Susan Stewart, *Crimes of Writing: Problems in the Containment of Representation* (Oxford: Oxford University Press, 1991), p. 110. See also Nick Groom, *The Making of Percy's Reliques* (Oxford: Clarendon Press, 1999), p. 101.

56 Davis, *Acts of Union*, p. 155.

57 Walter Scott, *Minstrelsy of the Scottish Border*, 2nd edn, 3 vols. (Edinburgh: printed for Longman and Rees, London, 1803), vol. I, p. cxxxii.

58 *The Poetical Works of Sir Walter Scott*, ed. J. Logie Robertson (London: Oxford University Press, 1906), p. 92.

59 Walter Scott, *Border Antiquities of England and Scotland*, 2 vols. (London: Longman, Hurst, Rees, Orme, and Brown, 1814–17), vol. I, p. xcv. For the geography of the Borders Wardens' jurisdiction, see D. I. W. Tough, *The Last Years of a Frontier: a History of the Borders During the Reign of Elizabeth I* (1928; Alnwick: Sandhill Press, 1987), pp. 1–29.

60 Scott, *Minstrelsy*, vol. I, p. lxvii. Scott gives a detailed account of Borders Law in *Border Antiquities*, vol. I, pp. lxxxvii–cxxvii.

61 Scott, *Minstrelsy*, vol. I, p. lxx.

62 For an account of the Scottish Militia Act and the opposition to it, see Kenneth J. Logue, *Popular Disturbances in Scotland, 1780–1815* (Edinburgh: John Donald, 1979), pp. 75–115.

63 Quoted in Logue, *Popular Disturbances*, p. 101.

64 Scott, *Minstrelsy*, vol. I, p. lvi. See also *Border Antiquities*, vol. I, p. xcv. 'Jeddart Justice' took the form of both hanging and drowning, and *The Monastery* makes ominous references to 'the black pool at Jeddart', evidently the scene of multiple judicial drownings. *The Monastery*, ed. Penny Fielding (Edinburgh: Edinburgh University Press, 2000), pp. 88 and 99. The phrase also appears in *Rob Roy*.

65 Scott, *Minstrelsy*, vol. I, p. 226.

66 Benedict Anderson, *Imagined Communities: Reflections on the Origins and Spread of Nationalism* (1983; rev. edn. London: Verso, 1991), p. 36.

67 Nicholas K. Blomley, *Law, Space, and the Geographies of Power* (New York: The Guildford Press, 1994), p. 29.

68 Charles Louis de Secondat de Montesquieu, *The Spirit of the Laws*, trans. and ed. Anne M. Cohler, Basia Carolyn Miller and Harold Samuel Stone (Cambridge: Cambridge University Press, 1989), p. 3.

69 Lettice, *Letters on a Tour*, p. 8.

70 James Plumptre, *James Plumptre's Britain: The Journals of a Tourist in the 1790s*, ed. Ian Ousby (London: Hutchinson, 1992), p. 104. In 1820, the structure Plumptre had crossed was replaced by a new Union Bridge, at that time the longest first suspension bridge in the world. In a neat exemplar of northern logic, the Scottish end of the bridge is south of the English.

71 Newte, *Prospects and Observations*, p. 395. John Carr similarly lists the residents of the Northumberland village of Billingham as 'petty tradesmen, carriers, smugglers, and poachers' without suggesting that these occupations belong in separate categories (*Caledonian Sketches*, p. 28).

72 Henri Lefebvre, *The Production of Space*, trans. Donald Nicholson-Smith (Oxford: Blackwell, 1991), pp. 38–9.

4 ANTIQUARIANISM AND THE INSCRIPTION OF THE NATION

1 Fairport's troublesome positions are set out by David Hewitt in his edition of *The Antiquary* (Edinburgh: Edinburgh University Press, 1995), pp. 447–8. Further references to this novel appear in the text.

2 Mike Goode, 'Dryasdust Antiquarianism and Soppy Masculinity: The Waverley Novels and the Gender of History', *Representations* 82 (2003): 52–86; p. 61.

3 Katie Trumpener, *Bardic Nationalism: The Romantic Novel and the British Empire* (Princeton, NJ: Princeton University Press, 1997), p. 6.

4 Arnoldo Momigliano, *The Classical Foundations of Modern Historiography* (Berkeley, Calif.: University of California Press, 1990), p. 54; Susan Manning, 'Antiquarianism, the Scottish Science of Man and the Emergence of Modern Disciplinarity', in Leith Davis, Ian Duncan, and Janet Sorensen (eds.), *Scotland and the Borders of Romanticism* (Cambridge: Cambridge University Press, 2004), pp. 57–76.

5 Ina Ferris, 'Pedantry and the Question of Enlightenment History: The Figure of the Antiquary in Scott', *European Romantic Review* 13 (2002): 273–83; p. 278.

6 For a helpful summary of the dispute, see Colin Kidd, *Subverting Scotland's Past: Scottish Whig Historians and the Creation of an Anglo-British Identity, 1689–c.1830* (Cambridge: Cambridge University Press, 1993), pp. 251–3.

7 John Pinkerton, *A Dissertation on the Origin and Progress of the Scythians or Goths* (London: George Nicol, 1787), p. 69.

8 Samuel Johnson, *A Journey to the Western Islands of Scotland*, ed. Mary Lascelles (New Haven, Conn. and London: Yale University Press, 1971), p. 115.

9 John Pinkerton, *An Enquiry into the History of Scotland Preceding the Reign of Malcolm III or the Year 1056*, 2 vols. (London: John Nichols, 1789), vol. I. p. 139. Pinkerton believed that modern Gaelic as spoken in the Highlands was a 'corrupt' language, 'quite full of Norwegian words' (vol. I, p. 137).

10 George Chalmers, *Caledonia; or, An Account, Historical and Topographic, of North Britain: from the Most Ancient to the Present Times*, 3 vols. (London: T. Cadell and W Davies, 1807–24), vol. I, p. 32. Further citations are to volume and page number and appear in the text.

11 Quoted in Hans Aarsleff, 'The Study and Use of Etymology in Leibniz', in *From Locke to Saussure: Essays on the Study of Language and Intellectual History* (London: Athlone Press, 1982), pp. 83–100; p. 86.

12 James Burnet, Lord Monboddo, *Of the Origin and Progress of Language*, 6 vols. (Edinburgh: A. Kincaid and W.Creech, 1773–92), vol. I, p. 406.

13 Thomas Newte, *Prospects and Observations on a Tour in England and Scotland: Natural, Œconomical, and Literary* (London: G. G. J. and J. Robinson, 1791), pp. 49 and 426.

14 William Wordsworth, *'Lyrical Ballads' and Other Poems, 1797–1800*, eds. James Butler and Karen Green (Ithaca, NY and London: Cornell University Press, 1992), p. 241.

15 Hilary A. Zaid, 'Wordsworth's "Obsolete Idolatry": Doubling Texts and Facing Doubles in "To Joanna"'. *Studies in Romanticism*, 36 (1997): 201–26; p. 203.

16 Wordsworth, *Lyrical Ballads*, p. 246.

17 Hugh Blair, *Lectures on Rhetoric and Belles Lettres*, 2 vols. (London: W. Strahan and T. Cadell, 1783), vol. I, p. 168.

18 Olivia Smith, *The Politics of Language, 1791–1819* (Oxford: Clarendon Press, 1984), p. 23. See also Murray Cohen on the relation of words and syntax in the eighteenth century: *Sensible Words: Linguistic Practice in England 1640–1785* (Baltimore, Md.: Johns Hopkins University Press, 1977). For the relevance of eighteenth-century language theory to Romantic poetry, see Richard Margraff Turley, *The Politics of Language in Romantic Literature* (Basingstoke: Palgrave Macmillan, 2002).

19 Yoon Sun Lee, 'A Divided Inheritance: Scott's Antiquarian Novel and the British Nation', *ELH*, 64 (1997): 537–67; p. 2.

20 Thomas Pennant, *A Tour in Scotland 1769* (Chester: John Monk, 1771), p. 287. For the composition of *Caledonia* through letters, see Charles Withers, 'Writing in Geography's History: *Caledonia*, Networks of Correspondence and Geographical Knowledge in the Late Enlightenment', *Scottish Geographical Journal*, 120 (2004): 33–45.

21 Gilbert Dyer, *Vulgar Errors, Ancient and Modern, Attributed As Imports to the Proper Names of the Globe, Clearly Ascertained: with Approximations to Their Rational Descents* (Exeter: G. Dyer, 1816), p. i. Further references appear in the text. For earlier connections between Celtic languages and Hebrew, see

Colin Kidd, *British Identities Before Nationalism: Ethnicity and Nationhood in the Atlantic World, 1606–1800* (Cambridge: Cambridge University Press, 1999), pp. 68–9.

22 Janet Sorenson argues that amid 'the legion of contexts and meanings of language [. . .] Johnson recasts any lack of linguistic "integrity" as a function not of the heteroglossic character of social language intra-nationally but of invasive foreign languages inter-nationally' with the result that 'the speakers of true English shrink to almost nil'. *The Grammar of Empire in Eighteenth-Century British Writing* (Cambridge: Cambridge University Press, 2000), p. 89.

23 Jonathan Bate, *The Song of the Earth* (London: Picador, 2000), pp. 223–5. Gilbert Dyer also supplies words 'which compose the roots of all the rivers in Britain and Europe, if not in the greatest part of the world'. *A Restoration of the Ancient Modes of Bestowing Names on the Rivers, Hills, Vallies, Plains, and Settlements of Britain* (Exeter: G. Dyer, 1805), p. 6. Yi-Fu Tuan points out the importance of river-names in the homogenisation of territory because 'the name can be said to have created the system, and not just the parts visible to observers on the ground, accessible to consciousness.' 'Language and the Making of Place: A Narrative-Descriptive Approach', *Annals of the Association of American Geographers*, 81 (1991): 684–96; pp. 688–9.

24 For the transition 'from demotic *ethnie* to civic nation' in the formation of nationalisms, see Anthony D. Smith, *The Antiquity of Nations* (Cambridge: Polity, 2004), pp. 194–201; p. 197.

25 For the cultural and political history of the Celt in the nineteenth century, see Sam Smiles, *The Image of Antiquity: Ancient Britain and the Romantic Imagination* (London and New Haven, Conn.: Yale University Press, 1994).

26 Chalmers is making a strong claim for the Scottishness of British law, deviating from earlier Unionist Scots depiction of Scottish law as a descent of English constitutional freedoms: 'When one dives into the Antiquities of *Scotland* and *England*, it will appear that we borrowed all our Laws and Customs from the *English*. No sooner is a Statute enacted in *England*, but, upon the first Opportunity, it is introduced into *Scotland;* so that our oldest Statutes are mere copies of theirs.' Henry Home, Lord Kames, *Essays Upon Several Subjects Concerning British Antiquities* (Edinburgh: A. Kincaid, 1747), p. 4.

27 John Lucas, *England and Englishness: Ideas of Nationhood in English Poetry 1688–1900* (London: The Hogarth Press, 1990), p. 47.

28 Linda Colley, *Britons: Forging the Nation, 1707–1837* (New Haven, Conn.: Yale University Press, 1992), p. 53.

29 Fiona Robertson, *Legitimate Histories: Scott, Gothic, and the Authorities of Fiction* (Oxford: Clarendon Press, 1994), p. 205.

30 Monboddo, *Of the Origin and Progress of Language*, vol. I, p. 406.

31 Lee, 'A Divided Inheritance', p. 554.

32 Judith Wilt, *Secret Leaves: The Novels of Walter Scott* (Chicago, Ill.: Chicago University Press, 1985), pp. 223–4, n. 13. *The Antiquary*, p. 375 n.

33 Tobias Smollett, *The Adventures of Peregrine Pickle*, ed. James L. Clifford, rev. Paul-Gabriel Boucé (Oxford: Oxford University Press, 1983), p. 662.

34 Shawn Malley, 'Walter Scott's Romantic Archaeology: New/Old Abbotsford and *The Antiquary*', *Studies in Romanticism*, 40 (2001): 233–51; p. 244.

35 Lee, 'A Divided Inheritance', p. 548.

36 David Jennings, *An Introduction to the Knowledge of Medals* (London: T. Fielding, 1764), pp. 56–7.

37 John Pinkerton, *An Essay on Medals* (London: James Dodsley, 1784), pp. 12–13. Further references appear in the text.

38 Joseph Addison, *Dialogues Upon the Usefulness of Ancient Medals* (n.p., 1726), p. 147. For a subtle untangling of Addison's dialogues, see David Alvarez, ' "Poetical Cash": Joseph Addison, Antiquarianism, and Aesthetic Value', *Eighteenth-Century Studies*, 38 (2005): 509–31.

39 Marc Shell, *Money, Language, and Thought: Literary and Philosophical Economies from the Medieval to the Modern Era* (Berkeley, Calif.: University of California Press, 1982), p. 1.

40 Shell, *Money, Language, and Thought*, pp. 1–2.

41 Richard T. Gray, 'Hypersign, Hypermoney, Hypermarket: Adam Müller's Theory of Money and Romantic Semiotics', *New Literary History*, 31 (2000): 295–314; p. 303.

42 Gray, 'Hypersign, Hypermoney', p. 301.

43 Patrick Brantlinger, *Fictions of State: Culture and Credit in Britain, 1694–1994* (Ithaca, NY and London: Cornell University Press, 1996), p. 92. For Scott's relations to Scottish banking systems, see Silvana Colella, 'Monetary Patriotism: *The Letters of Malachi Malagrowther*, *The Antiquary*, and the Currency Question', *Nineteenth-Century Studies*, 17 (2003): 53–71.

44 I am here in agreement with Caroline McCracken-Flesher's recent reading of the novel as she writes: 'there effectively is no past. For all Oldbuck's focus on antiquity, life is ever opening in the present.' *Possible Scotlands: Walter Scott and the Story of Tomorrow* (New York and Oxford: Oxford University Press, 2005), p. 43.

45 The word 'history', here restored in the *Edinburgh Edition*, is Scott's manuscript version and was replaced by 'antiquities' in the first and subsequent editions, probably a mechanical substitution on the part of compositors, proof-readers, or the printer James Ballantyne, to avoid a repetition in the next paragraph. The second 'history' works well as an example of parallelism, and, as I argue of the novel itself, makes a statement not only about the value of historical objects but also about the forms of historical narratives in general.

46 These transactions are described in greater details in David Hewitt's 'Essay on the Text', *The Antiquary*, pp. 359–60.

47 *The Letters of Walter Scott*, ed. H. J. C. Grierson, 12 vols. (London: Constable, 1932–37), vol. I, p. 522.

5 ULTIMA THULE

1 Katie Trumpener, *Bardic Nationalism: The Romantic Novel and the British Empire* (Princeton, NJ: Princeton University Press, 1997).

2 For an account of sea travel to and from Shetland, see Derek Flinn, *Travellers in a Bygone Shetland: An Anthology* (Edinburgh: Scottish Academic Press, 1989), pp. 1–4. For early visitors to Shetland, including Scott, see John M. Simpson, 'The Discovery of Shetland from "The Pirate" to the Tourist Board', in *Shetland and the Outside World 1469–1969* (Oxford: Oxford University Press, 1983), pp. 136–49.

3 Samuel Hibbert, *Description of the Shetland Islands, Comprising an Account of their Geology, Scenery, Antiquities, and Superstitions* (Edinburgh: Constable, 1822), p. 88.

4 Hibbert, *Description of the Shetland Islands*, p. 86.

5 On hearing of Scott's lighthouse trip in August 1814, Chalmers wrote to him with a copy of her printed book and a manuscript poem about the need for a further lighthouse on Shetland. She followed this up with a second letter the following January, anxiously inquiring if he received the poems, but no reply from Scott survives. National Library of Scotland MS 3885 and MS 3886.

6 Hibbert, *Description of the Shetland Islands*, p. 103.

7 John Pinkerton, *Dissertation on the Origin and Progress of the Scythians or Goths* (London: George Nicol, 1787), p. 202.

8 Arthur Edmondston, *A View of the Ancient and Present State of the Zetland Islands*, 2 vols. (Edinburgh: James Ballantyne, 1809), vol. I, pp. 111–12. Edmonston is referring to the Acts of Parliament of 1746 which brought feudalism to an end in Scotland.

9 Walter Scott, 'Voyage in the Lighthouse Yacht to Nova Zembla, and the Lord Knows Where', in J. G. Lockhart, *The Life of Sir Walter Scott, Bart.*, 6 vols. (Edinburgh: Robert Cadell, 1837), vol. III, pp. 136–277; p. 180. Further references appear in the text.

10 *The Voyage of the 'Pharos': Walter Scott's Cruise Around Scotland in 1814* (Hamilton: Scottish Library Association, 1998).

11 Alexander Pope, *An Essay on Man*, Epistle II, ll. 208–12. *The Poems of Alexander Pope*, ed. John Butt (London: Methuen, 1968), p. 523.

12 Scott is slightly misremembering Webster's *The Duchess of Malfi*, Act V, Scene 3, ll. 12–13.

13 Walter Scott, Robert Jamieson and Henry Weber, *Illustrations of Northern Antiquities from the Earlier Teutonic and Scandinavian Romances* (Edinburgh: J. Ballantyne, 1814).

14 George Chalmers, convinced that Shetland is Scandinavian in origin, sees the northern settlement of the Picts as fantastical: 'During late times, many of those edifices, in the Orkney, and Shetland, islands, and in Cathness, have been erroneously called Pictish castles, Pictish towers, and Picts houses, from a fabulous story, that attributes to Kenneth MacAlpin the impolicy of driving many of the Picts into the northern extremity of our island'. *Caledonia; or, An Account, Historical and Topographic, of North Britain: from the Most Ancient to the Present Times*, 3 vols. (London: T. Cadell and W. Davies, 1807–24), vol. I, p. 342.

15 Scott thinks Stevenson's earlier visit took place 'a year or two since', but the joke about grass growing on trees may have already been widespread since it

appears in Patrick Neill's *A Tour Through Some of the Islands of Orkney and Shetland* (Edinburgh: Constable, 1806), p. 93 n.

16 James Thomson, *Autumn*, ll. 860–5, *The Seasons* (London: J. Millan, 1730), p. 222.

17 *The Poetical Works of Sir Walter Scott*, ed. J. Logie Robertson (London: Oxford University Press, 1906), p. 703.

18 Gillian Beer, 'Discourses of the Island', in Frederick Amrine (ed.), *Literature and Science as Modes of Expression* (Dordrecht: Kulver Academic Press, 1989), pp. 1–27; p. 9.

19 In his own account, Robert Stevenson narrates an incident, unrecorded by Scott, which confirms this fractal geometry. The ship's cabin boy (prophetically named 'Jim' in anticipation of Stevenson's grandson's most famous novel) excitedly informs the party that an island has been sighted. After some discussion of what territory this might be, Scott himself observes 'Jim had indeed discovered an island, which however happened to be the island of Great Britain.' Robert Louis Stevenson, 'Scott's Voyage in the Lighthouse Yacht', *Scribner's Magazine*, 14 (1893): 492–502; p. 498. Great Britain, so far from being the Platonic island of which all others are mere imitations, is one of a random assortment of islands which might or might not be sighted at any given moment.

20 Hibbert, *Description of the Shetland Islands*, p. 85.

21 Alexander Peterkin, *Notes on Orkney and Shetland*, 2 vols. (Edinburgh: Macredie, Skelly & Co., 1822), p. 8.

22 Edmonston, *View of the Zetland Islands*, p. 144. Edmonston also includes the affecting detail that a Shetland author had written a poem on the subject of the seasons but had withdrawn it upon discovering that James Thomson had got there first (*View of the Zetland Islands*, p. 145).

23 Margaret Chalmers, *Poems* (Newcastle: S. Hodgson, 1813). The volume was poorly printed, and I have left uncorrected a number of obvious errors. Further references are to page numbers and appear in the text.

24 William Falconer, *Remarks on the Influence of Climate, Situation, Nature of Country, Population, Nature of Food, and Way of Life, on the Disposition and Temper, Manners and Behaviour, Intellects, Laws and Customs, Form of Government, and Religion, of Mankind* (London: C. Dilly, 1781), pp. 170 and 171.

25 Saree Makdisi, *Romantic Imperialism: Universal Empire and the Culture of Modernity* (Cambridge: Cambridge University Press, 1998), p. 9. Benedict Anderson, *Imagined Communities: Reflections on the Origins and Spread of Nationalism* (rev. edn, London: Verso, 1991), p. 24.

26 Edmondston, *View of the Zetland Islands*, vol. I, pp. vi–vii.

27 John Laing, *An Account of a Voyage to Spitzbergen* (London: J. Mawman, 1815), p. 54. Laing was a ship's surgeon on board the *Resolution*. His Malthusian perspective was a fairly common one to be brought to bear on the northern isles; cf. Edmondston, *View of the Zetland Islands*, vol. II, p. 150 and n.

28 Laing, *Voyage to Spitzbergen*, p. 55.

29 In a modern study of the spatial assumptions of geographical fieldwork, Matthew Sparke shows this as a gendered position: 'The field has been able to share and lock into the compartmentalization implicit in the *logos* of absolutized space by serving simultaneously as the feminized object of the masculine gaze, and the pictured place of communion with the actual or factual'. 'Displacing the Field in Fieldwork: Masculinity, Metaphor and Space', in Nancy Duncan (ed.), *Bodyspace: Destabilizing Geographies of Gender and Sexuality* (London and New York: Routledge, 1996), pp. 212–33; p. 218.

30 Falconer, *Remarks on the Influence*, p. 254.

31 John Sinclair, *The Statistical Account of Scotland 1791–1799*, eds. Donald J. Witherington and Ian R. Grant, 20 vols. (East Ardsley: EP Publishing, 1983), vol. XIX, pp. 444–5. Edmonston also extends the deleterious effects of tea-drinking to lower-class women but does concede that it is the 'inferior kinds of bohea tea which are used, and which seem to be the least pernicious variety of this herb.' *View of the Zetland Islands*, vol. II, p. 59.

32 Neill, *Tour through Orkney and Shetland*, p. 71. Neill shared Laing's concern about the tea-drinking proclivities of the Shetlanders and hopes that they might be 'encouraged to spend their scanty pittance on some more substantial and nutritive delicacy' (*Tour through Orkney and Shetland*, p. 92).

33 For female employment in the Shetlands, see Lynn Abrams, *Myth and Materiality in a Woman's World: Shetland 1800–2000* (Manchester: Manchester University Press, 2005).

34 The phrases in quotation marks are from the traditional song 'Tarry Woo' (which Chalmers may have encountered in Ramsay's *Tea-Table Miscellany*) and form part of the first stanza.

35 Adam Smith, *An Inquiry into the Nature and Causes of the Wealth of Nations*, eds. R. H. Campbell, A. S. Skinner and W. B. Todd, 2 vols. (Oxford: Clarendon Press, 1976), vol. I, p. 32.

36 Doreen Massey, 'Politics and Space/Time', *New Left Review*, 196 (1992), 65–84; pp. 80–1.

37 Dorothea Primrose Campbell, *Poems* (London: Baldwin, Cradock, and Joy, 1816), p. 1.

38 Campbell, *Poems*, p. 155.

39 J. E. Malpas, *Place and Experience: A Philosophical Topography* (Cambridge: Cambridge University Press, 1999), p. 35.

40 For the logocentric assumptions behind metaphoricity in geography in general, see Neil Smith and Cindi Katz, 'Grounding Metaphor: Towards a Spatialized Politics', in Michael Keith and Steve Pile (eds.), *Place and the Politics of Identity* (London and New York: Routledge, 1993), pp. 67–83.

41 Luce Irigaray, *This Sex Which is not One*, trans. Catherine Porter (Ithaca, NY: Cornell University Press, 1985), p. 154. For the significance of mirror images in feminist geography, see Gillian Rose, 'As if the Mirrors had Bled: Masculine Dwelling, Masculinist Theory and Feminist Masquerade', in Nancy Duncan (ed.), *Bodyspace: Destabilizing Geographies of Gender and Sexuality* (London and New York: Routledge, 1996), pp. 56–74.

42 Harriet Guest, *Small Change: Women, Learning, Patriotism, 1750–1810* (Chicago, Ill. and London: University of Chicago Press, 2000), p. 14. See also Dustin Griffin's account of Ann Yearsley in his *Patriotism and Poetry in Eighteenth-Century Britain* (Cambridge: Cambridge University Press, 2002), pp. 262–91.

43 Edmonston, *View of the Zetland Islands*, vol. I, p. 98.

44 This is in some ways recognisable as the kind of self-identification through a spatial imaginary which has been worked through by a number of contemporary feminist geographers. See Gillian Rose, *Feminism and Geography: The Limits of Geographical Knowledge* (Cambridge: Polity Press, 1993).

45 Maurice Merleau-Ponty, *The Phenomenology of Perception*, trans. Colin Smith (London: Routledge and Kegan Paul, 1962), p. 140. In the course of a longer discussion, Edward Casey succinctly sums up this idea of bodily experience as 'a sense of fit and of knowing one's way around'. *The Fate of Place: A Philosophical History* (Berkeley, Calif.: University of California Press, 1997) p. 231.

46 See, for example, Tim Ingold's conceptualising of landscape: 'each place embodies the whole at a particular nexus within it, and in this respect is different from every other. A place owes its character to the experiences it affords to those who spend time there – to the sights, sounds, and indeed smells that constitute its specific ambience. And these, in turn, depend on the kinds of activities in which its inhabitants engage. It is from this relational context of people's engagement with the world, in the business of dwelling, that each place draws its unique significance.' 'The Temporality of the Landscape', *World Archaeology*, 25 (1993): 152–74; p. 155.

47 Barbara Maria Stafford, *Voyage into Substance: Art, Science, Nature, and the Illustrated Travel Account, 1760–1840* (Cambridge, Mass. and London: MIT Press, 1984), p. 124.

48 In *The Pirate* (1822), which grew in part out his lighthouse tour, Scott was to offer a very different version of a female north. The novel represents its 'Northern Sybil', Norna, as a kind of demented Shetland antiquarian who, like *The Antiquary*'s Jonathan Oldbuck, lives surrounded by 'a confused collection of books of various languages, parchment scrolls tablets and stones'. *The Pirate*, ed. Mark Weinstein and Alison Lumsden (Edinburgh: Edinburgh University Press, 2001), p. 259. But whereas *The Antiquary*, as I argue in Chapter 4, validates Oldbuck's antiquarianism as a form of novelistic historiography, Norna is insane.

49 Dorothy Wordsworth, 'Floating Island at Hawkshead', ll. 27–8. Jennifer Breen (ed.) *Women Romantic Poets 1785–1832* (London: Everyman, 1992), p. 132.

50 Immanuel Kant, *Critique of the Power of Judgment*, ed. Paul Guyer, trans. Paul Huer and Eric Matthews (Cambridge: Cambridge University Press, 2000), p. 134.

51 For marginality in geography, see Edward Soja and Barbara Hooper, 'The Spaces That Difference Makes: Some Notes on the Geographic Margins of the New Cultural Politics' in Michael Keith and Steve Pile (eds.), *Place and the Politics of Identity* (London and New York: Routledge, 1995), pp. 183–205.

6 NORTHS

1 See Andrew Nash, 'The Cotter's Kailyard', in Robert Crawford (ed.), *Robert Burns and Cultural Authority* (Edinburgh: Edinburgh University Press, 1997), pp. 180–97. David Hill Radcliffe argues for the deviance of 'The Cotter's Saturday Night' from the neoclassical/peasant tradition in 'Imitation, Popular Literacy, and "The Cotter's Saturday Night"', in Carol McGuirk (ed.), *Critical Essays on Robert Burns* (New York: K. G. Hall, 1998), pp. 251–79.

2 Hogg was, of course, unable entirely to control his own media image and also appeared as the uneducated but loquacious character 'The Shepherd' in the *Noctes Ambrosianae*, a series of satirical and semi-fictitious conversations printed in *Blackwood's Edinburgh Magazine* between 1822 and 1835.

3 Peter Hallward, *Absolutely Postcolonial: Writing between the Singular and the Specific* (Manchester: Manchester University Press, 2001), p. xii.

4 For an interesting post-colonial reading of Hogg, see Caroline McCracken-Flesher, ' "You Can't Go Home Again": Hogg and the Problem of Postcolonial Return', *Studies in Hogg and his World*, 8 (1997): 24–41.

5 Walter Scott, *Minstrelsy of the Scottish Border*, 2nd edn, 3 vols. (Edinburgh: printed for Longman and Rees, London, 1803).

6 'Adam Bell' in James Hogg, *Winter Evening Tales, Collected among the Cottagers in the South of Scotland*, ed. Ian Duncan (Edinburgh: Edinburgh University Press, 2002), p. 75.

7 For the national tale, see Katie Trumpener, *Bardic Nationalism: The Romantic Novel and the British Empire* (Princeton, NJ: Princeton University Press, 1997), pp. 128–57. For Hogg's resistance to the national tale's ethnography, see Ian Duncan's introduction to his edition of *Winter Evening Tales*, pp. xxiv–vi.

8 Immanuel Kant, 'Dissertation on the Form and Principles of the Sensible and Intelligible World', in *Kant's Inaugural Dissertation and Early Writings on Space*, trans. John Handyside (Chicago, Ill.: Open Court, 1929), p. 59.

9 'John Gray o' Middleholm', in Hogg, *Winter Evening Tales*, p. 228. Further references appear in the text.

10 For Hogg's sources and analogues, see *Winter Evening Tales*, p. 569 where Duncan notes that the dream narrative Hogg uses is recorded in Robert Chambers's *Popular Rhymes of Scotland*.

11 Richard Sher, 'From Troglodytes to Americans: Montesquieu and the Scottish Enlightenment on Liberty, Virtue, and Commerce, 1649–1776', in *Republicanism, Liberty, and Commercial Society*, ed. David Wootton (Stanford, Calif.: Stanford University Press, 1994), pp. 368–402; p. 376.

12 Letter to William Robertson, 9 June 1777, *The Correspondence of Edmund Burke*, 10 vols. (Cambridge: Cambridge University Press, 1958–78), vol. III, ed. George H. Guttridge, p. 351.

13 John Pinkerton, *Modern Geography: A Description of the Empires, Kingdoms, States, and Colonies*, 2 vols. (London: T. Cadell and W. Davies, 1802), vol. I, p. iv.

14 William Robertson, *History of the Reign of the Emperor Charles V*, 3 vols. (London: W. Strahan, T. Cadell, 1769), vol. II, p. 431.

15 Adam Ferguson, *An Essay on the History of Civil Society*, ed. Duncan Forbes (Edinburgh: Edinburgh University Press, 1966), p. 24.

16 Pinkerton, *Modern Geography*, vol. I, p. iv.

17 Ferguson, *History of Civil Society*, p. 153.

18 James Hogg, 'The Adventures of Captain John Lochy', in *Altrive Tales*, ed. Gillian Hughes (Edinburgh: Edinburgh University Press, 2003), p. 91. Further references appear in the text.

19 Quoted in introduction to Hogg, *Altrive Tales*, p. liii. See also Hogg, *Winter Evening Tales*, p. xxx. Highly episodic, 'John Lochy' reads even more like a seventeenth-century prose romance with its cynical adventurer on foreign soil getting mixed up with historical warfare and offering a blurred picture of the authenticity of its narrator/author.

20 Nicola Chiaromonte, *The Paradox of History: Stendahl, Tolstoy, Pasternak, and Others*, rev. edn (Philadelphia, Pa.: University of Pennsylvania Press, 1985), p. 7.

21 Ferguson, *History of Civil Society*, p. 120.

22 See P. J. Marshall and Glyndwr Williams, *The Great Map of Mankind: British Perceptions of the World in the Age of Enlightenment* (London: Dent, 1982), pp. 61–184.

23 William Guthrie, *A New Geographical, Historical, and Commercial Grammar*, 3rd edn (London: J. Knox, 1771), p. 65.

24 J. G. A. Pocock, *Barbarism and Religion*, vol. II, *Narratives of Civil Government* (Cambridge: Cambridge University Press, 1999), pp. 330–45.

25 Alexander Pope, *An Essay on Man*, Epistle II, l. 15. *The Poems of Alexander Pope*, ed. John Butt (London: Methuen, 1968), p. 523.

26 Michel Foucault, 'Of Other Spaces', trans. Jay Miskowiec, *Diacritics*, 16 (1986): 22–7; p. 22.

27 Michel Foucault, *Power/Knowledge: Selected Interviews and Other Writings 1972–1977*, ed. Colin Gordon (Brighton: Harvester, 1980), p. 70.

28 But see also Sarah Moss, 'Romanticism on Ice: Coleridge, Hogg and the Eighteenth-Century Missions to Greenland', *Romanticism on the Net* 45 (2007). Available online at www.erudit.org/revue/ron/2007/v/n45/015816ar. html.

29 'Two versions of "The P and the Q; or, The Adventurers of Jock M'Pherson"', ed. Robin Maclachlan, *Studies in Hogg and His World*, 7 (1996): 87–101; p. 97.

30 Good accounts of the cultural meanings of Arctic exploration are Robert G. David, *The Arctic in the British Imagination 1818–1914* (Manchester: Manchester University Press, 2000), and Francis Spufford, *I May be Some Time: Ice and the English Imagination* (London: Faber, 1996). For Scottish involvement in the Arctic, see Ian Bunyan, *Polar Scots: Scottish Explorers in the Arctic* (Edinburgh: National Museums of Scotland, 1986), and Jenni Calder, 'Perilous Enterprises: Scottish Explorers in the Arctic', in Jenni Calder (ed.), *The Enterprising Scot: Scottish Adventure and Achievement* (Edinburgh: National Museums of Scotland, 1986), pp. 96–106.

31 *The Surpassing Adventures of Allan Gordon*, ed. Gillian Hughes (Stirling: James Hogg Society, 1987), p. 19. Further references appear in the text.

32 [James Wilson?], 'Account of Captain Scoresby's Observations on the Greenland or Polar Ice', *Blackwood's Edinburgh Magazine*, 2 (1818): 363–9; p. 363.

33 'Letter from an Officer Concerning the Polar Expedition', *Blackwood's Edinburgh Magazine*, 4 (1818): 193–8; p. 196. Communicated by the London publisher John Murray.

34 William Scoresby, *An Account of the Arctic Regions with a History and Description of the Northern Whale-Fishery*, 2 vols. (Edinburgh: Constable, 1820), vol. I, p. 110.

35 J. Hillis Miller, *Topographies* (Stanford, Calif.: Stanford University Press, 1995), p. 303.

36 For Symmes, see Spufford, *I May Be Some Time*, pp. 64–79.

37 'Letter from an Officer concerning the Polar Expedition', p. 193.

38 'Captain Parry's Voyage', *Blackwood's Edinburgh Magazine*, 9 (1821): 289–99; p. 295.

39 [David Brewster], 'Analysis of Mr Barrow's Chronological History of Voyages into the Arctic Regions', *Blackwood's Edinburgh Magazine*, 4 (1818): 187–93; p. 193.

40 Mary Shelley, *Frankenstein*, ed. Marilyn Butler (Oxford: Oxford University Press, 1993), p. 6. For Hogg's sources, see Gillian Hughes, 'Reading and Inspiration: Some Sources of "The Surpassing Adventures of Allan Gordon"', *Scottish Literary Journal*, 16 (1989): 21–34. In addition to its relationships with *Frankenstein* and *Robinson Crusoe*, *Allan Gordon* has clear echoes of 'The Ancient Mariner': like the mariner, Allan kills an animal in what he tells us is 'wholly a spontaneous act' (p. 13) and, in a direct verbal echo, finds himself 'alone on a wide wide sea' (p. 15).

41 Shelley, *Frankenstein*, p. 6.

42 Shelley, *Frankenstein*, p. 191.

43 Foucault, 'Of Other Spaces', p. 23.

44 'North-West Passage: Expedition under Captain Ross and Lieutenant Parry, in the Isabella and Alexander', *Blackwood's Edinburgh Magazine*, 4 (1818): 338–44; p. 339. Communicated by the London publisher John Murray.

45 'Captain Parry's Voyage', p. 293.

46 'North-West Passage', p. 339.

47 Laurence Sterne, *The Life and Opinions of Tristram Shandy, Gentleman*, ed. Melvyn New and Joan New (Harmondsworth: Penguin, 1997), pp. 159–60. The editors note that Sterne draws on the third edition of Thomas Salmon's *Modern History, or the Present State of All Nations* (1744), where winter in the northernmost latitudes is said to be nine months long, forcing the inhabitants to hide in caves. See p. 585 n. 13.

48 Mary Douglas, *Purity and Danger: An Analysis of the Concepts of Pollution and Taboo* (London: Routledge, 1966), p. 57.

49 Maggie Kilgour, *From Communion to Cannibalism: An Anatomy of Metaphors of Incorporation* (Princeton, NJ: Princeton University Press, 1990), p. 11. Ian

Duncan shows how cannibalism tests the limits of narration and, especially, narration's ability to absorb or incorporate its cultural past in Hogg's *Three Perils of Man*. 'Scott, Hogg, Orality and the Limits of Culture', *Studies in Hogg and his World*, 8 (1997): 56–74.

50 Scoresby, *Account of the Arctic Regions*, vol. I, p. 520.

51 John Franklin, *Narrative of a Journey to the Shores of the Polar Sea, in the Years 1819, 20, 21, and 22*, 2 vols. (London: John Murray, 1823), vol. I, p. 451. The problem of figuring cannibalism in Arctic narrative recurred in narratives of the last and fatal Franklin expedition of 1845. The Orcadian explorer John Rae's search for the lost expedition resulted in his reporting evidence of cannibalism, testimony vehemently resisted by the public.

52 Allan Cunningham, *The Songs of Scotland, Ancient and Modern*, 4 vols. (London: John Taylor, 1825), vol. I, p. 131.

53 Samuel Johnson, *A Journey to the Western Islands of Scotland*, ed. Mary Lascelles (London and New Haven, Conn.: Yale University Press, 1971), p. 146.

54 Introduction to Leith Davis, Ian Duncan and Janet Sorensen (eds.), *Scotland and the Borders of Romanticism* (Cambridge: Cambridge University Press, 2004), p. 3.

55 Mary Poovey, *A History of the Modern Fact: Problems of Knowledge in the Sciences of Wealth and Society* (Chicago, Ill. and London: University of Chicago Press, 1998), p. 228.

56 The classic account is Michael Hechter, *Internal Colonialism: The Celtic Fringe in British National Development, 1536–1966* (London: Routledge and Kegan Paul 1975).

57 Walter Scott, *Waverley*, ed. Claire Lamont (Oxford: Oxford University Press, 1981), p. 340.

Bibliography

PRIMARY

Acta Germanica; or the Literary Memoirs of Germany and the North, 2 vols. (London: G. Smith, 1742).

Adams, James, *The Pronunciation of the English Language Vindicated from Imputed Anomaly and Caprice* (Edinburgh: J. Moir, 1799).

Addison, Joseph, *Dialogues Upon the Usefulness of Ancient Medals* (n.p., 1726).

Aikin, John, *England Delineated* (London: J. Johnson, 1778).

Anderson, James, *Observations on the Means of Exciting a Spirit of National Industry Chiefly Intended to Promote the Agriculture, Commerce, Manufactures, and Fisheries, of Scotland* (Edinburgh: T. Cadell, 1777).

Baillie, Joanna, *The Dramatic and Poetical Works of Joanna Baillie* (London: Longman, Brown, Green, and Longmans, 1851).

Barbauld, Anna Lætitia, *Eighteen Hundred and Eleven, A Poem* (London: J. Johnson, 1812).

Bayly, Anselm, *An Introduction to Languages, Literary and Philosophical* (London: John Rivington, 1758).

Beattie, James, *Dissertations Moral and Critical* (London: W. Strahan and T. Cadell, 1783).

    Essays on Poetry and Music, As They Affect the Mind; on Laughter, and Ludicrous Composition; on the Utility of Classical Learning (Edinburgh: W. Creech, 1776).

    The Minstrel, new edn (London: Charles Dilly, 1784).

Blackwood, Edinburgh Magazine, 1817–35.

Blair, Hugh, *Lectures on Rhetoric and Belles Lettres*, 2 vols. (London: W. Strahan and T. Cadell, 1783).

Boswell, James, *The Life of Samuel Johnson*, 3rd edn, 4 vols. (London: Charles Dilly, 1791).

Burke, Edmund, *The Correspondence of Edmund Burke*, 10 vols. (Cambridge: Cambridge University Press, 1958–78).

Burnet, James *(Lord Monboddo)*, *Of the Origin and Progress of Language*, 6 vols. (Edinburgh: A. Kincaid and W. Creech, 1773–92).

Burns, Robert, *Notes on Scottish Song by Robert Burns: Written in an Interleaved Copy of 'the Scots Musical Museum' with Additions by Robert Riddell and Others*, ed. James C. Dick (London: Henry Frowde, 1908).

The Poems and Songs of Robert Burns, ed. James Kinsley (Oxford: Oxford University Press, 1969).

Burt, Edmund, *Burt's Letters from the North of Scotland, intro. by Robert Jamieson*, 2 vols. (Edinburgh: William Paterson, 1876).

Campbell, Dorothea Primrose, *Poems* (London: Baldwin, Cradock, and Joy, 1816).

Carr, John, *Caledonian Sketches; or a Tour through Scotland in 1807* (London: Mathews and Leigh, 1809).

Chalmers, George, *Caledonia; or an Account, historical and topographic, of North Britain: From the Most Ancient to the Present Times*, 3 vols. (London: T. Cadell and W Davies, 1807–24).

Chalmers, Margaret, *Poems* (Newcastle: S. Hodgson, 1813).

Churchill, Charles, *The Prophecy of Famine: A Scots Pastoral*, 2nd edn (London: Printed for the Author, 1763).

Cleland, John, *The Way to Things by Words, and to Words by Things* (London: L. Davis and C. Reymers, 1766).

Coleridge, S. T., *Coleridge's Poetry and Prose*, ed. Nicholas Halmi, Paul Magnuson and Raimonda Modiano (New York and London: W. W. Norton, 2004).

Colvill, Robert, *The Caledonians: A Poem* (Edinburgh: Printed for the Author, 1779).

Occasional Poems (Edinburgh: Walter Ruddiman, 1771).

Cunningham, Allan, *The Songs of Scotland, Ancient and Modern*, 4 vols. (London: John Taylor, 1825).

Currie, James, '*The Life of Robert Burns*', vol. I of *The Works of Robert Burns, with an Account of His Life*, 3rd edn, 4 vols. (London: T. Cadell and W. Davies, 1802).

Dunbar, James, *Essays on the History of Mankind in Rude and Cultivated Ages*, 2nd edn (London: W. Strahan and T. Cadell, 1781).

Dyer, Gilbert, *A Restoration of the Ancient Modes of Bestowing Names on the Rivers, Hills, Vallies, Plains, and Settlements of Britain* (Exeter: G. Dyer, 1805).

Vulgar Errors, Ancient and Modern, Attributed As Imports to the Proper Names of the Globe, Clearly Ascertained: with Approximations to Their Rational Descents (Exeter: G. Dyer, 1816).

Edmondston, Arthur, *A View of the Ancient and Present State of the Zetland Islands*, 2 vols. (Edinburgh: James Ballantyne, 1809).

Falconer, William, *Remarks on the Influence of Climate, Situation, Nature of Country, Population, Nature of Food, and Way of Life, on the Disposition and Temper, Manners and Behaviour, Intellects, Laws and Customs, Form of Government, and Religion, of Mankind* (London: C. Dilly, 1781).

Ferguson, Adam, *An Essay on the History of Civil Society*, ed. Duncan Forbes (Edinburgh: Edinburgh University Press, 1966).

Flinn, Derek (ed.), *Travellers in a Bygone Shetland: An Anthology* (Edinburgh: Scottish Academic Press, 1989).

Franklin, John, *Narrative of a Journey to the Shores of the Polar Sea, in the Years 1819, 20, 21, and 22*, 2 vols. (London: John Murray, 1823).

Gough, Richard, *Anecdotes of British Topography* (London: W. Richardson and S. Clark, 1768).

Grant, Anne, *Eighteen Hundred and Thirteen: A Poem* (Edinburgh: Longman, Hurst, Rees, Orme, and Brown, 1814).

Gray, Thomas, *The Complete Poems of Thomas Gray*, ed. H. W. Starr and J. R. Hendrickson (Oxford: Clarendon Press, 1966).

Guthrie, William, *A New Geographical, Historical, and Commercial Grammar* (London: J. Knox, 1770).

Herd, David, *Ancient and Modern Scottish Songs*, 2 vols. (London: James Dickson and Charles Elliot, 1776).

Hibbert, Samuel, *Description of the Shetland Islands, Comprising an Account of their Geology, Scenery, Antiquities, and Superstitions* (Edinburgh: Constable, 1822).

Hogg, James, *Altrive Tales*, ed. Gillian Hughes (Edinburgh: Edinburgh University Press, 2003).

 The Surpassing Adventures of Allan Gordon, ed. Gillian Hughes (Stirling: James Hogg Society, 1987).

 'Two Versions of "the P and the Q; or, The Adventurers of Jock M'Pherson"', ed. Robin Maclachlan, *Studies in Hogg and His World*, 7 (1996): 87–101.

 Queen Hynde, ed. Suzanne Gilbert and Douglas S. Mack (Edinburgh: Edinburgh University Press, 1997).

 Winter Evening Tales, ed. Ian Duncan (Edinburgh: Edinburgh University Press, 2003).

Home, Henry (Lord Kames), *Essays on Several Subjects Concerning British Antiquities* (Edinburgh: A. Kincaid, 1747).

 Sketches of the History of Man, 2 vols. (Edinburgh: W Creech, 1774).

Hume David, *An Enquiry Concerning Human Understanding*, ed. Tom L. Beauchamp (Oxford: Clarendon Press, 2000).

 Essays: Moral, Political and Literary (Oxford: Oxford University Press, 1963).

Jameson, Robert, *Mineralogy of the Scottish Isles*, 2 vols. (Edinburgh: W Creech and London: B. White, 1800).

Jennings, David, *Introduction to the Knowledge of Medals* (London: John Baskerville, 1764).

Jerningham, Edward, *The Ancient English Wake: A Poem* (London: James Robson, 1779).

 The Rise and Progress of the Scandinavian Poetry (London: James Robson, 1784).

Johnson, Samuel, *A Journey to the Western Islands of Scotland,* ed. Mary Lascelles (London and New Haven, Conn.: Yale University Press, 1971).

Kant, Immanuel, *Critique of the Power of Judgment,* ed. Paul Guyer, trans. Paul Huer and Eric Matthews (Cambridge: Cambridge University Press, 2000).

 'Dissertation on the Form and Principles of the Sensible and Intelligible World', in *Kant's Inaugural Dissertation and Early Writings on Space*, trans. John Handyside (Chicago, Ill.: Open Court, 1929).

Laing, John, *An Account of a Voyage to Spitzbergen* (London: J. Mawman, 1815).

Lemon, George William, *English Etymology; or, a Derivative Dictionary of the English Language* (London: G. Robinson, 1783).

Lettice, John, *Letters on a Tour through Various Parts of Scotland in the Year 1792* (London: T. Cadell, 1794).

McAdam, John Louden, *Remarks on the Present System of Road Making* (Bristol: J. M. Gutch, 1819).

Mackenzie, Henry, 'Surprising Effects of Original Genius, Exemplified in the Poetical Productions of Robert Burns, an Ayrshire Ploughman', in *The Lounger*, 3rd edn, 3 vols. (London: A. Strahan and T. Cadell, 1787), vol. III, pp. 278–89.

Macpherson, James, *The Poems of Ossian and Related Works*, ed. Howard Gaskill (Edinburgh: Edinburgh University Press, 1996).

Macritchie, William, *Diary of a Tour through Great Britain in 1795*, ed. David Macritchie (London: Eliot Stock, 1897).

Millar, John, *The Origin of the Distinction of Ranks*, 3rd edn (London: J. Murray, 1779).

Mitford, William, *An Essay Upon the Harmony of Language* (London: J. Robson, 1773).

Montesquieu, Charles Louis de Secondat de, *The Spirit of the Laws*, trans. and eds. Anne M. Cohler, Basia Carolyn Miller and Harold Samuel Stone (Cambridge: Cambridge University Press, 1989).

Neill, Patrick, *A Tour through Some of the Islands of Orkney and Shetland* (Edinburgh: Constable, 1806).

Newte, Thomas, *Prospects and Observations on a Tour in England and Scotland: Natural, Œconomical, and Literary* (London: G. G. J. and J. Robinson, 1791).

Pennant, Thomas, *A Tour in Scotland 1769* (Chester: John Monk, 1771).

Percy, Thomas, Preface to *Paul-Henri Mallet, Northern Antiquities; or, a Description of the Manners, Customs, Religion and Laws of the Ancient Danes, and other Northern Nations*, 2 vols. (London: T. Carnan, 1770).

Reliques of Ancient English Poetry, 3 vols. (London: J. Dodsley, 1765).

Peterkin, Alexander, *Notes on Orkney and Zetland*, 2 vols. (Edinburgh: Macredie, Skelly & Co., 1822).

Pinkerton, John, *Ancient Scotish Poetry*, 2 vols. (London: Charles Dilly, 1786).

Dissertation on the Origin and Progress of the Scythians or Goths (London: George Nicol, 1787).

An Enquiry into the History of Scotland Preceding the Reign of Malcolm III, or the Year 1056, 2 vols. (London: John Nichols, 1789).

An Essay on Medals (London: James Dodsley, 1784).

Modern Geography: A Description of the Empires, Kingdoms, States, and Colonies, 2 vols. (London: T. Cadell and W. Davies, 1802).

Plumptre, James, *James Plumptre's Britain: The Journals of a Tourist in the 1790s*, ed. Ian Ousby (London: Hutchinson, 1992).

Pope, Alexander, *The Poems of Alexander Pope*, ed. John Butt (London: Methuen, 1968).

Rousseau, Jean-Jacques, *Essay on the Origin of Languages*, trans. John H. Moran (Chicago, Ill. and London: Chicago University Press, 1966).

Scoresby, William, *An Account of the Arctic Regions with a History and Description of the Northern Whale-Fishery*, 2 vols. (Edinburgh: Constable, 1820).

Scott, Walter, *The Letters of Sir Walter Scott*, ed. H. J. C. Grierson, 12 vols. (London: Constable, 1932–5).

Poetical Works of Sir Walter Scott, ed. J. Logie Robertson (London: Oxford University Press, 1906).

The Antiquary, ed. David Hewitt (Edinburgh: Edinburgh University Press, 1995).

The Fortunes of Nigel, ed. Frank Jordan (Edinburgh: Edinburgh University Press, 2004).

Guy Mannering, ed. Peter Garside (Edinburgh: Edinburgh University Press, 1999).

The Heart of Mid-Lothian, ed. David Hewitt and Alison Lumsden (Edinburgh: Edinburgh University Press, 2004).

The Monastery, ed. Penny Fielding (Edinburgh: Edinburgh University Press, 2000).

The Pirate, ed. Mark Weinstein and Alison Lumsden (Edinburgh: Edinburgh University Press, 2001).

Rob Roy, ed. Ian Duncan (Oxford: Oxford University Press, 1998).

Waverley, ed. Claire Lamont (Oxford: Oxford University Press, 1981).

Border Antiquities of England and Scotland, 2 vols. (London: Longman, Hurst, Rees, Orme, and Brown, 1814–17).

Minstrelsy of the Scottish Border, 2nd edn, 3 vols. (Edinburgh: printed for Longman and Rees, London, 1803).

'*Voyage in the Lighthouse Yacht to Nova Zembla, and the Lord Knows 'Where'*', in J. G. Lockhart, *The Life of Sir Walter Scott, Bart.*, 6 vols. (Edinburgh: Robert Cadell, 1837), vol. III, pp. 136–277.

The Voyage of the 'Pharos': Walter Scott's Cruise Around Scotland in 1814 (Hamilton: Scottish Library Association, 1998).

Robert Jamieson and Henry Weber, *Illustrations of Northern Antiquities from the Earlier Teutonic and Scandinavian Romances* (Edinburgh: J. Ballantyne, 1814).

Shelley, Mary, *Frankenstein*, ed. Marilyn Butler (Oxford: Oxford University Press, 1993).

Sheridan, Thomas, *Lectures on the Art of Reading*, 2 vols. (London: J. Dodsley, 1775).

Sinclair, John, *Analysis of the Statistical Account of Scotland* (London: John Murray, 1826).

Observations on the Scottish Dialect (London: W. Strahan and T. Cadell, 1782).

The Statistical Account of Scotland 1791–1799, ed. Donald J. Witherington and Ian R. Grant, 20 vols. (East Ardsley: EP Publishing, 1983).

Skrine, Henry, *Three Successive Tours in the North of England and Great Part of Scotland* (London: P. Elmsly, 1795).

Smellie, William, *Account of the Institution and Progress of the Society of the Antiquaries of Scotland* (Edinburgh: William Creech, 1782).

Smith, Adam, *An Inquiry into the Nature and Causes of the Wealth of Nations*, ed. R. H. Cambell, A. S. Skinner and W. B. Todd, 2 vols. (Oxford: Clarendon Press, 1976).

Lectures on Rhetoric and Belles Lettres, ed. J. C. Bryce (Oxford: Clarendon Press, 1983).

Smollett, Tobias, *The Adventures of Peregrine Pickle, ed. James L. Clifford,* rev. Paul-Gabriel Boucé, (1964; Oxford: Oxford University Press, 1983).

The Expedition of Humphry Clinker, ed. Lewis M. Knapp, rev. Paul-Gabriel Boucé, (1966; Oxford: Oxford University Press, 1984).

Southey, Robert, *Journal of a Tour in Scotland in 1819*, ed. C. H. Herford (London: John Murray, 1929).

Staël, Anne-Louise-Germaine de, *De la littérature considerée dans ses rapports avec les institutions sociales, ed. Paul van Tieghem*, 2 vols. (Geneva: Librarie Droz, 1959).

Sterne, Laurence, *The Life and Opinions of Tristram Shandy, Gentleman*, ed. Melvyn New and Joan New (Harmondsworth: Penguin, 1997).

Stevenson, Robert Louis, 'Scott's Voyage in the Lighthouse Yacht', *Scribner's Magazine* 14 (1893): 492–502.

Stewart, Dugald, 'Account of the Life and Writings of Adam Smith', ed. Ian Simpson Ross, in Adam Smith, *Essays on Philosophical Subjects*, ed. W. P. D. Wightman and J. C. Bryce (Oxford: Clarendon Press, 1980).

Thomson, James, *The Seasons* (London: J. Millan, 1730).

Tytler, William, *Poetical Remains of James the First, King of Scotland* (Edinburgh: J. and E. Balfour, 1783).

Warner, Richard, *A Tour through the Northern Counties of England, and the Borders of Scotland*, 2 vols. (London: G. and J. Robinson, 1802).

Warton, Thomas, *The History of English Poetry*, 4 vols. (London: J. Dodsley, 1774).

Wilkes, John, *The North Briton*, 3 vols. (London: J Williams, 1763).

Wordsworth, William, *The Borderers*, ed. Robert Osborn (Ithaca, NY and London: Cornell University Press, 1982).

A Guide Through the District of the Lakes, in *The Prose Words of William Wordsworth*, ed. W. J. B. Owen and Jane Worthington Smyser, 3 vols. (Oxford: Clarendon Press, 1974), vol. II, pp. 123–458.

'*Lyrical Ballads' and Other Poems, 1797–1800,* ed. James Butler and Karen Green (Ithaca, NY and London: Cornell University Press, 1992).

SECONDARY

Aarsleff, Hans, *From Locke to Saussure: Essays on the Study of Language and Intellectual History* (Minneapolis, Minn.: University of Minnesota Press, 1983).

The Study of Language in England 1780–1860 (Minneapolis, Minn.: University of Minnesota Press, 1982).

Abrams, Lynne, *Myth and Materiality in a Woman's World: Shetland 1800–2000* (Manchester: Manchester University Press, 2005).

Albert, William, *The Turnpike Road System in England 1663–1840* (Cambridge: Cambridge University Press, 1972).

Alvarez, David, ' "Poetical Cash": Joseph Addison, Antiquarianism, and Aesthetic Value', *Eighteenth-Century Studies*, 38 (2005): 509–31.

Anderson, Benedict, *Imagined Communities: Reflections on the Origins and Spread of Nationalism*, rev. edn (London: Verso, 1991).

Ash, Marinell, ' "So Much That Was New to Us": Scott and Shetland', in Barbara E. Crawford (ed.), *Essays in Shetland History* (Lerwick: The Shetland Times, 1984), pp. 193–207.

Bainbridge, Simon, *British Poetry and the Revolutionary and Napoleonic War: Visions of Conflict* (Oxford: Oxford University Press, 2003).

Barrell, John, *The Idea of Landscape and the Sense of Place 1730–1840: An Approach to the Poetry of John Clare* (Cambridge: Cambridge University Press, 1972).

Bate, Jonathan, *Romantic Ecology Wordsworth and the Environmental Tradition* (London and New York: Routledge, 1991).

The Song of the Earth (London: Picador, 2000).

Beer, Gillian, 'Discourses of the Island', in Frederick Amrine (ed.), *Literature and Science as Modes of Expression* (Dordrecht: Kulver Academic Press, 1989), pp. 1–27.

Berry, Christopher J., ' "Climate" in the Eighteenth Century: James Dunbar and the Scottish Case', *Texas Studies in Literature and Language*, 16 (1974): 281–92.

Social Theory of the Scottish Enlightenment (Edinburgh: Edinburgh University Press, 1997).

Billinge, Mark, 'Divided by a Common Language: North and South, 1750–1830', in Alan R. H. Baker and Mark Billinge (eds.), *Geographies of England: The North-South Divide, Material and Imagined* (Cambridge: Cambridge University Press, 2004), pp. 88–111.

Blomley, Nicholas K., *Law, Space, and the Geographies of Power* (New York: The Guildford Press, 1994).

Bowen, Margarita, *Empiricism and Geographical Thought: From Francis Bacon to Alexander von Humboldt* (Cambridge: Cambridge University Press, 1981).

Brant, Clare, 'Climates of Gender', in Amanda Gilroy (ed.), *Romantic Geographies: Discourses of Travel 1775–1844* (Manchester: Manchester University Press, 2000), pp. 129–49.

Brantlinger, Patrick, *Fictions of State: Culture and Credit in Britain, 1694–1994* (Ithaca, NY and London: Cornell University Press, 1996).

Burgess, Miranda J., *British Fiction and the Production of Social Order, 1740–1830* (Cambridge: Cambridge University Press, 2000).

Butler, Marilyn, 'Burns and Politics', in Robert Crawford (ed.), *Robert Burns and Cultural Authority* (Edinburgh: Edinburgh University Press, 1997), pp. 86–112.

Buzard, James, 'Translation and Tourism: Scott's *Waverley* and the Rendering of Culture', *Yale Journal of Criticism*, 8 (1995): 31–59.

Casey, Edward S., *The Fate of Place: A Philosophical History* (Berkeley, Calif.: University of California Press, 1997).

Chandler, James, *England in 1819: The Politics of Literary Culture and the Case of Romantic Historicism* (Chicago, Ill. and London: University of Chicago Press, 1998).

Chiaromonte, Nicola, *The Paradox of History: Stendahl, Tolstoy, Pasternak, and Others*, rev. edn (Philadelphia, Pa.: University of Pennsylvania Press, 1985).

Cohen, Murray, *Sensible Words: Linguistic Practice in England 1640–1785* (Baltimore, Md. and London: Johns Hopkins University Press, 1977).

Cole, Richard C., 'James Boswell and Robert Colvill', *Studies in Scottish Literature* 16 (1981): 110–21.

Colella, Silvana, 'Monetary Patriotism: *The Letters of Malachi Malagrowther, The Antiquary*, and the Currency Question', *Nineteenth-Century Studies*, 17 (2003): 53–71.

Colley, Linda, *Britons: Forging the Nation, 1707–1837* (New Haven, Conn.: Yale University Press, 1992).

Craig, Cairns, *Out of History: Narrative Paradigms in Scottish and English Culture* (Edinburgh: Polygon, 1996).

Crawford, Robert, *Devolving English Literature* (Oxford: Oxford University Press, 1992).

Crawford, Thomas, *Burns: A Study of the Poems and Songs* (Edinburgh: Oliver and Boyd, 1960).

Daiches, David, *Robert Burns*, rev. edn (London: Deutsch, 1966).

Dainotto, Roberto M., *Place in Literature: Regions, Cultures, Communities* (Ithaca, NY and London: Cornell University Press, 2000).

D'arcy, Julian Meldon, *Scottish Skalds and Sagamen: Old Norse Influence on Modern Scottish Literature* (East Linton: Tuckwell, 1996).

Davidson, Peter, *The Idea of North* (London: Reaktion Books, 2005).

Davis, Leith, *Acts of Union: Scotland and the Literary Negotiation of the British Nation, 1707–1830* (Stanford, Calif.: Stanford University Press, 1998).

'At "Sang About": Scottish Song and the Challenge to British Culture', in Leith Davis, Ian Duncan, and Janet Sorensen (eds.), *Scotland and the Borders of Romanticism* (Cambridge: Cambridge University Press, 2004), pp. 188–204.

Ian Duncan and Janet Sorensen (eds.), *Scotland and the Borders of Romanticism* (Cambridge: Cambridge University Press, 2004).

De Certeau, Michel, *The Practice of Everyday Life*, trans. Steven Rendall (Berkeley, Calif.: University of California Press, 1984).

Derrida, Jacques, *Introduction to Husserl's Origin of Geometry*, trans. John P. Leavey Jr. (1978; Lincoln, Nebr.: University of Nebraska Press, 1989).

Of Grammatology, trans. Gayatri Chakravorty Spivak (Baltimore, Md. and London: Johns Hopkins University Press, 1976).

Douglas, Mary, *Purity and Danger: An Analysis of the Concepts of Pollution and Taboo* (London: Routledge, 1966).

Duncan, Ian, 'Primitive Inventions: *Rob Roy*, Nation, and World System', *Eighteenth-Century Fiction*, 15 (2002): 81–102.

'Scott, Hogg, Orality and the Limits of Culture', *Studies in Hogg and his World*, 8 (1997): 56–74.

Ferris, Ina, 'Pedantry and the Question of Enlightenment History: The Figure of the Antiquary in Scott', *European Romantic Review*, 13 (2002): 273–83.

   The Romantic National Tale and the Question of Ireland (Cambridge: Cambridge University Press, 2002).

Fiske, Roger, *Scotland in Music: A European Enthusiasm* (Cambridge: Cambridge University Press, 1983).

Flinn, Derek, *Travellers in a Bygone Shetland: An Anthology* (Edinburgh: Scottish Academic Press, 1989).

Foucault, Michel, 'Of Other Spaces', trans. Jay Miskowiec, *Diacritics*, 16 (1986): 22–7.

   Power/Knowledge: Selected Interviews and Other Writings 1972–1977, ed. Colin Gordon (Brighton: Harvester Press, 1980).

Frasca-Spada, Marina, *Space and the Self in Hume's Treatise* (Cambridge: Cambridge University Press, 1998).

Garside, Peter, 'Scott and the Philosophical Historians', *Journal of the History of Ideas*, 36 (1975): 497–512.

Gaskill, Howard (ed.), *The Reception of Ossian in Europe* (London: Thoemmes, 2004).

Giddens, Anthony, *The Consequences of Modernity* (Cambridge: Polity Press, 1990).

Glacken, Clarence J., *Traces on the Rhodian Shore: Nature and Culture in Western Thought from Ancient Times to the End of the Eighteenth Century* (Berkeley, Calif.: University of California Press, 1967).

Glendening, John, *The High Road: Romantic Tourism, Scotland, and Literature, 1720–1820* (Basingstoke: Macmillan, 1997).

Goode, Mike, 'Dryasdust Antiquarianism and Soppy Masculinity: The Waverley Novels and the Gender of History', *Representations*, 82 (2003): 52–86.

Gray, Richard T., 'Hypersign, Hypermoney, Hypermarket: Adam Müller's Theory of Money and Romantic Semiotics', *New Literary History*, 31 (2000): 295–314.

Griffin, Dustin, *Patriotism and Poetry in Eighteenth-Century Britain* (Cambridge: Cambridge University Press, 2002).

Groom, Nick, *The Making of Percy's Reliques* (Oxford: Clarendon Press, 1999).

Guest, Harriet, *Small Change: Women, Learning, Patriotism, 1750–1810* (Chicago, Ill. and London: University of Chicago Press, 2000).

Haldane, A. R. B., *New Ways through the Glens: Highland Road, Bridge and Canal Makers of the Early Nineteenth Century* (London: Nelson, 1962).

Hallward, Peter, *Absolutely Postcolonial: Writing between the Singular and the Specific* (Manchester: Manchester University Press, 2001).

Hartman, Geoffrey, 'Blake and the Progress of Poesy', in *Beyond Formalism: Literary Essays 1958–1970* (New Haven, Conn. and London: Yale University Press, 1970), pp. 193–205.

   'Inscriptions and Romantic Nature Poetry', in *The Unremarkable Wordsworth* (London: Methuen, 1987), pp. 31–46.

Harvey, David, *The Condition of Postmodernity* (Oxford: Blackwell, 1989).

Hechter, Michael, *Internal Colonialism: The Celtic Fringe in British National Development, 1536–1966* (London: Routledge and Kegan Paul, 1975).

Hughes, Gillian, 'Reading and Inspiration: Some Sources of "The Surpassing Adventures of Allan Gordon"', *Scottish Literary Journal*, 16 (1989): 21–34.

Ingold, Tim, 'The Temporality of the Landscape', *World Archaeology*, 25 (1993): 152–74.

Irvine, Robert P., *Enlightenment and Romance: Gender and Agency in Smollett and Scott* (Bern: Peter Lang, 2000).

Kaul, Suvir, *Poems of Nation, Anthems of Empire: English Verse in the Long Eighteenth Century* (Charlottesville, Va. and London: University Press of Virginia, 2000).

Kerrigan, John, 'Wordsworth and the Sonnet: Building, Dwelling, Thinking', *Essays in Criticism* 35 (1985): 45–75.

Kidd, Colin, *British Identities before Nationalism: Ethnicity and Nationhood in the Atlantic World, 1600–1800* (Cambridge: Cambridge University Press, 1999).

'North Britishness and the Nature of Eighteenth-Century British Patriotisms', *The Historical Journal*, 39 (1996): 361–82.

Subverting Scotland's Past: Scottish Whig Historians and the Creation of an Anglo-British identity, 1689–c.1830 (Cambridge: Cambridge University Press, 1993).

Kilgour, Maggie, *From Communion to Cannibalism: An Anatomy of Metaphors of Incorporation* (Princeton, NJ: Princeton University Press, 1990).

Lee, Yoon Sun, 'A Divided Inheritance: Scott's Antiquarian Novel and the British Nation', *ELH*, 64 (1997): 537–67.

Leerson, Joep, 'Ossianic Liminality: Between Native Tradition and Preromantic Taste', in Fiona Stafford and Howard Gaskill (eds.), *From Gaelic to Romantic: Ossianic Translations* (Amsterdam: Rodopi, 1998), pp. 1–16.

Lefebvre, Henri, *The Production of Space*, trans. Donald Nicholson-Smith (Oxford: Blackwell, 1991).

Linebaugh, Peter, *The London Hanged: Crime and Civil Society in the Eighteenth Century*, 2nd edn (London: Verso, 2003).

Livingstone, David N., 'Geographical Inquiry, Rational Religion, and Moral Philosophy: Enlightenment Discourses on the Human Condition', in David N. Livingstone and Charles W. J. Withers (eds.), *Geography and Enlightenment* (Chicago, Ill.: University of Chicago Press 1999), pp. 93–119.

The Geographical Tradition (Oxford: Blackwell, 1992).

Logue, Kenneth J., *Popular Disturbances in Scotland: 1780–1815* (Edinburgh: John Donald, 1979).

Lucas, John, *England and Englishness: Ideas of Nationhood in English Poetry 1688–1900* (London: The Hogarth Press, 1990).

'Places and Dwellings: Wordsworth, Clare and the Anti-Picturesque', in Denis Cosgrove and Stephen Daniels (eds.), *The Iconography of Landscape* (Cambridge: Cambridge University Press, 1989).

McCracken-Flesher, Caroline, *Possible Scotlands: Walter Scott and the Story of Tomorrow* (New York: Oxford University Press, 2005).

' "You Can't Go Home Again": Hogg and the Problem of Postcolonial Return', *Studies in Hogg and His World*, 8 (1997): 24–41.

McLane, Maureen, 'Ballads and Bards: British Romantic Orality', *Modern Philology*, 98 (2001): 423–43.

Makdisi, Saree, *Romantic Imperialism: Universal Empire and the Culture of Modernity* (Cambridge: Cambridge University Press, 1998).

Malley, Shawn, 'Walter Scott's Romantic Archeology: New/Old Abbotsford and The Antiquary', *Studies in Romanticism*, 40 (2001): 233–51.

Malpas, J. E., *Place and Experience: A Philosophical Topography* (Cambridge: Cambridge University Press, 1999).

Manning, Susan, 'Antiquarianism and the Scottish Science of Man', in Leith Davis, Ian Duncan and Janet Sorensen (eds.), *Scotland and the Borders of Romanticism* (Cambridge: Cambridge University Press, 2004), pp. 57–76.

Marshall, P. J. and Glyndwyr Williams (eds.), *The Great Map of Mankind: British Perceptions of the World in the Age of Enlightenment* (London: Dent, 1982).

Massey, Doreen, 'Politics and Space/Time', *New Left Review*, 196 (1992): 65–84.
Space, Place and Gender (Cambridge: Polity Press, 1994).

Mayhew, Robert J., *Enlightenment Geography: The Political Languages of British Geography, 1650–1850* (Basingstoke: Macmillan, 2000).
'British Geography's Republic of Letters: Mapping an Imagined Community, 1600–1800', *Journal of the History of Ideas*, 65 (2004): 251–76.

Merleau-Ponty, Maurice, *The Phenomenology of Perception*, trans. Colin Smith (London: Routledge and Kegan Paul, 1962).

Miller, J. Hillis, *Topographies* (Stanford, Calif.: Stanford University Press, 1995).

Millgate, Jane, *Walter Scott: The Making of the Novelist* (Edinburgh: Edinburgh Press, 1984).

Momigliano, Arnoldo, *The Classical Foundations of Modern Historiography* (Berkeley, Calif.: University of California Press, 1990).

Moore, Daffyd, *Enlightenment and Romance in James Macpherson's 'The Poems of Ossian': Myth, Genre and Cultural Change* (Aldershot: Ashgate, 2003).

Moretti, Franco, *Atlas of the European Novel 1800–1900* (London: Verso, 1998).

Moss, Sarah, 'Romanticism on Ice: Coleridge, Hogg and the Eighteenth-Century Missions to Greenland', *Romanticism on the Net*, 45 (2007). Available online at www.erudit.org/revue/ron/2007/v/n45/015816ar.html.

Muir, Rory, *Britain and the Defeat of Napoleon, 1807–1815* (New Haven, Conn. and London: Yale University Press, 1996).

Nash, Andrew, 'The Cotter's Kailyard', in Robert Crawford (ed.), *Robert Burns and Cultural Authority* (Edinburgh: Edinburgh University Press, 1997), pp. 251–79.

Nobbe, George, *The North Briton: A Study in Political Propaganda* (New York: Columbia University Press, 1939).

Nussbaum, Felicity A., *Torrid Zones: Maternity, Sexuality, and Empire in Eighteenth-Century English Narratives* (Baltimore, Md.: Johns Hopkins University Press, 1995).

Oliver, Susan, *Scott, Byron and the Poetics of Cultural Encounter* (Basingstoke: Palgrave, 2005).

Pawson, Eric, *Transport and Economy: The Turnpike Roads of Eighteenth-Century Britain* (London: Academic Press, 1977).

Pickles, John, *Phenomenology, Science and Geography: Spatiality and the Human Sciences* (Cambridge: Cambridge University Press, 1985).

Piggott, Stuart, *Ancient Britons and the Antiquarian Imagination: Ideas from the Renaissance to the Regency* (London: Thames and Hudson, 1989).

Ruins in a Landscape: Essays in Antiquarianism (Edinburgh: Edinburgh University Press, 1976).

Pocock, J. G. A., *Barbarism and Religion*, vol. II, *Narratives of Civil Government* (Cambridge: Cambridge University Press, 1999).

Poovey, Mary, *A History of the Modern Fact: Problems of Knowledge in the Sciences of Wealth and Society* (Chicago, Ill. and London: University of Chicago Press, 1998).

Porter, Roy, 'The Terraqueous Globe' in G. S. Rousseau and Roy Porter (eds.), *The Ferment of Knowledge: Studies in the Historiography of Eighteenth-Century Science* (Cambridge: Cambridge University Press, 1980, pp. 285–324).

Radcliff, David Hill, 'Imitation, Popular Literacy, and "The Cotter's Saturday Night"', in Carol McGuirk (ed.), *Critical Essays on Robert Burns*, (New York: K. G. Hall, 1998), pp. 251–79.

Reed, Arden, *Romantic Weather: The Climate of Coleridge and Baudelaire* (Hanover, NH and London: University Press of New England, 1983).

Robertson, Fiona, *Legitimate Histories: Scott, Gothic, and the Authorities of Fiction* (Oxford: Clarendon Press, 1994).

Rogers, Pat, 'North and South', *Eighteenth-Century Life*, 12 (1988): 101–11.

Rose, Gillian, *Feminism and Geography: The Limits of Geographical Knowledge* (Cambridge: Polity Press, 1993).

'As if the Mirrors had Bled: Masculine Dwelling, Masculinist Theory and Feminist Masquerade', in Nancy Duncan (ed.) *Bodyspace: Destabilizing Geographies of Gender and Sexuality* (London and New York: Routledge, 1996), pp. 56–74.

Rounce, Adam, 'Stuarts Without End: Wilkes, Churchill, and Anti-Scottishness', *Eighteenth-Century Life*, 29 (2005): 20–43.

Shell, Marc, *Money, Language, and Thought: Literary and Philosophical Economies from the Medieval to the Modern Era* (Berkeley, Calif.: University of California Press, 1982).

Sher, Richard, 'From Troglodytes to Americans: Montesquieu and the Scottish Enlightenment on Liberty, Virtue, and Commerce', in David Wootton (ed.), *Republicanism, Liberty, and Commercial Society, 1649–1776* (Stanford, Calif.: Stanford University Press, 1994), pp. 368–402.

Simpson, John M., *Shetland and the Outside World 1469–1969* (Oxford: Oxford University Press, 1983).

Smiles, Sam, *The Image of Antiquity: Ancient Britain and the Romantic Imagination* (New Haven, Conn. and London: Yale University Press, 1994).

Smith, Anthony D., *The Antiquity of Nations* (Cambridge: Polity, 2004).

Smith, Neil and Cindi Katz, 'Grounding Metaphor: Towards a Spatialized Politics', in Michael Keith and Steve Pile (eds.), *Place and the Politics of Identity* (London and New York: Routledge, 1995), pp. 67–83.

Smith, Olivia, *The Politics of Language, 1791–1819* (Oxford: Clarendon Press, 1984).

Soja, Edward and Barbara Hooper, 'The Spaces that Difference Makes: Some Notes on the Geographic Margins of the New Cultural Politics', in Michael Keith and Steve Pile (eds.), *Place and the Politics of Identity* (London and New York: Routledge, 1995), pp. 183–205.

Sorensen, Janet, *The Grammar of Empire in Eighteenth-Century British Writing* (Cambridge: Cambridge University Press, 2000).

'Internal Colonialism and the British Novel', *Eighteenth-Century Fiction*, 15 (2002): 53–8.

Sparke, Matthew, 'Displacing the Field in Fieldwork: Masculinity, Metaphor and Space', in Nancy Duncan (ed.), *Bodyspace: Destabilizing Geographies of Gender and Sexuality* (London and New York: Routledge, 1996).

Spufford, Francis, *I May Be Some Time: Ice and the English Imagination* (London: Faber, 1996).

Stafford, Barbara Maria, *Voyage into Substance: Art, Science, Nature, and the Illustrated Travel Account, 1760–1840* (Cambridge Mass. and London: MIT Press, 1984).

Stafford, Fiona J., *The Sublime Savage: A Study of James Macpherson and the Poems of Ossian* (Edinburgh: Edinburgh University Press, 1988).

Stam, James H., *Inquiries into the Origin of Language: The Fate of a Question* (New York: Harper and Row, 1976).

Stewart, Susan, *Crimes of Writing: Problems in the Containment of Representation* (New York: Oxford University Press, 1991).

Strout, Alan Lang, *A Bibliography of Articles in 'Blackwood's Magazine'* (Lubbock, Tex.: Texas Technical College Library, 1959).

Sutherland, Kathryn, 'Fictional Economies: Adam Smith, Sir Walter Scott and the Nineteenth-Century Novel', *ELH*, 54 (1987): 97–127.

'The Native Poet: The Influence of Percy's Minstrel from Beattie to Wordsworth', *RES*, 33 (1982): 414–33.

Taylor, E. G. R, *The Haven-Finding Art: A History of Navigation from Odysseus to Captain Cook*, new edn (London: Institute of Navigation, 1971).

Taylor, William, *The Military Roads in Scotland*, rev. edn (Colonsay: House of Lochar, 1996).

Tough, D. I. W., *The Last Years of a Frontier: A History of the Borders During the Reign of Elizabeth I* (1928; Alnwick: Sandhill Press, 1987).

Trumpener, Katie, *Bardic Nationalism: The Romantic Novel and the British Empire* (Princeton: Princeton University Press, 1997).

Tuan, Yi-Fu, 'Language and the Making of Place: A Narrative-Descriptive Approach', *Annals of the Association of American Geographers*, 81 (1991): 684–96.

Turley, Richard Marggraf, *The Politics of Language in Romantic Literature* (Basingstoke: Palgrave, 2002).

Walker, Robert, 'Apes and Races in the Scottish Enlightenment: Monboddo and Kames on the Nature of Man', in Peter Jones (ed.), *Philosophy and Science in the Scottish Enlightenment* (Edinburgh: John Donald, 1988).

Watson, J. R., *Romanticism and War: A Study of British Romantic Period Writers and the Napoleonic Wars* (Basingstoke: Palgrave, 2003).

Webb, Sidney and Beatrice Webb, *The Story of the King's Highway* (1913; London: Frank Cass, 1963).

Weinbrot, Howard D., *Britannia's Issue: The Rise of British Literature from Dryden to Ossian* (Cambridge, Cambridge University Press, 1993).

Wiley, Michael, *Romantic Geography: Wordsworth and Anglo-European Spaces* (Basingstoke: Palgrave, 1998).

Wilt, Judith, *Secret Leaves: The Novels of Walter Scott* (Chicago, Ill.: Chicago University Press, 1985).

Withers, Charles W. J., 'Geography, Natural History and the Eighteenth-Century Enlightenment: Putting the World in Place', *History Workshop Journal*, 39 (1995): 137–63.

Geography, Science and National Identity: Scotland since 1520 (Cambridge, Cambridge University Press, 2001).

'Toward a Historical Geography of Enlightenment in Scotland', in Paul Wood (ed.). *The Scottish Enlightenment: Essays in Reinterpretation* (Rochester, NY: University of Rochester Press, 2000), pp. 63–97.

'Writing in Geography's History: *Caledonia*, Networks of Correspondence and Geographical Knowledge in the Late Enlightenment', *Scottish Geographical Journal*, 120 (2004): 33–45.

Zaid, Hilary A., 'Wordsworth's "Obsolete Idolatry": Doubling Texts and Facing Doubles in "To Joanna"', *Studies in Romanticism* 36 (1997): 201–26.

Index

CAMBRIDGE STUDIES IN ROMANTICISM

General Editor

JAMES CHANDLER, *University of Chicago*